NICHOLAS ⸻

# The Cockney Whipping Boy

## A MEMOIR

Published by McQueen Publishers
mcqueenpublishers@hotmail.com

1st EDITION
Copyright © Nicholas McQueen 2024

Nicholas McQueen asserts the moral right
to be identified as the author of this work.
A catalogue record for this book is
Available from the British Library

Paperback ISBN: 978-0-9534508-3-1
Hardback ISBN: 978-0-9534508-4-8

McQueen Publishers would also like to thank our team for all
their hard work
Editor Kate Bohdanowicz
Book designer Andy Magee
Indexer Jack Turner
Cover Designer Ranae Kaira

Printed in the UK by CL Paper Sales Ltd
This paper has been responsibly sourced

Member of The Society of Authors

**This book is dedicated
to all the Cockneys.**

Wishing you the very best of luck.

*The Bible says one goat was sacrificed to the Lord and the other had all the sins placed on it and sent out into the world: a 'scapegoat'.*

*Whipping boys are known to have been used since the Knights Templars in Jerusalem. Since then, princes and future kings of England would have them. It was forbidden to strike a prince as they were given to us by God so to punish them, whipping boys would be beaten in front of the royal children instead. Whipping boys were usually the sons of noblemen and were given vast estates as payment for their services to the crown.*

# Contents

# Acknowledgements

I would like to thank my mentors who helped steer me through a sometimes difficult world in pursuit of happiness: George Last, Bobby Sulkin, Carole McQueen, Gianni Russo and my wife Paula. A special thanks to Liz Phillips for insisting I finish this book.

# CHAPTER 1

# One Night in the West End

My political career launched in a private room of a gentleman's club opposite the Bank of England in the City of London. It was 2014, and I was invited along to a meeting to see if it was possible to field a political party to tackle Lutfur Rahman, the Mayor of Tower Hamlets who had been accused of cheating the vote and asset stripping the borough he represented, which is the poorest in London. He'd been thrown out of the Labour Party for having unsavoury friends. Something had to change.

I was a perfect candidate for Tower Hamlets, which is the borough that covers the East End. After all, I was born in the East End and have been based there most of my life. If anyone knew this community, it was me. I wanted to see what this party had to say although as I'm not, and never have been, political, I wasn't sure if I'd want to be involved.

At the same time as our meeting, another gathering was taking place at another gentleman's club, the East India Club in nearby St James's Square. It was a retirement party for James Seymour, a master of Caterham public school, and was attended by the great and the good. A Canadian Supreme Court judge, the Right Honourable Mr Graeme Mew, gave a speech at the party, and recalled how Mr Seymour had taken a naughty schoolboy – a thief no less, who had stolen his peers' pocket money from the school safe – and dumped him in the East End of London, at a sleazy place that would have frightened this young lad. Everyone laughed and the speech was published on the internet for all to see.

The boy was me. Yes, it was me they were calling a thief, in public, me who they say had stolen everything from the children I ate, slept and lived with at Caterham boarding school. I can't think of a worse crime to be accused of, and to bring it up over 40 years later made it worse. It wasn't true.

I needed to set the record straight, not just for me but also for my late mother's memory. I could not allow these scoundrels to etch this lie into history, so I will tell the story about what really happened. It's never a good idea to reveal yourself in public but I feel I have no choice. When I embarked on this story I never expected to uncover so much.

# CHAPTER 2

# The East End

Before I can tell you about my life, you need to know where I come from. Historically, the East End of London, which is where I was born, was known to most people as the wrong side of the tracks, where danger lurks around every corner. Geographically, it's east of the old Roman wall in the City of London. As long as you're born in earshot of the Bow Bells in St Mary Le Bow Church at Cheapside inside the City of London walls, you're a Cockney, and by that I mean working class. There was a time when the Bow Bells could be heard for miles, but then the sound of horse-drawn carriages on the cobbled roads drowned out the chimes and they couldn't be heard more than a mile away.

The term Cockney goes back to 1362 and comes from the days when the working class waited at the gates of the City of London, selling laying hens to the bankers and well-to-do merchants travelling to and from the City. They'd get home to find they were not hens, but cocks – absolutely worthless, hence you've been Cockney'd. The Cockneys didn't just sell hens, they lined the City walls from Aldgate to Bishopsgate with their tables selling all sorts of merchandise.

Cockneys have their own language – Cockney rhyming slang – and their traditional food is pie and mash (not fish and chips), which consists of a minced mutton pie with mash potato covered in a green parsley sauce, which is called liquor, then salt, pepper and vinegar. We are proud people, whose ancestors built the City.

The French Huguenots arrived in the East End of London in the seventeenth century after escaping persecution from France. By 1700, it would be usual to hear French being spoken on the streets of Spitalfields. They flooded the area with their weaving skills, selling cloth and clothes, and building beautiful houses, many of which stand as museums today.

The lane that led from the Aldgate to the Bishopsgate was called Petticoat Lane, so called because it was rumoured its inhabitants would steal your petticoats at one end of the lane and sell them back to you at the other. It became famous for selling stolen property and one character who has gone down in history is Isaac 'Ikey' Solomon (c1787–1850), a fence and receiver of stolen goods. He was initially arrested for pickpocketing and was sentenced to transportation for life, but he escaped. After being re-arrested, he was heading for a long stretch in Newgate Prison when the carriage in which he sat made a detour down Petticoat Lane and his friends sprang the coach and released him. He was on the run for years before being re-arrested and transported to the Australian penal colony of Van Diemen's Land (now known as Tasmania). Charles Dickens modelled Fagin on him, in his novel *Oliver Twist*. Today, you will find Petticoat Lane Market but if you look for Petticoat Lane, you won't find it. In the nineteenth century, its name was considered too racy and was changed to Middlesex Street.

In Victorian times, The East End was becoming quite a dangerous place to live or visit. It was squalid, dirty, smelly and with a labyrinth of alleyways, which were crowded with people, many of whom were criminals and prostitutes. Money changed hands everywhere and respectable people avoided the area.

In 1860 two out of 10 houses in the East End were gin shops, with low counters so children could reach them. The area was a melting pot of people from all over the world, of all colours, backgrounds and religions, and there was a thriving Jewish community. People would jump merchant ships at London's East India Docks and settle in the East End, making it a fusion of cultures, with interesting people everywhere. The area became notorious in 1888 when the serial killer Jack the Ripper roamed the streets, murdering and dismembering women in the street. His identity remains a mystery today.

Petticoat Lane/Middlesex Street is still going strong today. The Roman City walls have long crumbled but the lines still exist. By this I mean the  invisible line that runs down the middle of Middlesex Street: one side is run by the City of London Police and the other by the Metropolitan Police. When I refer to Petticoat Lane I mean the whole area that takes in Middlesex Street, Wentworth Street, Cobb Street, Leyden Street, Toynbee Street, Goulston Street and Cobb Lane. The old neighbourhood has changed – one part by gentrification and the other by mass immigration. Things are not quite the same and there are very few Cockneys left. I'm proud to be a Cockney and I'm proud to have come from the East End.

I was 10 years old in 1972 when my mother, a local secondary school secretary, took me to my grandad's pub, The White Hart, in Aldgate East to live. My father had argued with my mother for the last time. She'd had enough.

We had two suitcases between us and we slept in one room near the top of the pub. My grandad was well known throughout the East End and he'd sit outside the pub in the mornings drinking coffee and smoking while a never-ending line of people would wait to shake his hand. My grandad, George Last, was a big man with hands like shovels, size 13 shoes and he always wore a suit and tie. Before becoming a publican, he was a prize fighter, unbeaten in the boxing booth, where all comers could try their luck with him to win £10. He'd had six professional heavyweight fights, winning the Directors Cup at West Ham football field in 1936. His boxing career came to an abrupt end when the Second World War broke out.

He was enlisted as a Physical Training Instructor Flight Sergeant in the RAF. He fought in Africa and helped liberate Italy and had the medals and the photos to prove it. He'd taught the airmen to box and play rugby. I still have the book he wrote: *The Art of Winning in the Ring*. He gave me my first lesson in boxing, and told me I'd now be able to defend myself, take control of the centre of the ring and keep them on the ropes. 'Jab and move, jab and move,' he would say.

The White Hart had been there since 1721 and was famous for being home to George Chapman who ran a barber shop in its basement at the time Jack the Ripper prowled the streets. Chapman was one of the main suspects. He was prosecuted for poisoning his wife and was executed for murder on April 7th. He was known to have visited New Jersey and committed Ripper-style murders there, and the story goes that after he was hanged, there were no more murders on the streets of Whitechapel. The Cockneys certainly believed he was Jack the Ripper as the story has been passed down through generations, and he certainly fitted the bill. Chapman, who was a Polish immigrant called Severin Klosowski, had worked as a junior surgeon before leaving Poland in 1887, a year before the murders began. He'd been spotted out in the middle of the night with his doctor's bag and the first murder took place no more than 50 feet from the back of the pub.

Chapman's barbers was now my play area. The atmosphere was eerie down there – chilly with a damp smell of sweet beer. I always looked over my shoulder when I went down there as I sensed that someone was behind me.

Next door to Grandad's pub was London's most famous Jewish restaurant, Bloom's. The owner, Sid Bloom, would always stop and chat before the day began. Sid Bloom was a very smart man, always in a Savile Row suit, shirt and tie. He and my grandad really looked the part. There was a little old man who sat in the doorway of Bloom's restaurant, selling beigels (bagels) and when he saw me he'd give me one for free. The salt beef would be sliced in the window for all to see, and rye bread and potato latkes were also on display. People would peer through the window, drooling.

Along the same row of shops was Albert's, the men's clothes shop, which sold smart attire; Wimpy (a burger joint), a jewellers and a sweet shop. I had everything I could wish for just under my new bedroom window. The only problem – aside from missing my dad – was that there was nowhere to play. The roads were busy with a never-ending line of speeding traffic, so after school I had to stay inside. It wasn't ideal. I just had to suffer it.

The weekends were a different story. On Saturday I'd go to Toynbee Hall drama club just round the corner in Commercial Street. Sometimes I'd meet friends and go on Red Bus Rover adventures: a ticket was valid on any London bus all day long. My friends and I would go all over the city, finding anything that was free, such as the Monument and museums, and then we'd go onto the Woolwich Ferry to play pirates. We'd spend hours going back and forth across the Thames and we'd jump on any bus, just to see where we'd end up.

Sunday was the highlight of the week. Early Sunday morning I'd go with my grandad and pick up the pickled herrings (rollmops), which he'd place on the saloon bar counter for free. I'd then help my nan make the cheese and pineapple sticks which would also be offered for free, as bar snacks. Then it was off to Petticoat Lane where I'd start at Club Row, the animal market full of puppies, cats, rabbits and unusual pets for sale. It was great going around touching and playing with them. The market was crammed with people, some carrying bags of goldfish in their hands, some getting photos taken with monkeys. There was so much going on, the atmosphere was amazing.

Then onto Brick Lane and the flea market with bric and brac, and people trying on old clothes hoping they'd fit. I loved looking at the army surplus gas masks, helmets and uniforms, I was fascinated by these items. After this I'd make my way to Cutler Street, to the coin and war medal market before getting to Petticoat Lane, which was my favourite place. The walk took me in a huge circle back to the pub just in time for Sunday lunch.

Petticoat Lane was famous for the auctioneers getting big crowds around their stalls, telling jokes and demonstrating new and wonderful inventions. Some threw china in the air, to show you how hardwearing the cups and plates were, and virtually – virtually – unbreakable. I still remember the names of the auctioneers: Jack sold dresses and Louis sold tea towels and towels, bundling them up into sets and selling them cheap. I'd never seen towels sell so fast. People would wave their money in the air trying to get the next cheap deal. It was all the fun of the fair for a 10 year-old-boy and I'd be entranced by the gyroscopes that balanced on a string or on the tip of your finger – the most intelligent spinning top of all time. My favourite stall was Bobby Sulkin's Dial-a-matic shred and chop vegetable machine. Bobby's son Graham told lots of jokes and I'd stand in the front of the crowd for ages watching him chop up vegetables and listening to his banter. I never understood the onion joke but the crowd roared with laughter every time.

There was free entertainment everywhere – balloons bigger than me for sale, bird warbler whistles, magic snakes that could crawl through your fingers and over your body – it was just an illusion as the fake snake was attached to a fishing line that you tied to your shirt button, and you'd be making it wriggle. The men gambling on the Chase the Lady card game always had a good crowd. Not only were there sights and sounds but the air was filled with the smell of fresh donuts, which was wonderful. I had to buy some every Sunday.

One particular Sunday, I was on my way home when I noticed a large box sitting on top of the rubbish pile beside the public toilets in Wentworth Street. Curious, I opened it to find a box of men's ties. They were brightly coloured, obviously new, and although I thought they were ugly, I decided to take them home and bring them back to Petticoat Lane the following week and sell them. I was excited all week. I couldn't wait to try my luck with my first business venture.

Soon enough it was Sunday again and I thought the best place to stand was opposite the Dial-a-matic stall. I placed a dozen ties over my arm and proceeded to shout like the other traders did: 'FIFTY PENCE OR THREE FOR A POUND.' It took 10 minutes before I made my first sale – three for £1. I was so excited putting the money in my pocket. Then, straight away, a man said he wanted seven for £2. I nodded emphatically. He went through the rucksack, picked seven, paid and walked off smiling, and I smiled too. As I put the two pound notes into my pocket, feeling very pleased with myself, I felt someone grab my shoulder.

'Oi. What do you think you're doing?' I looked up to see a policeman. I told him I was selling ties. He asked who I was working for and didn't believe me when I said 'myself'. He repeated himself again and again until Bobby came across from his stall. 'He's only a kid,' he said to the young copper. 'Anyway, he's standing on the City of London side of the street so you can't nick him, you're Met Police.'

'I'm only going to give him a warning,' he said, 'But if I see him again I will arrest him regardless of which side of the street he's on.'

The policeman went on his way and Bobby asked if I'd like an honest job, working on one of his four stalls as tea boy, a gofer. I jumped at the chance. He said I'd be paid £2.50 for working 7.30am–2pm and could start next Sunday. I was so happy. Three quid in my pocket and a job. I bought some dinky donuts and went home.

We would meet at 7.30am and set up the stalls. The other boys showed me what to do, getting all that was needed out of the storeroom (a basement in Middlesex Street), putting up the tables, uprights and sheets to cover the lot. Once it was up, we'd load the stalls with the stock ready for sale. It wasn't just the Dial-a-matic stall we had to set up. Bobby's wife Bessie sold fluffy toy dogs on her stall, Stuart's stall was in Wentworth Street, and he would sell jewellery out of a case under a sheet. Graham was selling the magnetic window cleaner, which would wash both sides of the window at the same time. Very clever.

Once everything was set up, I'd get the orders in for everyone's breakfast which I'd pick up at a local cafe. By this time customers were starting to arrive and the market was coming alive. The rest of the day my time was spent being a 'rick'. A rick is a plant. I'd stand in the crowd with the customers, listening to the sales pitch and when the demonstration finished and the salesman would say, 'Give me five pounds', I'd wave a five pound note and buy the item he was holding up. This triggered a buying frenzy. Never failed. When the crowd had dispersed I'd take my new purchases round to the back of the stall, drop them off and get more ricking money for the next demonstration.

I can still remember the overpowering smell of onions from Bobby's stall, as he tended to use onions the most in his demonstrations. It's a smell that made me want to cry. I didn't like working on Bessie's stall because while I liked her a lot – she reminded me of Diana Dors – I hated having to brush and fluff up the toy dogs to replace the ones she'd sold. I preferred working with Graham because we'd laugh all day.

At 2pm it was time to pack the stalls away and everything, plus left over stock, would be taken to the basement storage unit in Middlesex Street. You accessed it via a large metal chute and everything would slide down from the street, just like the one my grandad had for the beer barrels going into the pub cellar. Sometimes we had to push and shove to get to use the chute as everybody was in a rush to pack up their stalls. Bobby had built large cupboards inside the basement, and any he didn't need were rented to other stallholders.

I was actually paid £3, not £2.50. Yes, I got a pay rise. That was good money in the '70s for a 10 year old so I was always loaded. Bobby also gave me tips for life: 'Never rent anything unless you're going to cut it up and rent it in smaller pieces' was one tip. He'd also say, 'Money does not make money. A good idea and hard work makes money.' I didn't know what was more valuable, the wages or the life lessons I was getting. I loved working for Bobby. He told me he found all these super inventions in America and brought them to London. I thought about that a lot.

After the market all the child workers would look for treasure in the left over rubbish – we'd find decent stock, and money. It was just great fun playing in the rubbish. And there was rubbish as far as the eye could see – a carpet of rubbish. It was not a clean street. One Sunday, four of us child workers were laughing and playing Hot Bottle, where you play catch with a glass bottle. If you drop it and it smashes, you lose. All of a sudden two policemen came running out of nowhere and grabbed me – the others ran away – and they put me in the back of a police van, where they hit me and poked me until I cried. They wanted to know the other boys' names but I wouldn't tell. Eventually they let me go without a charge and I ran straight to the pub and told my grandad. The next day he complained to the inspector at Lemon Street Police Station and the officers got into trouble. It was a hollow victory though because after that Grandad told me I wasn't to play after work anymore.

Work was my hobby, where I'd earn money and learn about life. The people I'd meet would be from all walks of life. The market attracted people like a magnet.

A man who people called 'The Gambler' would shuffle up and down Petticoat Lane. He wore an old black coat tied around the waist with string, and his hands were black with ground-in dirt. If you mentioned any past horse race to him – any horse race, just tell him the date, time and location – he'd go, 'They're off' and recite the whole race. It was as if he was the commentator on the radio. They only had radios in the betting office in those days, and that's where street people, such as The Gambler, would take shelter from the rain and cold. After reciting two or three races he'd ask for a cup of tea, and we'd get him a cup willingly, thankful for the great entertainment he'd provided.

There was a man at Aldgate who had one leg and a crutch and the kids used to torment him mercilessly. They'd shout 'Grass' at him, and he'd chase after them with his crutch under his arm and no chance of catching them. The kids would yell: 'The Kray twins shot your leg off?' which wound him up. You never saw a man with one leg move so fast.

Another man was called 'Mr Time'. He was clean and tidy and always in a suit. The kids would ask, 'Got the time mate?' and he would pull up his sleeve, look at his watch and say, 'The time, time, time, time is the time, it's nine o'clock' and they would all laugh. They'd ask again and he'd repeat it over and over before he trundled off smiling. He was always happy.

The Captain marched everywhere with his arms swinging like a soldier. When he had to stop for traffic, he'd march on the spot, stand to attention, look left, look right, then march off again. He wore huge round glasses with orange lenses and a big black cowboy hat. If someone was in his way he'd march on the spot until his path was clear, then he'd march off again. We found this hilarious. He never smiled and looked at everyone with condescension. I never saw him speak to anyone and never heard his voice.

The characters were great, but there were also a lot of dodgy people too. Shoplifters, pickpockets and bullies and it didn't take long to recognise them and know who to stay away from. One man would walk around the market with a newspaper in his hand, go up to a stall, point at something on display with his free hand and flick another item into the newspaper quick as a flash while the stallholder was distracted.

I'd walk round proud as punch that I had a job. I always had money in my pocket but this was also my downfall as this was when I started smoking. I'd buy cigarettes from the sweet shop, despite being only 10. The shopkeeper would open a packet and sell them individually – they were called singles – and one cigarette was only 2p. Sometimes I'd buy a whole packet of John Player Special, which came in a shiny black packet, and share them with my friends. I'd also buy tobacco with liquorice cigarette papers and have a nice roll up, which left a lovely taste on my lips. A dreadful habit, but what else is a 10 year old going to spend their money on?

# CHAPTER 3

# Life Lessons

My dad started taking me boxing so I could fight other boys in the ring. 'Learning is doing,' my grandad would say. I trained and boxed for Poplar and District Boxing Club in the Roman Road, Bow. We'd train a couple of times a week and I really enjoyed it. Then, on fight nights, I represented the club, usually coming second – yes I lost but I still got a trophy. Alan Coverly, who was two years older than me, was a brilliant boxer. He'd lend me his velvet boxing kit to bring me luck. I thought I looked great. It was good to spend time with my dad because I was really missing him, but by then Mum had a new boyfriend and my dad had gone mad. He'd say terrible things about my mum and go on and on. It hurt to see him in pain but he was also turning me against my mum, brainwashing me into believing the break up was all her fault, and all women were no good. Not the kind of thing an impressionable young lad needs to hear.

One Saturday my grandad came down to breakfast and said he'd had a win on the horses and that I could have anything I wanted. I asked for a fishing rod as there was a fishing shop around the corner from the pub in Commercial Street and I'd often peered through the window, daydreaming about sitting on river banks and catching my dinner. So after breakfast we took the long walk down Commercial Street. Along the way he told me that in return for the fishing rod, he wanted me to remember some sentences. Of course I agreed. I would have remembered anything for a fishing rod.

The sentences were:

1) You're only as big as your enemies.
2) You don't ever do anything that stops you walking the high street with your head held high.
3) If you go somewhere, go first class or don't bother going.

4) Spend your money while you're young, It's no good to you when you're old.
5) Don't worry what people say about you. As long as they're talking about you, that's all that counts.

I repeated them back to him and he was pleased I'd taken them in. I didn't really get it at the time but I've never forgotten those sentences.

To my amazement, when we got to the fishing shop, he didn't just get me the rod, he got me the lot. The rod, reel, stand, bait box, hooks and a great big box to put it all in that turned into a seat. It was breathtaking for me. How lucky was I?

Shortly after, me and a friend of mine called Michael, who was the same age as me, travelled to Broxbourne in Hertfordshire to go fishing. We went by train from Liverpool Street Station, and boarded an old train with big heavy doors and twisty brass door handles that hurt your wrist when you open them. The carriage smelt stale and musky, the smell of countless adventures. We settled down and I had a smoke (much to Michael's disgust as he was a non-smoker).

I'd never been to Broxbourne, so on arrival we asked directions to the River Lea, which wasn't far. It was a spring day with billowing clouds threatening us with rain and blasts of intermittent sunshine. The air was fresh and clean unlike where we'd come from – London air was never clean. I remember struggling with the huge fishing box that contained all the equipment. Michael carried the rods and our packed lunch. We found a good spot on the river, tackled up, attached wriggling maggots to our hooks, tossed a few maggots into the river for luck, plunged our hooks in, sat back and waited. We were so excited. The water was clear and fish were sending bubbles up to the surface to indicate that they were coming and, sure enough, the floats went under and we caught our first fish.

We had found our hobby. We caught fish all day – gudgeon and perch. Catching your first fish is a great feeling, as is learning to get the hook back out of its mouth and putting the fish into the keep net. The beautiful River Lea was full of fish, the trees were reflected on the water's surface and the fresh smell of spring was in the air. I sat on the seat and lit a cigarette. What a great day!

A couple of weeks later I came home from school, St Mary's and St Michael's primary school in Stepney, to see my grandad sitting outside the pub with a cardboard box. Despite no-one in my family believing in God, they sent me to this Catholic school as it was the best in the area. But it wasn't an easy place. It was run by the Catholic nuns The Sisters of Mercy. If you misbehaved they'd ask you to hold out the palm of your hand and they'd smack it with a ruler and it would redden and sting. We wore shorts every day, even if it snowed and we were expected to go to church on Sundays, and it was noted if you didn't attend. I chose the 9am Mass because they had a live band with electric guitars and drums; it was really cool. They'd sing the prayers instead of reciting them. I'd take Communion and a good gulp of the wine. The wine was the bit I liked best as it kept out the cold. Once I had the job in Petticoat Lane I made the choice to work on Sundays so Mass and Confession was now at 6pm on Saturdays for me. Anyway, I saw Grandad with this cardboard box and as I got closer I could see a wire haired fox terrier puppy inside. 'Six weeks old,' he said. 'It's for you.' I was so excited I couldn't catch my breath. 'You better think up a name,' said Grandad as I peered into the box and saw this beautiful puppy with white fluffy legs a black saddle back, tanned ears and a white beard. It was love at first sight. Grandad told me he'd paid £5 for him so I needed to look after him well.

I named him Chippy because he liked to eat my chips, and he turned out to be the best thing about my childhood. We were inseparable and I trained him every day. Grandad had lost his dog a year earlier after intruders had broken into his pub and hit his poodle Tina with a hammer to stop her barking. They got into the safe and took the lot and Tina had to be put down. It was too much for Grandad to bear but Nan didn't want another dog so I think he bought me Chippy so he could have a dog around. But this dog was mine. I never had a leash for him – he would follow me everywhere. He really was my best friend.

I would walk Chippy opposite the pub in Itchy Park, which was once the site of the whitewashed church, St Mary Matfelon, from which Whitechapel gets its name. It was where the 'methos' hung out, drinking bottles of methylated spirits, men and women off their heads, fighting and arguing, and they all seemed to have bashed in faces. It was called Itchy Park because we were told they had fleas and were warned to stay away from them. Fleas can jump on you from six feet away and I didn't want Chippy to catch fleas. It wasn't a problem because when Chippy saw the alcoholics he'd lift the sides of his mouth to snarl, showing his teeth and adding a vicious growl. Chippy wasn't frightened of anything – he was a terrier with the heart of a lion. The drinkers never came close to us.

The park was filthy with cans and bottles, as well as debris and rubble from houses bombed in the War. I always had something to kick. Chippy reminded me of Tintin's dog, Snowy, who always liked adventure. Grandad told me that they used fox terriers down the docks, that the dockers would throw their dogs down the hold of the ships and they would kill all the rats, and this gave me a great idea. I would let Chippy loose on all the debris so he could find rats. We'd go hunting together. When he caught one he'd bite it, shake it, then throw it off dead. What fun!

The White Hart opened at 5pm and Grandad, Chippy and I would work the first hour in the public bar. This bar was mainly for the residents of Booth House, which was a hostel a few doors down opened by William Booth who was the founder of the Salvation Army. This was an army of Christians who helped people all over the world who had fallen on hard times. William Booth got a message in his ear from God saying 'help the heathen' so he did, and the Salvation Army is still going strong today. At 6pm, Little George, Grandad's head barman would arrive and he would run the bar until closing time. Little George had a glass eye and one night after my grandad told him to keep his eye on the till, he whipped his glass eye out and placed it on top of the till. I ran for my life. There was never a dull moment living in a pub aged 10.

The long public bar had 30 or more chairs lining the wall opposite, with small tables in front for the drinks. The chairs were always full and other customers would stand at the bar, which was always packed. The television was mounted high on a shelf so everyone could get a good view. Grandad would check the change

I was giving to make sure I'd added the drinks up correctly using mental arithmetic – it was a maths lesson in many ways. Nearly everyone smoked roll ups and some used snuff, and the air was thick with the smell. Once I found a tin of snuff left on a table so I had a try. Oh my God it nearly killed me. I was sneezing and choking with tears streaming down my face. Never again.

No-one talked to each other much, unlike in the saloon bar where everyone laughed and joked. To me the customers in the public bar seemed mostly sad. The reality of how sad life could become stared me in the face. I always chatted with the customers in the public bar, while I was pulling a pint of Double Diamond beer or putting a shamrock on a pint of Guinness. It made me feel so grown up, even though I was only 10. Some of the customers were ex-boxers and they were punch drunk, slow from repeated blows to the head and they slurred. They liked to chat about boxing. Grandad never got pummelled too much as he said he moved his head out of reach in the ring.

Once I asked a regular customer how he'd ended up in the hostel. He was a lovely man who came into the bar every day. He told me that he was an accountant and had gone to France on holiday with his family and on the first day they'd had a car crash and his wife and two young sons died. He'd survived by hanging on to the steering wheel, and he said the drink helped with the pain of losing them. I thought about that for a long time and never asked anyone anything personal again. Now I understood what my grandad had meant when he said, 'There for the grace of God go I. This is my charity work.' It could happen to any of us.

On Christmas Day, Grandad would open the public bar until 3pm and provide all the festive food – mince pies, pigs in blankets, the lot – for free. When I asked him why he opened on Christmas Day, he said these people had nowhere else to go and it's Christmas.

The methos weren't allowed in the pub, not because they had fleas, but because what they were drinking was nasty and they always ended up causing trouble. Anyone suspected of drinking meths would be followed to the toilet – you could tell because the smell after they'd urinated was awful and made you want to vomit. When Grandad caught one he would take a deep puff of his cigarette, place it in the ashtray on the bar, go to the door and put a wedge in it to keep it open, then pick the offender up by his lapels and punch him. He'd fly through the door and end up sprawled across the pavement outside. Grandad told me he was sending a message to the rest of them not to come here if they were drinking meths. It was also very dangerous because meths is flammable and you only needed to throw a cigarette down the urinal after one of the methos had peed and the whole place would blow up. How frightening. My mum told me that if I saw Grandad take a big puff of his cigarette and wedge the door, I had to run upstairs straight away. I said I would but there was no chance as I wanted to see the action.

The saloon bar was more expensive and this is where the City gentlemen would congregate. It was also used by Somali seamen, famous actors, and academics from Toynbee Hall, the world's first university-affiliated institution of the settlement, aimed at bringing rich and poor together. A place famous for creating social reform, Toynbee Hall is where Clement Attlee, one of our greatest prime ministers, once lived. The seaman told me stories of adventures, of Saladin, the famous Muslim warrior who'd given the Templar Knights a battle to remember. Somali warriors say, 'If you are sick for me, my knife will be your medicine.'

Their stories of faraway lands fired my imagination and made me want adventure. I'd listen as I helped Eileen, the pretty blonde barmaid with strong-smelling perfume, by collecting empty glasses and wiping any spilled beer off the tables. They'd sailed the world's seas and now it was time for them to spend their savings. They had loads of money and it would go over the bar like there was no tomorrow, while they laughed and joked as the jukebox played. The pub was full of Jews, Muslims and Christians and I never saw any racism. I didn't know there could be problems.

Some called the saloon the 'posh bar'. The bar was adorned with West Ham football memorabilia as West Ham was the Cockneys' team. I was once lucky enough to meet Bobby Moore, who was captain of West Ham and of England's 1966 World Cup-winning team. The year before arriving at the pub I'd been to a West Ham Christmas party with Grandad, and Bobby Moore gave me a big red fire engine as a present. Then, some time after the party but before I moved to the pub, I was getting Mum a loaf of bread from Al's corner shop, and I spotted Bobby Moore going into the Bishop of Stepney's house on Commercial Road. It was a big black door next to the East End Maternity Hospital where I was born. I rushed home to get my pen and paper for an autograph and I was back in five minutes. I waited next to the house for half an hour, which seemed like forever, hoping I hadn't missed him. I hadn't, and when he came out, I politely asked him for his autograph. 'Fuck off,' he said. I was shocked. Whatever happened inside the bishop's house wasn't good. I never liked football again. I still don't.

On Friday and Saturday nights, the saloon bar changed. Gone were the office workers, and in would come the ladies and gents, beautifully dressed in their finery. The ladies had big hairstyles and lots of jewellery, and the smell of tobacco smoke was replaced with perfume. In the corner was the pianola – an upright piano that played music if you fed it paper music rolls via a secret door and pressed the foot pedals. Whoever was pumping would move their hands over the keys to give the impression they were playing the chords. In those days the tunes would be *Roll Out the Barrel*, *Blue Spanish Eyes* and many others. I'd sing along at the top of my voice and on occasion I was allowed to pump the pianola. There were smiles and laughter everywhere.

Bloom's, the restaurant next door, didn't have a drinks licence so when any customer ordered a bottle of wine – or any kind of drink – the waiter would come into the bar and buy the drinks in the pub. There were always half a dozen waiters in white coats waiting for their orders and watching the news on the TV. They'd usually have a cigarette while they waited, and a quick drink. In fact sometimes they'd get engrossed in the news or the football. When they did, all hell would break loose as the head waiter would put his head round the door and shout in Hebrew or Yiddish at them and they'd scuttle out as quickly as their feet could carry them. Sometimes they'd bring me salt beef beigels and potato latkes, which were delicious.

If any big stars were dining in Bloom's the waiters would come and get me and introduce me to them, which made me feel so important. I met Telly Savalas, who was famous for playing *Kojack*. The waiter would say: 'Tell Nicholas, Telly,' and he'd reply,

'Who loves ya baby?', which was his catchphrase. I really enjoyed meeting him.

Mr Bloom's Irish valet Michael also stood in the bar after work. He was in charge of the parking and seemed important as everyone was giving him money. He did well because he always had a parking spot for customers.

Bloom's staff would throw the back door open to Gunthorpe Street, the alley that runs down the side of the pub where the entrance to the saloon bar is located. It's a well-known alley as Jack the Ripper murdered there. The Bloom's staff would use the back door to throw out old barrels of New Green pickling juice which would slosh down the alley, pass the pub entrance and to the drain. It stank and I worried that it would splash on my clothes. The rabbi was always at the back door and he'd give me a potato latke and scraps for Chippy. He was a jolly man and always seemed pleased to see me.

If I was sick with flu or a cold, Grandad would take me into Bloom's for lokshen soup. It's a chicken noodle type soup and is said to be Jewish penicillin, as it's supposed to make everything better. It does. If I was lucky I'd get an orange sorbet for dessert. It was amazing. I loved Jewish cuisine.

# CHAPTER 4

# Boarding School or Borstal?

The worst day of my life. It was a Wednesday and Grandad had given me 50p, sent me to Wimpy to have my dinner and told me to wait there while he nipped up to the London Hospital (now the Royal London). Sheffi, the owner of Wimpy, would always look after me, as would his wife. He was one of the first Asians to arrive in the East End and was married to a white woman. I went in there as often as I was allowed. Sometimes I even spent my own money in there.

I waited and waited until it started to get dark, then I went back to the pub. I couldn't find Grandad there, or Nan, or my mum. I never saw Grandad again. He'd died of a heart attack. He needed a heart bypass, but it hadn't been invented then. I read a prayer at his funeral in St Mary's and St Michael's Church. It was so full, guests had to stand in the street.

My mum had to step up to run The White Hart, which wasn't easy. She had my nan to look after as well as me, and she was a soft and placid woman now in charge of a tough East End pub. She had to learn quickly. She'd been a secretary at Robert Montefiore, a local secondary school, and she maintained the kids there were so naughty the pub couldn't be much harder. I didn't see much of her from that point and I wasn't allowed in the bar from then on.

This is when I began to go off the rails. I was now 11 and I'd passed the exam to go to Raine's Foundation School, the local grammar. My mum was proud of me, for once. It was the school she'd attended as a child.

I caught the bus home from school every day and had to walk past Woolworths and a jewellers run by a little Jewish man. Every day he would stand in his doorway and shout, 'I like the uniform' and then 'Shine your shoes: you can tell a man by his shoes.' He was a really lovely man. 'Mazel tov Nicholas,' he'd yell.

It was about the fifth week of Raine's when I was on my way home and expecting to receive the usual comments from the jeweller, but there was no-one outside his shop. Instead I saw white tape. My heart went into my throat – I knew that whatever had happened, it was bad. I went into the pub with my head bowed, and my mum took me upstairs. She said two men went inside the jewellers, pulled out a gun and told him to open the safe. He refused so they shot him in the leg. He still refused to open the safe so they shot him in the head. He was dead.

I felt immediate pain, like I'd been struck with something. Mum was very upset, as she was also his friend. She started ranting and telling me that if an intruder ever comes in the pub while I'm upstairs, don't try to fight them, do whatever they tell you, give them the safe key, and don't do anything stupid. 'I can get more money,' she said. 'But I can't get another son.' Of course I agreed.

I wasn't doing well at school. I was fighting and getting beaten by teachers, some days by Mr Spooner, who'd give me the slipper in his office, even when I'd just started school. Every time Mr Spooner hit me it was written in a book that recorded punishments. It wasn't long before my name was all over it. Mr Long, the PE teacher who was also the basketball teacher, hit the hardest. Every time he hit me with the gym shoe, I'd fly three paces and had to step back for more. I still liked him though.

At Raine's, they were breeding gerbils in the school laboratory and they were on sale at 25p each. I had a great idea of buying a pair, breeding them and selling them myself. I purchased a breeding pair and took them home in my pocket. By now I had a key to the top room in the pub, which was where I kept and smoked my cigarettes. I hung the key around my neck with a piece of string. The room had an old dressing table and I used the bottom drawer to make a home for my new pets knowing no-one could gain access to my room. It was too cold to keep them in the cellar.

I couldn't keep it secret for long though, and my nan was terrified when she found out. When she was younger she'd worked in an East London gin factory which had rats, and she'd never got over it. The rats would run along the heating pipes while she was working and nobody was able to catch them. Now she was petrified of all rodents and the very thought of them would have her tapping her feet, which amused me. I can remember telling her that if she kept on moaning at me for one thing or another, I'd go and get them. She'd clam up then. I still laugh when I think about it today – I was a naughty little sod.

I monitored the gerbils for months. No babies. No return on my investment. I just kept feeding them until one day I discovered they'd both died overnight. I was devastated. I'd grown fond of the gerbils and loved watching them run around the bottom drawer. I decided the best thing to do would be to say a prayer and give them a cremation in the pub furnace, which was used to fire the pub's oil heating system, and was downstairs in the kitchen. I wrapped my gerbils up in tissue and dropped them into the furnace. They instantly came alive and screamed for a second, then they were gone. No-one told me about hibernation! My nan had the cheek to smile. I was completely devastated, felt horribly guilty and stupid for ages.

I still worked for Bobby every Sunday and he always gave me little tips for life as he knew I was having a tough time with my grandad gone and my dad living away. I would not have missed my Sunday job for the world. Graham, Bobby's son, spent a lot of time training me to demonstrate the jewellery and magnetic window cleaner, and he'd let me practise in Petticoat Lane while he was having his break. 'You'll never go without money once you have the gift of the gab, son,' he said.

It was my first lesson in public speaking and street theatre, and just like everything else, practice makes perfect. I found it easy to pull the crowd, as people were shocked to see an 11 year old demonstrating on the street, so many stopped out of interest. I got more confident and my patter – with lots of Cockney rhyming slang – became more slick, all thanks to Graham. It was so much fun I loved it. The only thing I wasn't allowed to do was touch the Dial-a-matic shredding machine as they said I'd lose my fingers if I tried to use it. I've never touched one to this day.

Other traders started to ask me to work on Saturdays down Oxford Street. Two brothers, Needy and Greedy, flypitchers from the other end of Middlesex Street, told me to ask my mum for permission as my job would be looking out for the police while they flypitched (selling without a licence) the tomfoolery (jewellery). It was called 'working the tom'. They were going to pay me £5 for the day, which was massive. I asked my mum if I could go and she told me to tell them to take a running jump, but I couldn't bear to lose the opportunity to earn so much money in just one day (especially as I only received £3 for Sundays and cigarettes were just 40p a pack), so I told them I was allowed.

I got up super early on that Saturday morning and crept down the stairs with the pub keys, unlocked the pub door, carefully locked it back up and once outside posted the keys though the letter box. I got the bus to Oxford Street, the busiest shopping street in London, and found them. They were easy to spot as the two brothers had long blond curly hair and spoke with their hands all the time. We went to work. Needy and Greedy made me stand on a concrete planter on the pavement and look for police helmets as they were usually higher than everybody else's head and easy to spot. If I saw a helmet, I'd have to shout, 'Have it up' at the top of my voice. Greedy would then close the case full of jewellery and hide in a shop doorway, until the police had passed. Oxford Street was so crowded with people it was shoulder to shoulder, so I needed to be up on the planter. Sometimes the policeman would take his helmet off and creep along to try and catch us, but I was waiting for that too.

Needy would sit in what he called the saddle (a milk crate), open the case and start by banging up (selling). I'd never seen so much money accumulate so fast – 10 times faster than Petticoat Lane. These people in West London were rich. He'd shout: 'Forget about ten, nine or eight!' Then bang as he slapped a ream of tissue paper. 'Seven or six!' Bang as he slapped it again. People would start to get curious and a crowd would gather. 'Five or four!' Bang with more tissue. 'Watch what I'm going to do with another man's stock and property. While Mappin was in his Webb, I was in his warehouse!' Bang! By now there was always a full crowd.

'Item number one, the Dubarry drop pearl. We lost 10 men diving for these pearls. Forget five pounds, which is the value.

We're going to give these to you free of charge – no money to pay.' Then he'd show off the pearl pendant on a piece of black velvet.

'Item number two, the diamond-cut gold bangle bracelet. Forget 10 pounds. We'll add that to the sale for free, just for a bit of fun. Item three, the real gold locket. You put the mother-in-law's photo in one side and your pet dog in the other, shut it and see who wins.' The crowd would roar with laughter.

'Of course it's real gold madam it's been in the fridge all night. So there you have 20 pounds of jewellery but forget 20 pounds. Before the policeman comes, the first 10 customers give me five pounds only and if anyone asks you where you got them say you found them on a bus.'

Then the rick shouts, 'I'll have one' and all hell breaks loose, with money waving everywhere. It's a very clever way to sell things and great fun to watch. The actor Jason Statham started his career selling jewellery in Oxford Street.

All of a sudden my mum appeared screaming at the top of her voice: 'What do you think you're doing?' Needy was only about 18 years old himself but she still screamed at him: 'Couldn't you find a chimney to put him up? You should be ashamed of yourself.' She was still shouting as she dragged me off by my ear. Needy pulled some smirky faces but didn't argue back. Greedy went and hid in a doorway.

I still worked my Sunday job though.

Things were going from bad to worse at school. I was using my boxing skills too much, not learning, and refusing to do my homework because I was finding it difficult. I was also being rude to my mum until one day she flipped and sent me to live with my dad, with Chippy in tow.

I moved back to Albert Gardens in Stepney, which was where I once had a happy family, but now it was just me and my dad. I hardly saw him as he was working in the day as a black cab driver, and stayed out most nights at his girlfriend's. I was alone and pretty much looking after myself. I had to teach myself to cook (beans on toast), do the washing, housework and all the normal things adults do to keep on top of life. It wasn't easy but I just got on with it. My next door neighbours, Joe and Anne, would cook me a dinner every night and I was welcome to eat at the family table with their three kids, Joe, Sam and Chris. That's what being a Cockney is all about – helping each other. This family was the salt of the earth.

My relationship with my mum was at an all-time low. I was adamant that as she'd thrown me out, I wouldn't go back there. I was much closer to school – I could see it from my window, which saved a bus ride, but sometimes I chose not to go.

At that time the kids' clubs were very good. I'd go to Stepney Green school club most nights during the week. There was always something on. Wednesday was metalwork, fencing and car mechanics. The classes lasted until 8pm, and you could make all kinds of things but we made the stars used in kung fu, and other secret weapons. I enjoyed fencing and became pretty good at fighting with a foil. On Fridays it was disco time where we wore flared jeans, bell bottoms or Oxford bags trousers with the high waistbands and six or 12 buttons. I got my first love bite smooching to *Hey There Lonely Girl* by Eddie Holman.

One Friday, in the dimmed lights of the disco, I got grabbed from behind and saw a metal comb pass my eyes. I felt instant pain and knew I'd been cut across my face. I didn't see who it was. They most probably sharpened the comb handle in metalwork. My dad was very upset, but this was the East End, it was a violent place and you don't get second chances here. I saw young boys pick up hammers when they were fighting.

My behaviour, meanwhile, was getting worse at school and I was expelled. The government gave me a choice – boarding school or borstal? Which really wasn't a choice. I decided boarding school would be my best bet.

My friends and neighbours couldn't believe that I was being sent away at 11 years old. I wasn't even a criminal. But I suppose they thought it was for the best, after all I was looking after myself for most of the time. The saddest thing about leaving was that I had to give my faithful dog Chippy to my neighbours Joe and Anne. I knew they'd treat him like one of the family. They were great people and Chippy deserved to be well looked after, and it meant I would see him in the holidays.

I told Bobby what had happened and he sat me down and explained it could be a good thing, an opportunity. 'Your job will always be here,' he said. 'Just turn up and work when you're home.'

# CHAPTER 5

# The Smell of a Schoolboy Battle

We only had a few weeks to prepare. My dad bought the uniform, sports kit, trunk and tuck box and even a Sunday suit. I looked at the trunk in disbelief, sitting at the bottom of my bed, slowly filling up with clothes. I really didn't want to go. I liked having no rules and being my own person, and I knew things were about to change drastically. My dad kept moaning about how much it was all costing. There was so much kit, even towels and a travel rug. My mum sent me a carrier bag of biscuits to put in my tuck box, and a new lock for it.

Then it came, the day I'd been dreading. We loaded everything into my dad's black taxi and off we went. I can still remember how sick I felt, sicker than I'd ever felt before. It took an hour and a half to get to Caterham in Surrey, then the long drive down Harestone Valley Road which was the last mile of the trip. We then turned left into the drive of an enormous house surrounded by woods. It was called Mottrams after a former headmaster, and this was where the preparatory school boarders aged 8 to 13 lived – all boys, no girls.

We pulled up close to the entrance and I could see the chaos. Trunks, kids, parents everywhere, everybody rushing about. We got our stuff out the taxi and went inside. The headmaster, Mr Churchill, was waiting to greet us and he introduced us to his wife, who was the matron, and Nick Johnston. Mr Johnston was my housemaster, a tall man well over 6ft, who played county cricket for Surrey. He seemed pleasant enough and he helped us with the trunk upstairs to my dormitory, which was called Foxborough. It had five beds and was between two masters' rooms. I could smell the fresh paint on its light blue walls, and the carpet was a hard wearing wiry type of red tile.

I hugged my dad goodbye. Mr Johnston assured him that I was going to be fine, and that was it, my *Tom Brown's School Days* had begun, and boy was I dreading them. The boys introduced themselves in well-to-do accents. I thought, 'Oh my God, they're all posh.' They explained that everybody used last names only. I wasn't Nicky anymore, I was now McQueen. Then one of the boys proceeded to show me around the building. With its highly polished wood-panelled walls it was just as intimidating as I'd imagined. I was shown the dining hall, which smelt of cooking. We then went outside where the same posh boy proudly showed me the extensive grounds, explaining that we were only allowed to go here or there. There were boundaries, you just couldn't see them. I felt tense. Up until this point I'd never really had any boundaries, I could go pretty much wherever and whenever I pleased. I was a city boy and this remote countryside made me feel vulnerable. The whole place seemed cold and soulless and I couldn't see myself having any fun here.

We then went to the tuck box room, where there were rows of boxes, all with locks. The tuck boxes were placed on shelves from floor to ceiling, and loads of kids were sitting on their boxes, talking about their holidays and eating their treats. I was shocked to see them making hot drinks using the hot water basin taps, I thought they'd make themselves sick. I found a spot for my tuck box and put it in place.

I soon learnt that the masters rarely came in here, and so the children could be themselves without fear of punishment. The school attracted kids from all over the world and you got to hear their stories. Some were following family tradition and were third and fourth generation Caterhamians, being put through this strange ritual of education. There because their father had been educated there. Once I'd been in there a while I found it hard to believe that these parents knew how horrible these places were, and yet still sent their children to them. At least my dad didn't know, so I couldn't blame him. Our family didn't know anyone who'd been to boarding school.

My mum had filled my tuck box with all sorts of biscuits and drinks. I'd hidden my 10 Number Six cigarettes and box of matches in one of the packets of biscuits. I was craving a cigarette but I hadn't even unpacked yet. I didn't want trouble on my first day. I went back to the dorm and finished unpacking and then the trunk was taken away and the biggest nightmare of my life began. I felt abandoned, unwanted and really sad.

The bed had a straw mattress. I couldn't believe it. It took me ages to manage to sleep on it. The whole place was strict and like something out of the previous century. The day began at 7am, when we made our beds – I was shown how to fold bedsheets properly, with hospital corners – then we straightened up our travel rugs. The travel rug was the one thing that gave us an identity in the dorm, and mine was a McQueen tartan rug. Then it was inspection time. Mrs Churchill, the matron, would wait at the bottom of the huge polished wood staircase and check our hands, shoes, hair, teeth and behind our ears. The junior matron was ever so young compared to Mrs Churchill, and not as tough. Her room was opposite Foxborough. She would monitor us washing ourselves in the bathroom and I didn't like that at all as I was used to privacy. There were two baths in the middle of the room with lots of sinks around the walls and she would sit on her chair sewing buttons onto the boys' shirts, and she'd supply fresh underwear, socks, shirts and things like that when we needed them.

After washing, we were off to the dining room for a cooked breakfast, before we headed over to the day school block. Day boys were not allowed to go into Mottrams as it was our home.

After school it was back to Mottrams, where a cup of strong tea was waiting, then it was free time, then dinner. The meals were very good, nothing like the school slop we were fed in the East End. We were allowed to have our favourite spreads on the table to eat with bread after our meal. I was amazed at all these different spreads – Marmite, peanut butter, and all sorts. I only knew jam. Then it was time for prep, which was homework. We'd sit in the dinner hall in silence for an hour and a half, just working. The master would sit at the front, marking homework until he got up and took a stroll to stretch his legs. You asked him a question at your own peril. The best way to communicate with someone was to write a note. When you finished your work you were allowed to read a book. Then it was to the tuck box room, quick smoke in the toilet, then off to bed.

School was six days a week, with free time on Wednesday and Saturday afternoons unless you got 'gated', which meant detention. On Sunday we had an extra hour in bed and a day of Christian stuff. The school was based on Protestant values and it was very different for me as I was raised a Catholic. I didn't know the songs. Sunday was always a very long day, and the day I thought of home a lot, and the day I realised my freedom had been taken away. I missed playing on the Woolwich Ferry, travelling to Broxbourne, the Red Bus Rover tickets, Petticoat Lane, Bobby, Graham, and my wages.

As soon as I'd arrived at Caterham, I was sent to the school barber. It was 1973 and my hair was long, as that was the fashion. I got into the queue and waited patiently. As the first victims trooped out, I saw what their haircuts looked like. Shocking! Then it was my turn. The barber had a London accent so when he told me to sit in the chair, I told him I didn't want a cut, just a trim. I thought that when he heard my accent was the same as his, he'd be more understanding, but he couldn't have cared less and just started with the electric razor. It was over in less than 60 seconds, but there wasn't even a mirror so I couldn't see what he was doing. When I did finally get a look at myself and saw he'd cut the lot off and left a mop of hair on the top, I felt I'd been robbed. I was horrified. The worst part was the two inch gap behind the ears. I hated this barber, not because I was vain but because he didn't give a hoot and the cut was so fast. He should have been put into the *Guinness Book of Records* for the worst and fastest haircut of all time. I now felt very ugly and dreaded my friends at home seeing me like this.

The boys in my dorm were different to me as they were so posh, but they were great kids and they'd remain my friends for my entire stay. They 'initiated' me by pancaking my bed, which is when they pull the bottom sheet up from the bottom and tuck it round the top to look like the top sheet, so when you try to get in, it's like an envelope. Sometimes I'd wake up with my hand in a cup of water and toothpaste on my wrist, because they were trying to make me wet the bed. Pillow fights were great fun, even though the pillows were as heavy as sacks of potatoes; when you hit someone with the pillow they went flying. Most kids had a torch to read under the covers late into the night. Sometimes we even got out the Ouija board.

I was the only new boy and on my first day of school the maths teacher Mr Moore introduced me to the class. All the kids knew each other and I was surprised at how many were day boys – they outnumbered boarders 10 to one. It took about five minutes for me to realise they were far ahead of me in maths. Right away I knew I was in trouble. A boy walked up to my desk and asked to use my ruler, but when I went to get it off him at the end of the class, he said it was his now. We stood there, both grasping one end of the ruler and pulling it until it snapped, to which he shouted, 'Hillside McQueen!' I had no idea what he meant until other kids explained this was the rallying call for a fight up in the woods on the hill. I'd only been at school for one lesson!

The hillside had one huge tree in the middle of the woods, the canopy of which sprawled 100 feet wide with nothing below except a carpet of brown leaves. This was the duelling spot. The rest of the hillside was dense with bushes, treehouses and dens made by boarders and strictly off limits to day boys. I looked around and could see some sweet spots for a smoke.

I took the high ground on the hill to gain the advantage and lifted my fists. About 50 lads had gathered in a circle and were shouting and cheering. No teachers came by – they must have known what was going on and obviously seemed to let it go on. It didn't take me long – two jabs then the strong right hand pushed up from my right thigh, just like Grandad had taught me. This sent him rolling down the hill with leaves flying, which kicked up a damp rotten smell. This was the smell of a schoolboy battle.

All I heard in my first week was 'Hillside McQueen!' in posh accents. It felt like all the day boys wanted a piece of me. I spent every breaktime of my first week on the hillside until they'd had enough. I never lost. It was only ever the day boys, never the boarders, and the boarders started to become like brothers to me. I didn't know what it was like to have brothers, so to me this was as close as I was ever going to get.

I lasted two weeks at school. The homesickness pain, which was an ache in my stomach, had kicked in after a couple of days. I woke with what felt like a painful dense hole inside and the only time it shifted was when I was playing sport or doing an activity. After two weeks I'd had enough, so I got up and ran for my life. It wasn't planned at all, it was though I'd woken up running and I just ran and ran. I didn't even start to think until I was half way to town. It was too late to turn back so I just had to continue. I bunked the train at Caterham Station, arrived in London and caught a bus from London Bridge to home. I was so pleased to be back in the East End, even if my hair did look ridiculous.

I got home and waited for my dad, and when he arrived I told him I wasn't going back. It took a couple of days for him to persuade me that I had to. 'Be a man,' he said. 'Or they'll put you in a detention centre.' That made me think. He said the school was going to train me to be a gentleman and give me an education. 'Then you can do anything you want in life,' he said. He told me I hadn't given it a fair chance. Eventually, he resorted to old-fashioned bribery, promising me a holiday to America if I stuck it out.

I went back to Caterham in my dad's black cab. As we drove up Harestone Valley Road the dense hole in my stomach came straight back, but I knew I had to carry on and give this so-called opportunity a try.

After being back for four weeks the beatings began. I was getting beaten with gym shoes on a regular basis; every teacher took their turn to beat me. I was put into detentions, made to run before breakfast and write lines in huge numbers. I realised I was being used to keep the other boys in order – I was a whipping boy. The masters seemed to have no conscience with me, inferring that I could take it as I was a tough East End lad. The fear of punishment was as bad as the punishment and they'd make an appointment for the beating so I had to wait for it. I decided I would not fear it. I remembered what my grandad said: 'A coward dies a thousand times, a hero only dies once.'

The worst punishment (from talking in prep) was from Mr Robinson-Fuller, a house master from the other side of Mottrams. The first time he issued me and another boy a cold shower punishment, everybody turned round and looked at us with fear in their faces. You could hear the children actually stop breathing. This meant he was coming for us at 6am the next morning and we had to wear our white gym kit. The other boy slept next to me, and woke me up at 5.45am and we changed. I had no idea what was going to happen. At 6am precisely we heard him coming along the creaky corridor and he stood in the doorway, a skinny man, very well spoken with a trimmed moustache, and he said, 'Right, let's go.' I thought I was going for a cold shower next door in the bathroom to our dorm but he led us out of the building. I was petrified. Dawn was breaking and we were being led across the field on a dirt path to the main building. My intuition was telling me not to go.

I turned to my friend. 'Are we getting raped here?'

'It's OK, 'he said. 'He's only going to throw cold water over our penises.'

I froze. That's not right, he can't do that.'

'Yes he can. That's what we do here McQueen.'

I thought, 'Is this the way Protestants behave? The Sisters of Mercy only hit us with rulers.'

It was a bright morning and there was a chill in the air. It felt like forever to reach the day school and the old unused shower cubicles. When we arrived, he told us to take our clothes off then stand in the shower. It was a dirty filthy place and there we were naked and already very cold. A few minutes later he came back with his suit jacket off, shirt sleeves rolled up past his elbows and carrying two red fire buckets full of cold water which had been left out all night. He then threw a bucket of water over each of our private parts, which by the look on his face and the noises he made gave him sexual gratification. We didn't look at each other. We were ashamed and degraded. After he'd finished his torture we dried off and he took us back to our dorm. In order to get us there, we had to pass the junior matron's room, Mr Moore's room, Mr Johnston's and Mr Bellamy's. It beggars belief that this could go on. But go on it did.

This form of torture became a regular occurrence and it felt as though it was always me whether I'd misbehaved or not. I was obviously his favourite, and it was always with another boy, a younger child of around eight or nine, whom I would now have to reassure that they would be OK, knowing full well that, like me, they would be scared stiff and scarred for life.

It usually began with a sleepless night for me. We were always taken in twos across to the day school block, and it was still dark most of the time, sometimes foggy, eerily silent and always with the smell of damp countryside in the air. I'd have goosebumps but I never knew if they were due to cold weather or fear. Robinson-Fuller would carry homework that he had marked in prep, alongside other books, and he'd walk in front of us as we followed him sluggishly. We really didn't want to go. He did this every single morning and each night left two fire buckets of water outside the school building. Sometimes they'd have frozen in the cold winter weather. After I'd stripped naked and stood in the old, nasty shower, I'd stand to attention and imagine I was a British soldier being tortured by the Japanese in a concentration camp. Because it was torture. This was the start of my psychological blocking. The more terrified the small boys were, the more it pleased him, so I wasn't going to give him that. He'd throw some water over my penis and some over the other boy's, taking it in turns, eking it out while he exploded with pleasure, twitching on his face and neck, which would then cause his arm to twist. It was horrible to watch.

We boys never made eye contact but I could see some shake uncontrollably. I'd look deep into Robinson-Fuller's eyes, watching his sickness consume him, but I knew he couldn't see me, just my penis. I knew that if he tried to rape me I would dig my fingers into his eyes, and I would do it without mercy.

Afterwards, I would ask if the other boy was OK and I'd hear a whispered 'yes' but we still didn't make eye contact. We never spoke of it afterwards. Robinson-Fuller would then go back to his room for 30 minutes. I wonder why? He'd also come into the bathroom on bath night and ogle us. Even today, my memories and dreams are full of the little eyes of my roommates peering over the bed sheets in true fear, watching me being taken away again, not knowing if this was the day that I was going to be raped, or that they were going to be next.

It wasn't until I reached puberty that he stopped getting me from my bed. Obviously I was getting too old for him. I would still get up early and watch him from my window taking the little boys across the dirt track and I'd always check that both those boys came back. He'd have two boys every day without fail. I no longer had the cold shower treatment but Robinson-Fuller still beat me in French lessons. I hated him! And guess what? I don't speak French.

He wasn't the only sadistic bastard of a teacher. All the boys had to swim naked in the school pool, and jump in and out like it was normal. I thought it was some type of freak show and I didn't want to be part of that, so I'd do anything to avoid swimming, even though I swam well and enjoyed it, with trunks on. The master in charge could not hide his pleasure watching all the little boys. I know. I watched his eyes.

Some teachers were alright. Mr Bellamy was a junior house master who taught me Latin, although I couldn't figure out why I needed to learn Latin. His room was on the other side of my dorm. He was a lovely bloke, really patient. He also taught me photography and he had a dark room next to my dorm. We'd process black and white photos using bromide. I enjoyed that even though it smelled bad. I'd stroll around the school taking pictures. One day a ball I was playing with got stuck on the school roof so I climbed up and got it with my friend, taking snaps all the way. I still have to laugh about that, as it would have been a certain beating if I'd been caught.

And aside from the beatings, school wasn't all bad. I had lots of friends to play with and we'd make camps, do activities and play sports while trying to squeeze in as many smoke breaks as possible, congregating in one of the treehouses. We'd make elderberry wine and leave it in the bottle to ferment – schoolboy hooch – it tasted disgusting but it did make you merry. We'd snack on wild leeks from the hillside. Everything was so different here. I learned so much from my new brothers, like how to make a fire with a magnifying glass using the sun, and how to play many different board games. Keeping busy was the only way I could avoid the homesickness pain and put the torture I'd endured to the back of my mind.

When there was a full moon, it would pull us like it pulled the tides. We turned into the Foxborough Commandos. We all knew that some Caterham boys had escaped from Colditz Castle during the Second World War. It was actually mentioned in the John Mills film *The Colditz Story* that Colditz was similar to Caterham. If you could survive Caterham you could survive Colditz. If they could do it then, so could we.

So we planned the Mottrams escape. The five of us in our dorm would get up at 3am. Our gear was ready as one of the boys would sort out coffee, torches and woolly commando hats. We'd go to bed with our pyjamas on over our clothes for a quick change, then off we'd go, with military precision. The masters slept either side of our room so we had to be precise with our footsteps as there were some creaky floorboards – one foot wrong could blow the mission. But we knew every creak in the old floorboards.

We'd slip past Mr Bellamy's room to go down the masters' back staircase, then creep along to the tuck box room, unlock the door then out the window with commando rolls. We'd leave the window ajar for our return, then exit the grounds, military style again. Once we got to the woods we'd sigh with relief as we could talk without worry from this point on. We usually started giggling hysterically, half out of nerves as it would be a certain whipping if we were caught. Torches on, then towards the building site of the M25, the motorway that circles London, which was being built at the time. The shadows and snapping branches made it really scary in the dark. You could smell the countryside and always hear wildlife, with owls hooting and rodents scurrying.

The M25 was being built through the night and there was always heavy machinery going, and all the diggers and trucks had lights on. We'd be high on the hill watching the action. I'd smoke a cigarette while the others would set up the picnic. We laughed for the whole two hours, playing ball and just feeling really naughty. Then we'd make our way back so we were back in our beds for 6am. We never got caught.

One term I got there to find they were all going fishing and I'd forgotten the rod my grandad had bought me so I decided to nip home and get it. I'd planned it so they wouldn't miss me. Off I went to Caterham Station, bought a ticket to London, arrived at the pub where I kept my fishing gear in the cellar, passing Eileen the barmaid in the bar where she commented: 'It's Little Lord Fauntleroy.' I had no idea who she was on about. It was a three-hour round trip and I returned to the school without getting caught.

But the next day my mum turned up. The bar staff had squealed on me. Mum was upset that I was obviously not being supervised. I was brought before the headmaster Mr Churchill who gave me six of the best with a bamboo cane, which he kept hung on his wall for all to see. It was banned in the state schools, but not here! It hurt like mad and I didn't think I'd be able to sit down for days. Plus, I wasn't allowed to go fishing. I never confided in my parents again.

The time went slowly for me at Mottrams but soon enough it was time to move to the main school. Me and my friends were all worried, as this was where we were going to mix with the big kids, 13 to 19 year olds. We'd heard about the stories of fags and bullies. But nothing could be worse than what I'd experienced here. Could it?

# CHAPTER 6

# The Cavey

I was in the back of my dad's taxi again, on my way back to Caterham, daydreaming about what fun I'd had working for Bobby and Graham over the holidays and how much money I'd saved up. Then we reached Harestone Valley Road and the painful dense hole was back in my stomach. I was already a whipping boy. If the class was disruptive it was me dragged to the front for a beating. I was called 'Cocker' because of my London accent, they laughed at me because my dad was a taxi driver and their dads were wealthy company directors, ambassadors, army colonels and top professionals. I was the only one in the school with a Cockney accent. They made comments like, 'What's he doing here?' Everybody knew I was there on a charity basis and I felt that their parents were not happy having a Cockney near their children. Or was it because I was a Catholic? The only Catholic in the school.

Even though Mottrams had not been easy, I was sad to leave Mr Bellamy and Mr Johnston who had given me a lot of their time when I needed it. I didn't know men like this in the East End. They'd answer all manner of questions and they seemed to have all the answers. Anyway, onwards and upwards.

Mr S. R. Smith was the headmaster of the main school. He was an ex Lions rugby player who always wore a black cape. Mr John Jones was my house master, and he was backed up by Mr Jim Seymour. There were four houses and I was put into Townsend House. I was placed in a dormitory with more than 30 boys of mixed ages. I was pleased to have my brothers from Foxborough still sleeping next to me as it was reassuring that we were going through this together. I could not get the word 'colditz' out of my head for a long time.

The dorm was full of bunk beds, with a huge bathroom at the end with about 20 sinks. The sixth formers had cubicles along the corridor – they were the prefects who helped manage the smaller children. The prefects also had the power to beat us with a gym shoe, if they could justify it. There was no way I was going to let another kid beat me with a weapon. I wasn't going to be fagged either – which meant having to clean the older boys' shoes or run errands for them. I just wasn't going to put up with that. Not me, no way, I was from the big pond.

The first day in my dorm I was amazed to see four boys doing backward rolls and then lighting their farts with a lighter to make explosions. It was disgusting but they were crying with laughter. Sometimes the boys would make whips out of the towels – they'd wet the tip so it would make a loud crack when it was whipped. I was told if it got your leg it could actually cut you. I wouldn't play that game. Nor would I play the fainting game. This is when they'd do 30 squats then someone would bear hug their tummy and they'd pass out. Oh my God!

Being at the main school meant we got more freedom. We had passes to go into town where there was a Wimpy, which was my comfort food. It wasn't quite Cockney pie, mash and liquor but it brought back all the memories of Grandad, Sheffi and Aldgate and they were happier times. I'd be able to get passes to the Purley Cinema and Croydon's shopping mall, the Whitgift Centre.

Academically I wasn't doing well. I'd carried on just how I'd started, which was bottom of the class. I struggled to keep up and it was an uphill battle just to finish the prep. It wasn't until I reached adulthood that I realised I was dyslexic and most probably had a touch of ADHD (Attention Deficit Hyperactive Disorder) as well, but these things weren't heard of back then.

Nevertheless, the extra-curricular activities were great and we even had a TV in our common room. The grounds in the main school were huge, with a swimming pool, where we could swim with our trunks on. There were squash courts, tennis courts, rugby and hockey pitches. There was even a shooting range up at Beech Hanger, another boarding house on the hill.

There were loads of fantastic after-school clubs: Air Training Corps, the debating society, the Christian club, the model aeroplane club and chess club. I joined them all as it helped my homesickness and eased my pain. When I joined the Air Training Corps, I was given a military uniform and a Lee Enfield bolt action rifle with real bullets to be used at the range at Beech Hanger. I became a crack shot and found something I was good at other than rugby. I spent any spare cash on extra bullets so I could practise. I wanted to join the RAF and thought that if I was a good shot, I'd have a better chance of getting in. The club taught me how to march and I had to study for an aviation exam which I found very difficult. My flight sergeant used to help me cheat – I loved him for that – and I became a leading cadet. The night exercises were great fun, with 50 children fighting for the flag, bundling one another as we ran through the woods in the dark.

The debating club taught me to lie, which wasn't crucial for me because I can fight so I tend not to lie. The debating game starts with you being given the argument for and against, and you don't know what side you're going to get. You pick it out of a hat and then you give a convincing argument, even when you don't believe it. That's politics. One day a big debate was taking place in the school hall and there were more than 100 boys, the headmaster and his police guests. The motion was 'Should the police get more powers?' Well, it all sounded a bit one sided to me so, when it was the audience's time for questions, I got up and told them that where I live every wall is emblazoned with the words 'George Davis is innocent', and that's because the police can be corrupt and tell lies. The police can even beat children and there was no way they could deny it because I knew that first hand. So I said I think we should be careful about giving them any more power.

The headmaster nearly choked. His little red face got redder and redder and his eyes bulged at me. I laughed for ages. Of course I'd made a big mistake telling the truth, because the truth hurts. George Davis was a well-known bank robber of Irish descent living in the East End. He'd been found guilty of robbing the London Electricity Board offices in Ilford in 1974 and a year later, based on dubious police evidence, he was imprisoned for 20 years.

Immediately, his supporters launched a blistering campaign to free him, which included digging up Headingley cricket pitch to stop the England vs Australia match in August 1975. One of his supporters – Peter Chappell – was jailed for it. Roger Daltrey of The Who wore a T shirt with 'George Davis is innocent' on the front and Sham 69 sang about it. In 1976 Davis' conviction was overturned and he was released.

I did well in chess club because I'd been taught by my fishing mate's dad in London. Michael's dad was a unionist who taught me to play three moves ahead, bring your opponent into the trap and then checkmate. The posh kids hated that I could beat them at chess.

I was told I was the naughtiest boy the school had ever had and I was beaten to a pulp every day by them all. Mr S. R. Smith would say, 'Mr McQueen you're here again. Touch your toes', and he'd proceed to cane me with the most painful stick of all time. Fuck me did it hurt. It was a much bigger cane than Mr Churchill's. I didn't think I was bad, I was just all boy – smoking, fighting, never bullying, just defending myself or others, mainly victims of the bullies. Nothing had changed. I was still the whipping boy. I had detention after school most days (I was gated for three months ahead), I wasn't allowed off the premises and was given chores as a punishment. I even got two beatings in one day, which I thought was a disgrace.

By this time I was conditioned to take punishment as part of my normal daily life. I'd been sexually tortured in prep school and now I was being physically abused in main school. I didn't feel pain anymore. The teachers bounced chalk board rubbers off my head if they heard talking in class, not because it was me who was chatting, it was just how it was. I was punished in case I did anything. In rugby, the master called me over and then said to the rest of the boys: 'This is what you're going to get if any of you mess around in my class.' Then he began to demonstrate what he called 'bicycle wheels'. He got hold of my short sideburn and started to twist the hairs round and round until I was on my tip toes and the hairs started to pop out of my head. Fuck, the pain was excruciating!

Mr Richmond Pickering was the most frightening looking teacher. He reminded me of Henry VIII, only his beard was bright red and he was much larger. He always wore the black cape and board and looked like he was straight out of a Dickens novel.

When he walked, the cape would flow around him and if anybody got in his way he'd walk straight through them without stopping. After some time I got to know him, and yes he beat me, but I liked him a lot.

Again the beatings were scheduled with appointments, and waiting for the appointment was as painful as the wallops, but it also gave me the opportunity to put on two extra pairs of Y fronts to cushion the blows. I don't think these brutal punishments were intended to be used as daily medicine, I think they were supposed to be deterrents, but I felt it was misused. Especially with me. I was the whipping boy whose daily floggings were intended as a warning to other boys to keep them under control. I was too ashamed to tell my parents what was happening and I felt like they'd given up on me. When I went home in the holidays, I was alone with no adults to guide me. Despite promising to take me to America for sticking with school, when I was 13 I got home to find my dad had gone to America for two weeks with his friend Eddie and left me on my own. What was he thinking? Where was his head?

I was naughty because it released my adrenaline and it eased my pain, but I tried to be a good person. I was very respectful. I was being trained to be a gentleman, and trained to act appropriately and I knew it. I couldn't have been that bad because the masters always asked me to serve the public the truffles and coffee at school shows and concerts. I always turned up for my beatings on time and I was never rude to anybody that I can remember, except once when I woke up with my bed clothes being ripped off me by Mr Jones – the other boys were already up. I had a huge erection poking through my pyjamas and Mr Jones was laughing and pointing at it. I jumped out of bed with all the boys laughing and I shouted, 'If you do that to me again I'll punch you.' Mr Jones melted in shock. It was out of character for me to threaten a master but after Mottrams I swore that if anyone went near my penis again, I'd defend myself. I was still half asleep. I'm sure I paid the price for threatening a master that day.

Apart from the horrific things that I had to endure, there was a lot of fun at school. We were never short of boys to make up a team to play rugby or cricket. The other kids taught me a lot because they came from all over the world and they filled my head with stories of exciting places. This was the privileged part of my education; I learnt far more from the kids than I did from the teachers. I couldn't wait to get travelling.

I spent my spare time volunteering at the mental hospital, St Lawrence's, as part of my Duke of Edinburgh award. St Lawrence's was on Caterham Hill, a half mile walk up a country lane, a walk I must have done a thousand times and sometimes in the dark (which was a great time for me to have a smoke). As well as the hospital, I also went to the hill to play rugby as the school owned rugby pitches there, which we'd use for training as only the most important games were played on the home field. The Catholic church I attended was also nestled on the hill alongside a public recreation ground.

The hospital was intimidating and scary. Built in Victorian times as an asylum for the extremely mentally ill, the patients wore head guards to stop them smashing their heads on the walls. The rooms were padded and the smell was horrendous – urine and faeces. It was upsetting to see humanity in such a state, to me it was a real window to hell. I helped organise the Friday disco. I was usually the disc jockey and more often than not the patients would want the same record played over and over again – they really enjoyed themselves. The staff had to stop them getting too amorous with one another.

Adults at home kept telling me that these were the best days of my life (if only they knew what I was being put through), and I found those words so depressing because if these were the best days how bad was life going to be? Now, looking back, I know they were definitely the worst years of my life. And we wonder why some kids kill themselves. I struggled every day with the lifestyle and the beatings, and the nightmares I was having trying to block the memories of Robinson-Fuller were preventing me from being able to learn. And as I was already at the bottom of the class, this wasn't good.

The boarders were not as academically gifted as the day boys, but they were much stronger. Even the younger boarders who were very small would stand their ground to the very end. Like trained boxers, we boarders would get back up even when it looked impossible, and we would carry on. Boarding school had hardened my heart and my emotions but it wasn't until later on in life that this piece of the puzzle made sense to me.

One day the school was casting for a new show – *Joseph and the Amazing Technicolor Dreamcoat*. I went for a role. The director, head boy Graeme Mew, made me sing along to the piano and then cast me in the small part of Reuben Joseph. I was shocked because at my primary school, St Mary's and St Michael's, when we had to sing Christmas Carols for our parents the teacher said my voice was so bad that I'd put the whole class off, so they made me mime. My poor mum had to sit there and watch me mouth the words. I thought Graeme Mew was going to get himself into trouble with my casting.

I soon became Graeme's assistant, helping with all aspects of getting the show ready – lights, sound, even costumes. The facilities were far better than Toynbee Hall, which is where I'd had my first theatrical experiences. I worked on all aspects of the show and little did I know that Graeme's training was going to come in handy for me later in life.

Sport took away my homesickness. I was wicket keeper in cricket, goalkeeper in hockey and I was playing number eight in rugby and playing for my house and the school. The rugby teacher who had demonstrated bicycle wheels on my sideburns made me the appointed hitman, which meant I had to identify the best player in the opposing team and then hurt him, so he didn't go for the ball anymore. It was get the ball or scare them off the ball, it didn't matter which. It worked because we became champions of the school league but I broke a boy's arm and two boys' collarbones in one season and I'm not proud of that. I was told that a few years earlier, a boy died on the home field after being kicked in the head. Apparently he went off, stood for five minutes then dropped to the floor and died. Once I got sent off for fighting at half time while sucking my oranges. My friend Latham was in charge of the oranges and I always got an extra one.

We were playing all the posh boarding schools in Surrey. After beating Dulwich College and getting back to our dorm in Caterham, I was in bed when I heard someone shout that they'd taken a bag of Dulwich rugby shirts as souvenirs and one was for me, and it was up on the heating pipe. I said I didn't want it.

The next day an appointment was made for the whole rugby team to be caned for stealing the shirts. Now, by this time I was a professional at being caned and while the rugby team was tough, they'd never had this. I got myself prepared by putting on three pairs of underpants, and a big belt (because if he missed, it struck your lower back), and I picked the tenth spot in the queue of 15 for the whipping. I thought the headmaster might be tired by then, but he would get stronger towards the end – a sprint finish. I couldn't tell the boys my tricks because they might catch me.

It went according to plan. One strike hit the belt, and there were five blows on my cushioned pants so it wasn't too bad. Some of the lads who'd never been caned before now knew what I had to put up with. I'd never seen so many watery eyes leaving the headmaster's office. Later that evening the fullback said he'd pulled his pants down to get undressed for bed and saw that every stroke had cut his buttocks. They'd bled and dried but as his pants came off, all the wounds ripped open and there was lots of blood and pain. I felt so guilty for not telling him my trick. He was most probably scarred for life.

Boarders were allowed home one Saturday night every six weeks. As much as I looked forward to it, I knew it was just a torment, because as soon as I got home it was time to return to school, and the homesickness pain. The summer holidays were eight glorious weeks. In those days the summers were the hottest on record. For me it went from one extreme to another – no adult supervision while I ran about London and then being under the tightest scrutiny at school. Bobby always gave me my job back, just like he'd promised, and I was back in Petticoat Lane, my community, and I loved it.

After setting up the stalls I'd take everyone's order for breakfast. I'd go to the Jewish cafe under the stairs at the top of Wentworth Street to get cold egg and tomato rolls for the Jewish boys, then off to Mick's cafe to get my favourite bacon and tin tomato subs. There was always a queue. Mick kept a big bowl of tinned tomatoes in the oven and fresh bacon would be flipped in front of you. He had the best seedy sub rolls from Kossoffs bakery. Thinking about it now, I could just eat one. While I was on my way lots of traders would shout, 'Nicky? You going cafe?' You could see them drooling as they also wanted a Mick special bacon roll.

Maurice and Kalifa had a picture and mirror stall nearby, so if I had to wait for my order I'd chat to them for a while. Benny and Albert would be walking up and down collecting the rent money for the stalls – they rented hundreds of stalls out and they'd get the methos to put them up for the stallholders. In return, they'd let them sleep in the storage yard and give them bottles of meths. Carpool, a Cockney Sikh boy, was also selling pictures and we always had a laugh. Barry would pass with his trolley of brown paper bags with wholesale prices for the traders, shouting, 'Carrier! Carrier!' He never stopped for long in case the market inspector nabbed him, and if he needed to shoot off, he'd change his cry to 'Wet paint! Wet paint!' You never saw people jump out of someone's way so fast. I had all the fun of the fair and at the end of the day Bobby gave me £3. Great!

The punk rocker shop was also there. My mate Tony worked there and he got all the tickets for the concerts. Tony worked for Micky French (RIP) and Margaret the owners, who both had the peroxide blond punk look. There were crowds outside their shop they were all heavily made up, fans of the Sex Pistols, the Damned, The Clash and The Stranglers, they would stand there posing, trying to look cool. Ten days before I was due to return to school in Caterham, on August 27th 1975, the Provisional IRA planted a bomb in the Caterham Arms pub, which was a regular of the Welsh Guards stationed at Caterham Barracks. I watched the news in disbelief to learn that the bomb had been placed under a bench inside the pub and no warning was given. The bomb exploded at 9.20pm injuring 33 civilians and 10 off-duty Welsh Guards, three of whom lost limbs. The blast blew the pub's roof off. It signalled the end of the truce with the British Government and the start of a long bombing campaign. I was now starting to realise how much hatred there was between the religions. I still went to Mass on Sunday rather than sit in school – I would do anything to get a pass out of that place, just to breathe freedom and to smoke a cigarette on the way. It was also a chance to see girls of my own age, and sit near to them in church.

I was so desperate to get out of school I even signed up to go to opera with Mr Jones. A group of 10 of us would go to the London Coliseum and other West End theatres quite regularly. It was a taste of London I could not refuse. We'd wear our Sunday suits and go in the school minibus with Mr Jones driving. In the interval, if you were late getting back to your seat they'd lock you out or, more to the point, they locked the teachers in, which allowed me to have a good drink up at the bar. Of course I loved going to the opera and staggered back every time.

Mr Jones, aka 'The Goose', liked all classical music. He was a pianist and had a harpsichord and a clavichord in his room. They're like miniature pianos but a bit tinny and twangy, and they'd remind me of the pianola at my mum's pub and the fabulous nights we had singing around it. He'd play for me quite regularly while I sat on his bed listening. One Wednesday, I was instructed to run around the hockey pitch with the class after lunch. I had a bit of a cold but I didn't want to go to the matron at the sanatorium, as the last time I'd been there with a cold she kept me there for three days. It was hell being trapped there, isolated from my friends in a separate building that was like a mini hospital with three wards consisting of 10 beds in all, and it stank of disinfectant. The matron was about 70 and I'd put money on it that she'd been military trained. So this time I decided to get under my bed and take a nap. I knew no-one would miss me, as I did this sometimes, using my travel blanket to keep me warm. It was my siesta.

As I walked into my dorm I was confronted by a day boy who was older than me. I'd already been told he'd been selling drugs in the playground, and my brothers had warned me to keep away from him. I didn't know anything about drugs then. It appeared that he was in there looking for things to steal. I asked what he was doing and he got in my face and demanded to know where the safe was. I didn't respond (I actually had no idea if or where there was a safe) as I was speechless from shock. This time he turned aggressive. 'Where's the fucking safe?' he demanded. He was much bigger than me, his eyes were like big red saucers and white foam was all over his mouth and spraying on my face. I remembered what my mother had told me to do if anyone asked for money. 'We haven't got a safe,' I said. He was moving fast. 'Where's Seymour's room?' he spluttered, asking after the master. I knew I was in serious trouble and I pointed to Mr Seymour's room.

My mum had trained me for this, but it wasn't going well. I couldn't move my legs or talk properly, and as tough as I thought I was, I was frozen to the spot. 'You're cavey,' he said to me as he went into the room. Cavey is Latin for 'beware' and is used by public school boys as a term for look out. He was inside the room for what felt like four seconds and he must have had a hammer or tool to get into the safe. When he came out, I was still rooted to the spot. He then said: 'If you say a word, it's you who's going to take the blame' and he shoved something into my side pocket of my blazer and ran. The whole thing lasted around 30 seconds.

I felt in my pocket and pulled out £70. Oh my God! After the blood had returned to my legs, I chased him to give him the money back but he was taller and faster and I lost him. Now I wanted to vomit (how I wished I'd gone to see Matron). I was like a headless chicken and didn't know what to do. The Inner London Education Authority had me under the threat of borstal if I messed this up. I just couldn't think. I ran to the phone box in cloisters and called my friend David in London, as he was as honest as the day was long. I told him what had happened and asked him desperately to help me. Quick as a flash he said he'd get the train right now, meet me on the hillside and post the money back and then no-one will be any wiser. 'Don't worry about the junkie,' he said. 'He'll be apprehended by tonight, because he's fucked up, OK?'

I went straight to the woods to wait, and like the good friend he was, and still is, he came. He took the cash, the smoking gun that was going to frame me, and I went back to my dorm where all hell had broken loose. I was ashamed that I'd been outwitted by this boy. He was good. No way was this his first time, he was too slick. He was the first person I'd ever seen on drugs but I couldn't tell what he was on. My possessions were searched twice – they even exposed the film in my camera to see if the money was inside. Of course they thought it was me, the poor Cockney, Catholic, whipping boy.

I was traumatised, and feeling sick. Mr Seymour was pacing around, panicking. He was only 25 himself but it was his fault for keeping the safe in his room. The junkie was one of his students, and he'd attacked me with full knowledge of the safe. I didn't know about the safe and nor did any of my dorm brothers. It must have been insured but there was no security whatsoever. I felt by keeping a safe in such close proximity to us boys, we were vulnerable to being attacked and that I, and the others, should have been protected from something like this happening. Those were my thoughts, and as much as I wanted to tell Mr Seymour what had happened I knew I would pay just like always, even though I was innocent, and a victim.

Three days later, my friend David told me the following day he was taking time off his after-school job stacking shelves in Sainsburys to post the money back. He realised if it was posted with an East London postcode on the envelope, the school would know I had something to do with the robbery, so he was going to post it from the outskirts of London.

That evening Mr Seymour asked me to accompany him to his TV room, where he used to let us watch *The Sweeney*, but this night I could see the plainclothes police downstairs in the carpark. Remember, I'm trained to spot police, and I knew they were coming up for me. My head felt like it was exploding. I pulled open the door and tried to run but Mr Seymour had placed the school's two biggest rugby players on guard at the door. I rushed through and they tackled me rugby style and my legs went up over my head. I landed on the tip of my shoulder and there was a loud crack as my head hit the concrete floor. This flattened a part of my skull and gave me an injury for life. I was pinned to the floor and dragged back into the room screaming in pain.

I sat in agony as I was interrogated by the police, without being read my rights. I can remember to this day screaming like a crazy person. I was having a total breakdown. I told the truth, and was informed that they'd apprehended the other boy who'd been caught buying clothes and records in Caterham town. Apparently he'd stolen £13,000 and told them about me and they wanted the money that was put in my pocket.

I was taken away in a police car to David's house in the East End and I got the money from David and gave it to Seymour. Then they drove me to my mum's pub, even though she was no longer my legal guardian as that was my dad, and Mr Jones. Mr Seymour went in, told her I was a thief, came out, told me to get out of the police car and they left. I went in and it was the first time I'd seen her for years. She looked at me in disgust and told me to go away and that was when my childhood ended.

I was still concussed, on the street late at night with nowhere to go. I find it hard to believe my mother, or any adult, would do that to a child. My thoughts were suicidal. I waited in the park at Albert Gardens until my dad got back and then I got a beating.

I thought the school would understand that I was the victim, not the culprit, especially after they got the £70 back. But no. Some weeks later I got the message that they didn't want me back. I'd been expelled. I was also told that I had to attend the police station in Caterham. In the meantime my dad had disowned me and would no longer talk to me. He believed my story, but he'd beaten me because I'd let them steal my education from me and he felt he'd wasted all that money on uniforms. Four weeks later my mother accompanied me to the police station for an interview. It was a four-hour return trip and we sat on the train facing each other without saying a word. I was really depressed.

When we arrived at the police station we sat down with a young policeman who told us the school, and the police, were going to prosecute me and I needed to sign a caution if I wanted it all to end today. The policeman said it was not his decision but the order had come from the bigwigs upstairs who had a good relationship with the headmaster. My mum told me to sign because she didn't have time to go to court or police stations as she had a pub to run. The school had already expelled me so she thought there was no point me not signing.

I glanced at the policeman who was shaking his head and mouthing to me not to sign it, and then I realised it was all corrupt. I was a scapegoat. Why would they do this to the victim of a crime? A child? I had absolutely no chance with these people and I should be thankful they didn't put drugs in my pocket. But under pressure from my mum I signed it, and by doing so I allowed these people to crucify me. I felt as though I'd been nailed to a cross and dumped in a sewer. And you can't swim in a sewer with someone else's cross nailed to your back.

I was branded a thief, a safe robber who steals from his friends, his community, the people he eats and sleeps with. This is vile by anybody's standards, but especially by Cockneys. In prison this kind of thief would be seen as the worst.

After this, no local school or place of learning would allow me through their door, especially as Caterham wrote to them with spiteful 'references' about me. So the police and the school board made special provision to keep me at my dad's flat in Albert Gardens with a fortnightly visit from the police. They'd taken away my rights to an education before I'd even sat my O Levels. I hadn't even prepared for the mocks yet. I wished my grandad was still alive as he wouldn't have let this happen to me. But then I remembered all those sentences he'd drummed into me.

The next time Caterham had a sports day that was open to the public I went along, and took a pretty girl I was dating at the time. We walked around the school and I had my head held high. I didn't feel ashamed because I was the innocent party. I could have been suffering with concussion that terrible day – my skull has a dent in it until this day – but who cares? I was the Cockney poor boy, just a whipping tool for the privileged. I was the patsy.

My friends, my so-called brothers, turned their backs on me and that really hurt. The people that did this to me ran for cover because they couldn't look me in the eye. I found out that the junkie boy was reinstated and sat his O Levels, so he received his credentials to go on with his life. His father was important, apparently, one of the old school Caterhamians. I don't know if it's true but I heard he paid all the stolen money back. I thought there was more to this than meets the eye. Boarders are brought up too well to have done something so scummy and this dirties us all. The history is incorrect, the junkie day boy did it. It was not one of us, it was one of the mummy's boys.

The father of Caterham School, Rev John Townsend (1757–1826), was a hero of mine and he must have been turning in his grave. Like me, Rev Townsend was from East London, a Cockney born within earshot of the Bow Bells. Like me, he would have played around the Whitechapel Bell Foundry, which was full of craftsmen known for making the world's finest bells: Big Ben, Bow Bells and the American Liberty Bell (which cracked due to damage sustained while crossing the Atlantic in a storm). The Whitechapel Bell Foundry even made the bell for the opening of the 2012 London Olympics, before casting its last bell in 2017.

Most children know this nursery rhyme from 1744, which comes to mind when you pass the foundry:

> *Oranges and lemons*
> *Say the bells of St Clement's.*
> *You owe me five farthings*
> *Say the bells of St Martin's.*
> *When will you pay me?*
> *Say the bells of Old Bailey.*
> *When I grow rich*
> *Say the bells of Shoreditch.*
> *When will that be?*
> *Say the bells of Stepney.*
> *Oh I do not know*
> *Say the great bells of Bow.*
> *Here comes a candle*
> *To light you to bed.*
> *And here comes a chopper*
> *to chop off your head.*

John Townsend devoted his life to helping the poor and society's outcasts. In 1792, he founded the London Asylum for the Deaf and Dumb, the first deaf school for children of the poor. In 1807, he helped set up the London Female Penitentiary to house and rehabilitate repentant prostitutes, and in 1811 he started a boarding house for working class boys in South London and made it available free of charge. This was later moved to Caterham Valley where it was stolen by the richer families to become the Caterham School of today. When I was there, I was the only Londoner in the whole school. There's a statue of Rev Townsend at Caterham, and so there should be. I can't believe he wasn't knighted.

I played rugby, cricket and hockey for Townsend House, and played proudly with my heart. I attended Christian club (even though I was a Catholic) and I helped out at the mental hospital. Do you think that's the type of child who'd do safe cracking in his spare time? I don't think so.

So yes, I believe Rev Townsend would have been horrified to see how I'd been treated by his school, where sexual torture and physical abuse of small children took place and everyone turned a blind eye. The headmaster, the teachers and the trustees made sure I couldn't stand back up. For some reason they felt the need to keep me buried. They knew exactly what they were doing when they expelled me – they made me their scapegoat. They'd been paid well by the state to give me a good chance in life but they did the opposite. I lost my legal right to an education and my right to see what it's like to have a job – nobody would give me a job with my criminal background. I lost my dreams, my good name, my honour and my reputation. If I'd been a day boy this wouldn't have happened to me, especially if I was from one of the privileged families of Caterham Valley.

On top of everything, by being in boarding school I'd grown apart from my dad. My personality had changed and we found it difficult to relate to each other. Family politics had become something I found difficult to understand as I'd been away too long. Caterham had taught me to bottle up my emotions and I had to reach deep inside to find the will to hang on. I wanted to kill myself. Jump from a building and end this excruciating pain. I wasn't even bothered if I got murdered on the dangerous London streets. It took a lot of soul searching and dark thoughts before I decided I wasn't going to kill myself. I had nothing to worry about as I was already a dead boy walking, with nothing in life and so, nothing to lose. I decided to get some alcohol. I remembered my grandad told me it stops the pain.

# CHAPTER 7

# Bright Lights, Big Dreams

I was 15 years old and although I was living with my dad, I seldom saw him. I had to fend for myself, and find a way to eat and clothe myself. That meant going back to my Cockney ways, back to the gates of the City of London, where they say the streets are paved with gold. Back to Petticoat Lane where I stood in the gutter with a bread tray filled with trinkets for sale. I watched my brothers from Caterham, the friends I'd sat in class with, come to gloat at my misfortune, believing I deserved it as I was a thief and a scumbag. Time passed slowly. I was left with absolutely nothing, just pain. I'd see Chippy my dog when I had dinner with Anne and Joe's family, as they were about the only people who didn't turn their back on me. They'd grown attached to Chippy and could provide for him, so I couldn't take him back.

I'd get stock on credit at Tommy Bird Wholesalers in Commercial Street. I'd pay £3 a dozen for towelling men's socks, tea towels and ladies briefs, then I'd go on the knock. I'd knock on all the doors in the area selling three items for £1. People were really friendly and I'd take money at every door. I had other lines too, and when I'd made £15 profit I'd go home to my empty flat.

The weekends were different; the street markets were buzzing and it was a time when cash was king. There was no such thing as credit cards on our streets. One day I cut my school trunk in half and made two big trays. It hurt me to do that because I knew I'd never use the trunk again for the purpose it was made. Then I was on the number 15 bus and off to Petticoat Lane. Once there I loaded the trays with the stock and stood in the middle of Middlesex Street. I didn't have a stall or a licence – I was too young to get one. When the market inspector or police came along I'd run and hide behind a stall. If I got caught by the police I'd be charged with obstructing the Queen's highway or selling without a licence, or both. I had a good little business – bar the fact I spent a lot of time in court getting fined – as the office girls who filled the street in their lunch breaks from noon to 2pm wanted all my bargains. I'd sell out then get back off to Tommy Bird, who was always puffing on a cigar, and pay my bill.

Next door was Sami and Salam, where Sami would sit spooning instant coffee directly into his mouth from the jar. Reuben and Emil were Tip Top Wholesale and they were always willing to give me credit. I'd pay my credit accounts off then get more gear and get back on the bus home to deliver my orders around the houses, then home to my flat.

I lived at the top of a Georgian house in Albert Gardens (formerly Albert Square, just like in *EastEnders*). There's a beautiful park in the middle of the square. The park keeper was deaf and didn't speak and took no nonsense from drunks or naughty kids. He kept the park spotless and safe for everyone to use, unlike how it is today. Flowers popped up everywhere, it was always pretty and colourful. I knew everyone in the square because I was always knocking on doors selling things. Looking back now I'm sure some people just bought from me because I was a child and trying to earn some money, plus I had the gift of the gab. I'd use all the chat from the market. 'I'm not doing this to make money, I'm doing this to make friends,' I'd tell them as they opened their doors. 'Honest, it's not stolen, it's just not been paid for yet.'

The world loves a bargain, a smile and a laugh. I was surviving, even though I knew my life was ruined as far as most people were concerned. I had to convince myself it had just changed direction, just as long as I could stay out of trouble. I'd heard stories of kids starting as tea boys and after a lifetime of work they ended up running the company, and I kept that thought close to me, but it was difficult as I couldn't even get a job as a cleaner. My fifteenth year seemed to last forever.

I had a good idea for the Sunday market at Petticoat Lane. I wheeled Old Joe's barrow down Wentworth Street (Old Joe used it to move his goods from his car to his stall and when he was finished I could use it). Then I set it up like it was a real stall. My mate XL Tel (Extra Large Terry) was my partner. He was also 15.

We set the stall up on the pavement, opposite Jack, bold as brass as if we were allowed to be there. We sold socks, pants, ladies knickers, boxer shorts, all kinds of hosiery and even cigarette lighters. We sold anything the other stalls didn't sell. We couldn't afford to have any complaints from the other stall holders because we weren't supposed to be there, and when the toby – the market inspector – came along, I'd give him £5, and he'd nod and take it.

What a result. It would cost £20,000 to buy a stall and we had one for free! It was a cash machine, outside the public toilet and next to the chicken slaughterhouse, which stank. 'Where there's muck there's money,' Terry would say. We had a great time. The customers varied from grandmas to young girls, Nigerians and Ghanaians with empty suitcases that they'd fill up to take home and re-sell. This is where I first met Paula. Paula bought half a dozen pairs of our best knickers, cotton gusset of course. I'd become an expert in knickers by then. I asked her if she'd like them delivered after 8pm. 'Dream on,' she said. Some of the stall holders knew Paula and you couldn't miss her, she was slim with long braids down to her waist. She looked exotic.

Life's what you make it and this was our stall every Sunday. We loved the hustle and bustle of market life, and being cheeky chaps with our funny oneliners: 'It's cheap enough to throw at the cat to make the baby laugh.' I could earn a week's wages in one day, but more than that I was mixing with the salt of the earth, like Joe and the other people of Petticoat Lane.

I was drinking a lot though, to numb my pain. I was under age but I was spending my money in the pubs and clubs and getting drunk as often as I could. It was mostly great fun but it was tinged with sorrow. I blamed Caterham for throwing me into the gutter. I couldn't get the cross off my back, and it got heavy at times. I'd pass the West End theatres I used to frequent when I watched the opera and the like, and think of my housemasters that did this to me. I turned my back on God. There can't be a God if this can happen to an innocent child.

By the time I was 16 I was drinking more and raising hell but thankfully that junkie at Caterham had turned me off drugs so that was a positive. The East End was alive and kicking with people coming from all over to drink in our pubs and party. It was great.

The Black Boy pub in Stepney Green with Barry as the landlord was my spot. I was in there all the time, that's if I wasn't in The Hackney Cab, The White Hart, The Globe, Tipples or one of the other disco bars. It was better than Shoreditch is today. You had to push people out of the way to get into the pub, and push your way to the bar and, with music thumping and young people dancing and talking, it was just one big buzz. There were up-and-coming Glam Rock stars everywhere. Then it was off to Hackney dog track for Cherry's disco. It was a great experience living in East London in the '70s, as long as you could avoid getting hurt in pub battles. The fights would more often than not end with glasses being used as weapons – that was an ugly business.

I met a man called Steve McGuinness in Petticoat Lane, while I was demonstrating the Click-o-matic clothes brush. I'd found a warehouse that was full of these brushes. I'd paid 38p each and I'd sit on a milk crate in the middle of the market and cover myself in cotton wool. I'd wear brown corduroy trousers as they'd show up the fluff more effectively. When I was covered, I'd use all the same jokes and street theatre techniques to show how good the brush was for removing the fluff. 'Give me one pound a brush,' I'd yell and I'd sell at least 10 every time, but the supply was coming to an end. Steve McGuinness told me he had a job for me selling his stock, of which there was an endless supply. Steve owned a massive wholesale warehouse called Stretch Deal, and let me have as much credit as I wanted. He was such a kind generous man and he really looked after me – he even gave me the goods on a sale-or-return basis.

It wasn't long before the sewer washed me up to Soho to sell stuff – jewellery, love beads, anything – in the week days. It was busy there, full of tourists even at night and there was always money to be made. Soho in the 1970s was the armpit of London. It was the red light district of London's West End, full of prostitutes, pimps and sex predators. It was a dangerous place, especially for a child. I knew I wasn't going to survive this place being an angel so I had to change for the worse. Violence doesn't solve anything, so I'd been taught, but in Soho acting violent solved everything. You get your way and you stay safe – if they think you're dangerous you get left alone .

Being able to access a variety of goods from Steve meant I was able to sell so much, and I'd work until it started to get dark. I was earning more than I'd ever earned and it was my first taste of good money. I was only 16 and listening to the stories of the people of Soho, I soon realised that I wasn't really so bad off. I developed empathy for them, but also perspective and it helped me get over sadness and feelings of being hard done by. Some people really do have bad luck. I decided my glass was half full.

Soho and Piccadilly attracted waifs and strays from all over the country, and behind the dazzling lights and shiny neon signs, it was a sad place. Runaway children who'd been abused at home now displaying signs of mental illness; boys selling themselves to men in the toilets of Piccadilly Underground Station. I was too frightened to go down there to get a tube, let alone use the toilet. Staying in the public eye was the only way to stay safe. I stayed away from the fruit machine shops as they were full of sex predators. I only used buses. I'd hang out in Berwick Street Market because I knew the traders there – some were from the markets that I'd worked at before. Herbie the stall boy, the Scott brothers, Eddie Sweets, Ronnie Flowers and Lance, Jason, Martin and others. I knew I was safe there. I learnt a lot about humanity in Soho. I learnt that all people have a value and, as tough as it seems, you must hang on for tomorrow or maybe the day after tomorrow but life can turn on a sixpence, and it does.

As I've said before, the secret of flypitching is to make your customer laugh – then they'll buy even if they didn't want to. You need to entertain them to build up a crowd. It's street theatre, black market sales. It's not a criminal offence, it's a misdemeanour. But what fun. The money was very good in the summer and Christmas periods. I could earn most people's weekly wage in a day. The best flypitchers taught me the ropes and one of those was Micky the Waff. He wore white trousers and a Hawaiian shirt, had a big head of blond curly hair and was always chasing the girls. I had such a laugh with him. When pretty girls went by, he'd say: 'You're the best I've seen all day and I've been looking. What are you doing tonight?' Then he'd ask for their phone number. He spent so much time chatting up girls we lost out on making money.

Lenny Horse Blanket always knew where to go to work. Erith, Dartford, unusual spots in London, and never without a good product. Davey was always suited and booted, a smart man known as a money-getter. The characters were wild and varied, they were the gentlemen of the streets and markets. Dave used to tell me, 'No harm being a fool. It's when you don't know you're a fool, you're going to get yourself into trouble.' In other words 'know yourself'. Street philosophy, you can't beat it. When things are rough, some would say, 'When the soles of your shoes wear out, you're on your feet once again.' I never stopped laughing and it's the best tonic, a good laugh. That's the cheeky Cockney chap, full of wit at the most trying of times. 'We're not here to make money, we're here to make friends.' These flypitchers would just reel it off, creating laughter and fun everywhere and, on reflection, I wouldn't have missed it for the world. When I think about it, I just smile. We had a special skill pulling the crowd from nowhere – it's like a magic money maker.

I didn't have the paperwork to prove I was educated as I hadn't got any qualifications. So I'd have to prove it another way, somehow, someday. I realised that Caterham had done a good job on teaching me how to behave correctly and how to learn things for myself. However, word had spread around the pubs of the East End and everyone knew what had happened to me, and no-one believed my innocence. They all thought I was a safe robber, a thief, a low life and there was nothing I could do about it. I was an outcast, someone who couldn't be trusted, and I stopped being invited to a lot of places. It must have been the biggest lie Caterham ever told. Or do they have a graveyard full of skeletons? Hitler once said the bigger the lie the more people are likely to believe it. Some say lies are for fools, but I honestly thought – in fact I knew – I would prove them all wrong one day. They say the truth always comes out in the wash.

In a perfect world I should have still been in school but as we know the world is far from perfect. In fact, I didn't have it too bad. I had money in my pocket, freedom, a zest for life and a party that never stopped. House parties everywhere, party, party and more drink – it was just a great time.

Sometimes I'd go up to Soho to see John Pierre, who ran the club Le Kilt in Greek Street. I'd often go on Sundays as you couldn't get a drink after 10.30pm on Sundays in the East End (whereas there were more than 200 illegal nightclubs in the West End). I still felt the need to stay drunk so I'd go off to Le Kilt where John Pierre had all the drinks under the bar and you could party all night. There were lots of other clubs, such as VIP, Mazurka and Candy Box. I was welcome, even though I was under age. Everyone there knew me including the people on the door. If I encountered any problems they'd stick up for me.

Now at this point, my life took a different direction. I'd been out in the clubs most nights, from the East End to the West End, drunk, and having a whale of a time with my best friend, a fellow EastEnder. We went everywhere watching each other's backs. One day his family rang me with some bad news. My friend had walked into a nightclub in Regent Street, one we'd frequented many times together, but this time he was alone. A Rastafarian man had thrown his arm over my friend's shoulder from behind and stabbed him in the stomach with a carving knife. He then twisted the knife, opening him up from one side to the other. Guns were also discharged as the chaos enfolded. His family told me he was in hospital on a ventilator, and it looked like he'd survive, but I couldn't go and see him because he was being guarded by armed police. It was attempted murder. I was very lucky that I wasn't with him. I was truly shocked. All I could think of was Fagin in the film *Oliver!*, telling his young charges, 'Boys we are moving.'

I was given the news on a Saturday and that same day I bought a ticket for California, which left on the Monday. I'd been saving money for a trip to California for ages. I liked the look of it on TV: I was a *Rockford Files* fan and dreamed of living on the beach. I just wanted to see it with my own eyes and after my dad broke his promise to take me to America I decided to save up and make the trip on my own. I had planned to go in a few months but my friend's attack made me bring it forward. That Sunday, I was working down Petticoat Lane with XL Tel and I explained that I wouldn't be around for a while. I also happened to see Paula and we got chatting. I'd been thinking about her a lot, even though she was in her twenties and I was 17. l asked her how she'd got on

with the underwear I'd sold her, but she went shy and told me she
didn't want to talk about that. I asked her what she did for a living
and she told me she was the manager of an employment agency.
I couldn't believe my ears – she was a really nice girl with a good
job. She told me she could get me a better job but I told her I was
quite happy on my stall. I asked her if she'd like to come for a drink.
She said she didn't drink but wouldn't say no to a meal.

I explained that I was going to California on holiday the next
day and I'd see her when I got back. She might not have believed
me but I knew I'd be true to my word. I had to get her out of my
system either way as I couldn't stop thinking about her. We
exchanged numbers.

# CHAPTER 8

# American Sunday Sauce

I had the money and the visa for America, I just had to get my gear packed. My Aunt Linda used to be a croupier and had given me a bunch of phone numbers of her friends in California who were croupiers and bunny girls working for Hugh Hefner's Playboy emporium, and she said they might let me stay with them for free. I was so excited. On Monday morning, I made my way to Heathrow Airport for my direct flight to Los Angeles. I felt really lucky as the plane was nearly empty so I made a bed out of the four middle chairs, laid down on them and managed to get some sleep on the 13-hour flight.

When I got off the plane and into Immigration I was quizzed about why I didn't have a hotel booked. I showed the officer my travellers cheques and said I was going to Disneyland. He nodded and said, 'Welcome to the United States of America.' I felt great. I'd made it! He stamped my passport and I went through security, and then I got to the billboard advertising hotels. You pick up the phone and they come and collect you for free and take you to the hotel, which is what I did. The hotel was in Inglewood and when I settled in I realised it was dodgy, with prostitutes hanging about. I needed some sleep after a long trip so I ignored it.

The next morning I rang some of the numbers Aunt Linda had given me and her friend Janie came to get me. Janie was shocked that I was in a dangerous hotel in a bad part of town by the airport. She took me to her apartment in Hollywood Hills, which is where a lot of the film stars lived. I couldn't believe I was there: my adventure had begun. Janie was really good to me and let me stay with her as it was a lot safer, and she directed me to all the tourist spots. I went with her to her yoga class the next day and Paul Michael Glaser who played Starsky in *Starsky & Hutch* was the instructor. I thought I was seeing things. Yoga wasn't for me, so I sat and watched. Michael was so down to earth and a really nice guy but I had to stop myself from calling him Starsky.

The next day, me and Janie went to Le Dome restaurant and had drinks with Adam Faith who was a singer but I knew him as the star of the TV series *Budgie*: another Brit enjoying the great state of California. I was surprised and shocked at how well-spoken he was. Gone was the Cockney accent he had on the TV.

After a few days Janie dropped me at a stunning house belonging to her friends Charlotte and Mia in Pacific Palisades. It was a multi-million dollar property with a figure-of-eight swimming pool and a guest suite for me. A far cry from Albert Gardens. Charlotte had three sons, Robert, who was my age, and twin boys Tim and Tom who were a bit younger. I had the greatest times with these guys. I even went to school with them, sat in class and nobody seemed to care. It was a relaxed system that seemed to welcome visitors. Nothing like Caterham. I stayed with them for three weeks, we hung out in all the cool places and went surfing regularly. That's when I realised the surfing wars that took place between the valley against the hills – I was with the hills – as they argued over who owned the waves. But it was nothing like what was going on in London, it was fine. We even went to Mammoth Mountain for a weekend ski trip and stayed in a luxury condominium on the slopes. I was getting spoilt and it was no surprise that I was falling in love with the American lifestyle, not to mention the sunshine.

I was sad to leave them but I needed to continue my trip. I wanted to see as much of California as I could. I travelled to San Francisco and stayed there a few days seeing the sights: Alcatraz, Fisherman's Wharf and the trams, but it wasn't as much fun as being with Charlotte, Mia and the lads. I was alone. Then I went on to Las Vegas, sleeping overnight on Greyhound buses to save money on accommodation. I was still worried about my mate on the ventilator, and feeling guilty that I was having such a fantastic time.

When I arrived in Las Vegas, Aunt Linda's good friend Kim Krantz, who was a well-known actress and showgirl, was waiting for me. It was so hot. She took me to her beautiful home, with pool, just a stone's throw from the Strip and introduced me to her children, Jeff, Jodie and Kerry, and her husband Danny. Danny was a wise guy from New York, or so Kim told me, and we got on like a house on fire. We never stopped laughing. He was an entertainments manager at the Flamingo Hilton, which is where the mobster Bugsy Siegel, who helped develop the famous Las Vegas Strip, got gunned down. Danny taught me some gambling tricks so I'd have a chance of winning in the casinos. It worked, and I still use his system today.

Danny worked in Las Vegas when the Mob was running things and the corporations kept him on because of his contacts in the entertainment industry. He was retired now but his family had ticket offices in the hotels all over Vegas, for the shows, boxing etc., so he kept his hand in. Danny wasn't just smart, people liked him. He knew all the important people in Las Vegas, and he was known for hosting dinner parties in the Bugsy Siegel suite.

He married Kim in 1957. She had gone to Las Vegas to marry a cowboy but fell in love with Danny instead. Kim was a Minsky's Burlesque showgirl and friends with Bugsy Siegel. The Mob guys said she had great drapes, whatever drapes are, and I loved her – drink in one hand, cigarette in the other and a great husky voice with never-ending stories of interesting people. They even put her picture on a $100 chip at the Riviera Hotel. She appeared in many films, including *Casino*. If they were filming in Vegas, she was in it.

Danny got me free tickets for lots of shows. He said that although I got in for free, in order to get a good booth at the show I needed to tip the maitre d' as I entered the venue. It's something I always did. It brought back memories of my grandad who taught me about tips and how, if I wanted it to impress my guests and gain instant celebrity status when I walked into a restaurant, it was important to pay what he called the tip 'to induce promptness'. You gave a tip when you entered and made it big enough to get the waiter's attention. This method was created by the Victorians but for some reason the meaning has been lost and the Americans now tip at the end of the meal, which is really the service charge.

The promptness tip worked every time. I would fold the money, place it in the centre of my hand, then shake the maitre d's hand, passing the notes to them discreetly. Then the waiter would review the booking and find my name. From then on it was, 'How was your starter Mr McQueen?', 'Can I get you something else Mr McQueen?' and so on. Waiters would hover around my table when everyone else in the place couldn't get a drink. For sure it's worth the extra expense, it works every time. What fun.

Today, millions of people live in Las Vegas but back then Danny and Kim were two of the first 35,000 residents. Kim was also a New Yorker, with stories that would keep you amazed for hours. Things were changing. I was having fun and feeling better about life, especially as I'd heard my mate was off the ventilator. It might have been the new friends I was making, the glorious sun, or just the American people in general, but I was feeling better, that was for sure, better than I'd ever felt. And, I wasn't getting drunk.

Not wanting to outstay my welcome, two weeks after I'd arrived I told Danny and Kim I was going back to California. It was a wrench. I could have stayed in Vegas a lifetime. So I was delighted when Danny persuaded me to stay another week because the following Sunday we were going to Gianni Russo's house for what they called Sunday sauce (but was Sunday lunch to me). Gianni was a famous Hollywood actor who played Carlo Rizzi in *The Godfather*. Carlo marries Vito Corleone's daughter Connie and one of his best scenes is when he fights Connie's brother Sonny, played by James Caan, at the dustbins. He eventually gets garrotted in the car. According to his book, *Hollywood Godfather*, Gianni said he didn't have to act too much as he grew up in Little Italy and had worked for the Mob from being a kid. More importantly, he was instrumental in ensuring the *Godfather* trilogy was made when it ran into trouble with the New York Mafia. It helped that Gianni was best friends with Frank Costello, the real Godfather. As *The Godfather* was the greatest film of all time, I couldn't believe it when he'd told Danny specifically to 'bring the English kid along'.

That Sunday we got ready and arrived at Gianni's at noon. He had a large beautiful house situated in La Paloma Drive, in an upmarket part of Las Vegas. His Bentley sat on the drive, and Kim parked their Lincoln Continental beside it. As we entered, a party was already in full swing, with a house full of Italian Americans with those unmissable New York accents. Women were dotted around chatting to each other, all beautifully dressed as though they'd just returned from Sunday Mass. Kids were running around playing and the men were in the kitchen laughing and joking. I thought there were about 30 adults and a dozen kids – a full house. I was introduced to Gianni and thanked him for the invitation before leaving him to chat with Danny, and heading off to mingle. I didn't want to encroach on their catch up or hang around Gianni looking star struck. I don't like to put myself on anyone.

As I entered the kitchen I noticed these big guys with New York accents all cooking on a large hob, one ring each, poking fun at each other over their cooking abilities, bumping shoulders and pushing each other in a friendly way. The smells were making my mouth water with excitement. Then all these different dishes – garlic prawns, pasta sauce, ravioli – were plated up on saucers and sent around the house to the guests who were eating them informally. One of the guys said to me, 'Can you cook, kid? You look interested.' I shook my head with a smile and he said, 'Real men cook. Don't you forget that.' Then the guy next to him said, 'So why you cooking then?' and they all started laughing and bumping into one another, like a scene from *The Sopranos*. Back then the men in the East End didn't cook – the women did – and I couldn't cook to save my life. The only male cook I knew was the TV chef The Galloping Gourmet, Graham Kerr.

I was given my first saucer of three which I ate slowly. So delicious. The other guys wanted me to taste their dishes and say who was the better chef. I'm not that stupid, and I said they were all fantastic. Honestly, that was the truth. I couldn't fault any of it. I went into the lounge with my plates, found a chair, and a lady brought me a glass of red wine. I sat there as the kids ran in and out – it was a real family day, really enjoyable. Gianni came over to me making sure I had everything I needed. He told me this was the typical Italian American Sunday sauce. We then walked towards the dining room and he said, 'Nicky, you sit next to me.' I couldn't believe it. I sat next to him, opposite Danny and Kim, as Gianni sat at the head of the white table that seated 26 people. The kids went into the kids' dining room and the women started to serve a roast beef meal to each of us with all the trimmings, and it was matched with good red wine on the table. A perfect lunch.

The conversation was surreal. They talked about the actress Julie Andrews, who I knew from *The Sound of Music* and *Mary*

*Poppins*, and her brother, who was a pilot stuck south of the border trying to get a visa into the States. Over dinner, they tried to put a plan together to get him across and it brought back my memories of wanting to be a pilot and how I had to put my dream aside due to a lack of qualifications and an incomplete education. Gianni seemed interested in me as it transpired that we had a lot in common – we were both from poor neighbourhoods, and had both sold things on the street. As the wine flowed, I told him about the class system in Britain. How we had working class, middle class and upper class, and you can tell which class people are from straight away, just by the accent. He said they didn't have that in the USA. 'We have the American Dream,' he said, 'No class system here. You can have anything you want if you're prepared to work hard.'

He told me about his life, how he'd started off selling pens on the street corners, then went to work for the US Army in one of their barracks as a demolition builder. His job was to use wheelbarrows to remove rubble from the barracks then dump it in the skips outside the main gate. Every time he went past the guard on the gate, the guard would run a fork through the rubble and say, 'What you stealing today?'

'Nothing,' responded Gianni.

Then he told me he'd worked there for three months and stole 18 wheelbarrows. We really laughed.

This day changed my life. It made me realise that anything was possible. I wasn't going steal wheelbarrows, I was going to work hard and chase the American Dream. Gianni Russo had inspired me, and rather than believe my life was ruined, I could dream once again. The after-dinner conversation turned to the building of the Renaissance Hotel, which Gianni owned – no problems with the gambling commission, all legal investments.

A few weeks later, at another Sunday sauce, five guys turned up outside Gianni's house and opened fire with automatic weapons, spraying the house completely. The bullets even went in the kids' dining room. Everyone dived to the floor, women and children included. Luckily no-one was hurt,  and lucky that it wasn't the day me, Danny and Kim were there. Luck doesn't knock on your door, you need to look for luck – it's out there but you need to stay lucky in this life.

The reason for the unwelcome visit was because mobster Anthony 'Tony the Ant' Spilotro wanted the souvenir concessions at the Renaissance Hotel. He'd approached Gianni, as he couldn't put his name to it due to his relationship with some of the outfit, not to mention his psychotic behaviour around Las Vegas – it's really not that big a place to behave badly. However, Gianni had said no. Spilotro wasn't even allowed in the hotels, let alone do business in them. In *Casino*, Joe Pesci's character of Nicky Santoro is based on Spilotro, with Robert De Niro's character based on his mate Frank 'Lefty' Rosenthal, the gambling genius.

Anthony Spilotro's luck had run out. What happened to him and his brother was portrayed realistically in *Casino*, when they were stripped to their underwear by their friends, baseball batted into a grave alive and then buried. What a grisly end. Three days later the police were given the location of their grave, and the message was sent.

Gianni was not only in *The Godfather,* he also went on to appear in *The Godfather Part II, Seabiscuit* and more than 40 Hollywood films. He became a producer and a singer – trained and styled by Frank Sinatra himself. His childhood was similar to mine in that it was less than perfect, but he achieved so much. He proved to me you can make it if you go for it and work hard. My eyes were opened wide.

On the plane back to London, I promised myself that I would stay out of trouble, work my socks off and come back to America with enough money to make a new start. Gianni had given me a new strength. I knew I should really be still in school, but that wasn't going to happen so work I must.

I was 17, back at my stall in Petticoat Lane and the markets of London, having fun and with everything to play for. True to my word, I contacted Paula and we started dating and enjoying each other's company. She introduced me to her eight-month-old daughter Carly and explained that she'd escaped a violent relationship. It wasn't long before things started to get serious between us. I felt as though I'd been struck by lightning. We belonged together and I couldn't imagine life without her.

I took a stall in Berwick Street in Soho as I knew the community there. I set up an underwear stall selling lingerie, dressing gowns, socks, all cut price compared to the expensive West End stores. I did very well. A lot of the ladies of the night would buy from me. They spent a lot of money with me – Paula made sure I didn't offer a delivery service. On occasion I'd see old school friends who were now working for the Metropolitan Police, and we'd chat about our days as boarders. Many of my old friends had joined the police force.

Paula and I moved into a flat in Hoxton. I loved her, and her baby. Paula was shy but tough and intelligent. I had to tread carefully and treat her very respectfully. Life was good. I had some problems with my family, and it didn't help that Paula was six years older than me, a mother and mixed race. There weren't many mixed couples in those days and I'd get the odd racial slur from both sides. Black friends of mine would say she was betraying black people being with me, and white friends would ask what I was doing with her. All behind our backs of course, but I got to hear as the East End is a small place. I didn't care and still don't. Back then there was more racism, classism and ignorance than now. Paula and I are both Cockneys who love and enjoy each other's company, and we both enjoy pie and mash. We just have different skin colour. If someone doesn't want the green sauce on their meal, it means you need to look a bit closer at them.

Life was good for a bit but I was drinking again and one day, when I was 20, Paula and I had a big row and she threw me out of the flat with three black bags of clothes. I didn't have anywhere to go and I didn't want to tell my parents because I didn't want to hear them say, 'I told you so.' So I took my clothes to a friend's house, put them in his spare room and we went out drinking. I was running with the boys, trying to sort out my next move but after three days my friend told me to come and get my clothes as they were too smelly and his wife was going crazy. I was put out – I didn't smell! But when I went to get them, the stink hit me. Paula had given me a bag of rubbish with my two bags of clothes. I wasn't pleased but I did my best to repair the relationship – I sent her flowers and put money through the letter box every Friday for the baby.

# CHAPTER 9

# The Gold Rush

I used to have fun running the stall, no two days were ever the same, but one day it started to rain and it kept on raining for six weeks. I didn't think it was ever going to stop. The damage to my stock, and the wear and tear on my body was starting to get me down. Then I heard of a gold rush. My mate Dave, who lived in Sydney, sent me messages that the streets there were paved with gold. He was selling on the street and earning a fortune, and he didn't even have to mention the beaches and glorious sunshine. Paula was still working at the employment agency but as we were no longer a couple, and I had nowhere to live, I decided to seek my fortune Down Under.

When I got to Australia, Dave's brother-in-law Steve, and his wife, put me up. They lived in a Sydney suburb called Neutral Bay and Steve had a big store in Pitt Street, an indoor market in the city. I worked there to start with, then after a few weeks, at night, I worked as an auctioneer in Kings Cross, using the same old jokes and selling the same old stock. I worked with Paul and Jamie who were also from London, and they showed me around Sydney. Kings Cross was the same as Soho with the lights, prostitutes, tourists and nightclubs. After work we'd go to the Texas Tavern, and the Aircrew club bar upstairs.

I went from strength to strength money wise, which was a good job because my phone bills to Paula were expensive. I'd work the Paddy markets in Flemington on Sundays, and the Haymarket in Sydney during week days – it was just like Petticoat Lane. I worked all the hours I could, using the same style of selling to entertain the customers so that even if they didn't want what I was selling, they'd still buy it because I'd made them laugh. They called it 'spruiking' in Australia – someone who holds forth in public and gives a good spiel. To me, it was theatre and when it was time, I just switched into action. I was on stage.

It didn't take long to leave Steve and his wife's house and I lived in a suburb called Woollahra, with my house mate Malcolm. It was a nice place, and the prime minister also lived there. My grandad had a lot to answer for when he said I should go first class or not at all, but even though it was a higher standard of living, it was still cheaper than London. I sent money home to Paula and the baby. We'd made up on the phone and she was shocked that I'd left London. I explained that if I was going to be homeless I might as well be homeless in sunny Australia. But I was far from homeless – I had a beautiful home, new friends, endless work, lots of money and glorious sunshine. The only thing missing were my loves – Paula and Carly. I could also see a lot of potential here, especially if I was prepared to work hard. Jamie, Paul and I were waiting for the Commonwealth Games to start in Brisbane. A million people would be at the Games, with lots of money to spend, and we had a plan. I was chasing the American Dream, but in Australia.

I wanted to bring Paula and Carly over from London once I had enough money from the project that Jamie, Paul and I were planning. Paula had finally forgiven me and I was missing my little family terribly. It reminded me of the emotional torment I'd endured at school, which I'd been trained to bottle up. I knew it had damaged me due to my nightmares and excessive drinking, but it had also made me strong.

Jamie, Paul and I had printed our own version of the Commonwealth Games programme and had 'Souvenir' printed on the front of it, to get around the copyright. The real programme had 'Official' on it and was 10 Aussie dollars. We were not trying to copy their programme, this was our version.

We got the timetable from the newspaper, and all the articles were copied from library books. Then we stuck the lot in a scrapbook, took it to a printer and got our booklet printed – it cost 10 cents a copy. We sold each one for $2. We rented an American motorhome, a small Winnebago, loaded it up and off we went to the Gold Coast, along with an Irish guy called Danny, who Paul and Jamie had employed to help us. Was Brisbane going to be the city paved with gold? It took us two days to get there, and the motorhome was full to the brim with stock, with just enough room to sleep. I got the bed above the cab, it was really comfortable.

We got to the Queen Elizabeth II Stadium in a suburb of Brisbane called Nathan, and went to work. The Games started on September 30th 1982, with 46 nations taking part, and a 13 metre mechanical kangaroo called Matilda as the star of the opening ceremony. We'd brought white coats to make us look official. I was stationed at the coach arrivals, Jamie the car park and Paul the train station. Danny would ferry the stock to our positions because it was difficult to park the motorhome close to the venue.

I was nearly killed in the rush! I couldn't hand them out quick enough. I was surrounded with customers 10 to 15 deep, all waving $2 bills at me. It was a sell-out. Like pennies from heaven. Better than my wildest dreams. The other boys had the same result and we made a frantic phone call to the printer in Sydney to start the presses, as we needed as many programmes as they could supply. We couldn't take the money fast enough.

We were already in profit by the end of the opening ceremony, and we were now making huge profits at the event stages – cycling, swimming events etc,. It was to last another 10 days and I knew I was going to earn enough money to bring Paula and Carly over, and get a lovely home. I was so excited, and so were the rest of the guys. We were doing better than we'd ever imagined. I rang Paula that evening and told her of my success, that we sold nearly the 10-day supply of programmes in one day and only had a few thousand left. I'd been phoning Paula regularly, keeping her updated with what I was doing.

Then the inevitable happened. The Australian Federal Police (AFP) arrived – they're like FBI. They crept up on us in plain clothes, each of them sucking lollies, pulled out their guns and arrested us at gunpoint. We were handcuffed for trading within 5km of the Games unlicensed, which was a new law brought in days before the event, and of which we had no knowledge. We wouldn't have done it if we'd known.

They took us to the police station and beat us up until we gave them the information they wanted. Where was the van? Where did we live? Where were our passports? Once they had all the information, and all our programmes, they told us they thought we were linked to the Mafia. That's why they were so heavy handed, and that's why it was the AFP dealing with us and not the local police. I told them the Australian Mafia were into gambling and prostitution not selling programmes. They were not amused.

Handcuffed, we were taken to the Brisbane Watch House, which is a prison attached to the police station. Watch houses are common in Australia and this was the biggest in Queensland. I hadn't planned for this and I was sweating, not just from the sunburn I'd received after standing outside for two days in extreme heat, but from the feeling I was in real big trouble. The police really didn't like us.

The watch house was in the middle of Brisbane, a skyscraper with no windows, just a huge metal gate on the ground for the vans to deliver prisoners. We were put into a cage with loads of others, it was big enough to hold about 30 people. Our handcuffs were removed as we went in, and this was where we waited to get issued a cell. The admission desk was manned by six women. There must have been 100 TV screens above it on the wall, watching every corner of every cell in the building, including the toilets. This was why it was called a watch house.

After a few hours spending time with a lot of unsavoury characters in a giant cage, we were taken into the lift and up to the cells. It must have been about the eighth floor and we were taken to the cells in twos. Luckily for us we were opposite each other and as it was cagelike on the front of the cell, we could all talk to each other. There were no windows but it was still hot. I couldn't sit down. I walked round and round the tiny cell until I got on the other's nerves. The police had already informed us that, unlike in Great Britain, we were guilty until we proved our innocence – they didn't like Brits coming there and taking the piss. Apparently we sent their ancestors there for stealing loaves of bread (no mention of the murderers and rapists). Now it was payback. I froze. We were in trouble and could expect five years imprisonment.

By now we were starving but under Aussie law they didn't have to feed us in police custody. At 6pm, the Salvation Army came with soup – 'helping the heathen'. Thank God for the East End. A trolley was pushed down the aisle between the rows of cells, with a squeaky wheel, serving the prisoners soup and a bread roll. If you dropped the roll you'd have cracked the floor, that's how stale and hard the bread was. The soup looked like water with bits in, so I asked the guy serving it what soup it was. 'Soup, soup matey,' he replied.

Someone with an Australian accent shouted from another cell: 'You need to float the roll in the soup matey, so you can eat it.' It was the worst meal of my life, but I ate it. All I could think of was the convict Papillon (real name Henri Charrière) in the film of the same name saying, 'Eat everything they give you. You need as much strength as possible.' Charrière (1906–1973) was a French criminal wrongly convicted of murder and sentenced to a life of hard labour at Bagne de Cayenne, the penal colony of Cayenne in French Guiana known as Devil's Island. He escaped in March 1944, along with four others.

We were upset with our treatment as we were only market traders, not real criminals, and we got arrested with carrier bags of hard-earned money. Alright, maybe not hard earned. We had a huge amount of cash between us.

After a steward's inquiry, we were given a big wad of our cash back and we started to order takeaways. It was the best-tasting Big Mac I've ever had in my life. This was the first time I'd ever really been hungry. We were lucky to be two in the cell – other cells were full of Aborigines, and it was standing-room only for them. There was definitely a hint of racism about it. The Aborigines drove me crazy with their continual singing: 'All we are saying is give us our land.' They'd been arrested for demonstrating at the Games, demanding their land rights, and squashed into these cells. They were very placid considering how badly they were treated. It was a shame to see it.

We stayed in the watch house for three days while the police raided our addresses in Sydney and recovered our passports. Then they sent word that we'd be held in prison until our court date, which was after the Games had finished. We were going to be sent to HM Prison Brisbane, which was a category A prison known as Boggo Road Gaol. This was going to be an experience. Boggo Road Gaol was the last remaining penal prison – once the hanging prison – full of ghosts of the executed and renowned for the abuse to the inmates. It was the most feared prison in Queensland. My schoolmasters had always said I'd end up in prison, and they were right.

# CHAPTER 10

# Boggo Road Gaol

Boggo Road Gaol opened in 1883 and was thought to be named after the boggy quagmire on which it was built. The biggest and most notorious prison in Queensland, known for its poor conditions and brutality, its stark red brick walls dominated the Brisbane skyline. We went through the huge gates and weren't let out of the prison van until the gates were firmly closed behind us. We were marched into admissions, stripped searched, disinfected, then given uniforms and a pair of sandals. You only got boots if you'd been there a while and were trusted with a job. The bluey grey cotton clothes were a bit big for me and I must have looked as terrible in them as the other three did. Paul was making jokes but I felt like Papillon again, as though I was in some sort of bad film. I think I was still in shock.

Off we were marched to our single cells and given a book of the rules that also had a list of punishments and consequences for breaking the rules. For instance, if you got caught exercising in your cell, the punishment would be either three days bread and water in solitary confinement – otherwise known as the black hole – or seven days solitary with food instead. Your choice.

My cell was on the second floor and empty apart from the bed which was metal framed and as old as the prison. I had to make it up but I didn't bother with hospital corners. The place stank of 100 years of sweaty prisoners, and now it was me in that bed, with nothing but a set of rules welcoming me to Boggo Road. The part of the prison I was in was built like a U block, with the bottom of the U fenced off to make the communal yard. Guards were on all the roofs, armed with automatic rifles.

We were the only English prisoners and the guards and the inmates called us the Poms. I was given two explanations for this

– one that it was an acronym of 'prisoners of mother England' but also because we looked like pomegranates after we'd been in the sun. I could tell they didn't like us. The Aussie language was similar to English in many ways – 'tinnie' was a can of beer, 'whinger' was a moaner, 'dinkum' was genuine – but a lot was abbreviated, so it was 'brekky' for breakfast, 'Crimbo' for Christmas, 'ambo' for ambulance and so on. It got on my nerves as I had to work it all out.

The day started at 6am when the door would open. By this time, I'd have already raised the mattress to air it, and folded all the sheets. Then I had to stand to attention outside the cell on the landing so they could take the roll call. I'd step forward and salute when my name was called. What a performance. Paul's cell was opposite mine and I could also see Danny and Jamie – they were not looking happy. On the first morning, when the prison officer did the roll call from the middle of the yard, shouting out all the names in turn, each prisoner took one step forward, stood to attention then made a military salute and shouted 'Here!' Paul stepped forward and did a Benny Hill salute. The prison officers went mental. They ran up the stairs and gave him a kicking as they dragged him down the metal staircase and took him away. I never saw him again that day.

During the day we chatted with the other inmates in the yard and they told us stories of the ghosts that lived in the prison, mostly the executed murderers. They said one ghostly prison officer would appear, talk to the inmates then disappear again. He must have liked the job when he was alive to keep on coming back. I'm not scared of ghosts but these tales didn't help me warm to the place. We could go to our cells any time of day, until 8pm, and then we'd be locked in until 6am the next morning. I could hear the guard (I'm assuming it was the guard as I could hear someone) directly above my cell crunching around all night on the shingle roof. The guard was armed with an automatic rifle – we were told he would shoot to kill if he needed to.

On the second day, Paul saluted correctly, so they obviously hurt him for taking the piss. The heat was unbearable. There were lots of lifers about and we were told by others that a spate of rapes was happening in the toilets. Every time we went to the toilet we all went together. I've never spent as much time around toilets.

A rumour went round that we were bank robbers because four British bank robbers had recently been arrested and were caged somewhere in Queensland. We decided to keep the truth to ourselves – being mistaken for dangerous bank robbers might help us survive this very dangerous place. Everything ended with a beating in this prison – it reminded me of Caterham. The regime was very abusive but I had skills to navigate this kind of environment because I was institutionalised as a kid. I avoided being punished by keeping my head down and not making eye contact with the authorities. However, my mates did on occasion get hit. The prison authorities wanted the prisoners to get fat and lazy, so they would be less of a threat to the guards. The guards looked like gym lovers, all pumped up with steroids, and every meal we had – all four of us would eat together in the dining room that held 100 people – came with half a loaf of cut bread for each person. I was getting fat, and the heat made my cell like a sweatbox. Everywhere we went I felt the eyes of all the real criminals on us. We were the new boys, which made us targets. I hoped I didn't have to defend myself like I did on the hillside, but if I had to, I was ready.

Right in the middle of the yard was a wooden structure with a bamboo roof and a TV underneath, and we'd spend most of our time watching the communal TV and chatting to the other prisoners. They were all smiling and being extremely friendly, but they were trying to find our weaknesses. We were all too shrewd for that. Some even told us they were there for parking tickets – yeah right, in a category A prison? They more than likely killed their mum and dad. The Aborigine prisoners would walk about the yard grabbing tropical bugs and roach-like beetles and put them in their mouths. You could hear the crunch of the bug exploding as they bit into it.

I was not enjoying prison life at all. I'd ended up in a penal colony just like Ikey Solomon from Petticoat Lane. The only difference was I'd paid to get there.

We went to court two weeks later. First we spent an hour with our court-appointed attorney who, after looking at our case, informed us that we were guilty until we could prove our innocence. So he instructed us to plead guilty. He told us to expect the worst – they don't like smartass Poms coming here and breaking the law. We were taken to the dock in the court and sat down to wait. Then the judge came in and we had to stand up. When he got to his chair, I thought he'd sat down but he was still standing. He was tiny. I thought to myself, 'Here we go, big man in a little body – Napoleon syndrome I'm going to prison for life.' But as it turned out he was really lovely. He was a bright man. He thought the programme was well written and great value for money. He recommended we use our literary talents for legal purposes. He sentenced us to time served and instructed the police to give us our money back. Yippie!

We thanked him and then Immigration jumped on us, arresting us for working on non-working visas. Back to the court cells. More interrogation, passport stamped out and we were going to be deported back to Blighty. But, after a few hours Immigration decided to let us leave under our own steam because we had return tickets. So the four of us went to collect our campervan in the prison car park.

Once we were all on board we drove up to the huge prison gates which seemed to take an age to open. Inch by inch, we could see more of the outside world. We were blinded by brilliant sunshine. Paul, who was driving, turned the radio up and I will never forget the sound of Dexy's Midnight Runners singing *Come On Eileen*. As we pulled through the gates to start our trip back to Sydney we were screaming with joy, and singing along, feeling elated.

When we got back to Sydney, I realised I'd had enough of Australia and I missed Paula. It hurt when I had to put down the phone on her after our long chats. It's no fun being alone. So I did what the authorities wanted me to do: I got on the first plane home.

Despite my 'deportation', I've been back to Australia many times since because we Brits get given a new passport number every time we lose a passport, or if one runs out. The rest of the world only seems to track the numbers and most countries issue their citizens with a number for life but we don't. Thank you Britain.

Boggo Road Gaol closed in 1992, due to the terrible abuse of prisoners and the dreadful inhuman way in which they lived. I can vouch for that. In the 1980s prisoners rioted, staged rooftop protests and went on hunger strike to campaign for better living conditions, and eventually they were heard and it was closed. It became a museum with guided tours and history re-enactments, and you could even spend the night there, locked in your haunted cell. Although now temporarily closed, the plan is to reopen it as a permanent tourist attraction. I don't think I'll be rushing to book my tickets.

# CHAPTER 11

# McQueens

I arrived back in Britain to find my mother had moved pubs; she now had the tenancy of The Magpie pub in New Street, Bishopsgate. Built in 1520, it was thought to be the birthplace of Shakespeare's contemporary, the actor Edward Alleyn, who went on to found the College of God's Gift, which is now Dulwich College public school. The Magpie is mentioned in Daniel Defoe's 1722 book *A Journal of the Plague Year,* and in the eighteenth century it was known as a meeting place for Freemasons, and they still met there when my mother took over the licence. It was in an area that was now called Cutlers Gardens, in the heart of the banking district in the City of London. Top marks for my mum. We were now getting on better. She had accepted Paula, even though she was a bit older than me and multi-racial, which unfortunately was a problem for some people then. Paula is multi-racial – her father is black African and her mother is white and Jewish. Paula doesn't like being called mixed race as she maintains there's only one race, the human race. Personality is what's important, regardless of colour or religion. Racism comes from both sides, it doesn't have a colour, it's an illness. I was in love, but more to the point I was being loved like there was no tomorrow, it really empowered me to 'go make one' as we say in the East End. Get out there, work hard and achieve something.

In 1983 I sold my Berwick Street stall as I needed to get out of Soho. It wasn't where I wanted to spend my life. I persuaded Paula to leave her job so we could work together to try and build something for our little family. I took a flower stall in Cutlers Gardens, Bishopsgate, as I'd made contacts in Mum's new pub and heard of the opportunity. It was situated in the covered arcade outside the hairdressers, dry but still cold – the cold is good for the flowers and at least we'd be out of the rain. Working outside can become soul destroying if there's too much rain. I was excited about the future as I rolled my three barrows full of Dutch flowers to my pitch. I'd visited Holland to see how they sold flowers and they had pre-made hand-tied bouquets ready to go. No waiting, no talking, just pick one up and pay. It was a perfect system for busy Londoners, so I used it.

The landlord was Standard Life and I had to pay a large legal bill for the contract, which came with a deed and a map where X marked my pitch. The City is where all the banks are, and all the money. That's why they say it's paved with gold. Bob Cottey and Tony Uphill were the managers and they also provided me with a storeroom, so I could keep everything safe at night.

Paula and I had been studying flowers and plants at home like mad so that we were knowledgeable about our stock. I was absorbing it like a sponge, treating it as though I was back in prep at Caterham, and most of the text was Latin. I knew I was trained to sit for hours and self-learn. Latin didn't scare me. Thanks Mr Bellamy. I soon became an expert on horticulture and my creative talents made the pitch a floral feast for the eyes of the bankers with their deep pockets as they arrived for work. I'd made a big barrow by hand and it was really pretty. A relative of mine worked as a porter at Covent Garden Flower Market and had introduced me to lots of people there to help get me cheap flowers. My mate Steve gave me references so I could get credit accounts – he was now a big wholesaler in the East End selling to all the market boys. My company – McQueens – was off.

At first I started buying mixed parcels of Dutch flowers from the night porters. They'd unload the artic lorries arriving full of stock for the florists – they told me that it was a mixture of good flowers called weeds. I thought they were left over flowers and these were what I would buy, paying £300 instead of £1,000. I could sell them for £2,000, which was cheaper than anyone else. I was told the flowers were a bit older than the fresh ones but nobody would know the difference. (It took me a while to discover that these flowers weren't left over, the porters had just pinched a couple of fresh bunches from every order. When I found that out I stopped buying them.)

I was up at 3am on my buying days and then I'd embark on the most wonderful drive in the world, along the Embankment with all the twinkling lights reflecting onto father Thames, inhaling the early morning air, which is a very different smell to when the traffic arrives. I'd cross over the Thames at Vauxhall Bridge and into the market, park up and walk through the huge plastic double doors that kept it chilled inside. Boom! The smell hit you like a bat to the nose. It was the size of a football stadium with no barriers, just lines on the ground showing which company owned what stock, and it was so busy, it always felt like the middle of the day, even at 4am. I'd see the night porter and get my flowers and then walk around the market ordering more flowers and whatever else I needed. I'd then find my day porter by shouting 'Ian!' Then the next guy would shout 'Ian!' and so on until Ian would be in front of me. I'd present him with my list of companies, as well as my van keys. He'd then take his barrow around picking up my stock shouting 'McQueens!' Only porters were allowed to use barrows – everyone else had to carry what they could. Union rules. When he finished he would meet me at the cafe and give me the van keys back. The van would be fully loaded and ready for the trip back to the City.

Back to Cutlers Gardens and time to set up the show, cut and stand the flowers in water, then sit back and wait for the customers. This was a good time for me to read up on the plants because I was getting orders for hanging baskets, window boxes and all sorts.

The management at Cutlers Gardens had given me a licence with a map showing an X marking the spot where I was allowed to trade, but at weekends Cutlers Gardens was closed so I put an extra X on the back wall of Cutlers Gardens, which was in Petticoat Lane. The extra X was about four stalls width, so on Sundays Paula and I worked that whole corner. We sold flowers, plants and we also had hardboard models of life-size famous people and the royal family that my childhood friend Graham had given me. The tourists would stand next to the hardboard models and I would snap them with an instant Polaroid camera. The photos looked so realistic that I had lines of people waiting. I also had four photographers working for me: Timmy, Mason, Chrissy and Paula.

One day as I was working, four boys from Caterham gave me a walk by. One of them said, 'Alright' but they didn't stop, even though I'd sat next to one of them in class for four years. They did a slow walk by and just looked at me – looked down on me. They didn't say anything else but you know the look. They made me so upset. I only look down on someone when I'm helping them up.

It wasn't long before the City of London Police asked to see my licence. I duly showed it them, and the map with my X, and the extra X, and they told the market inspectors I was on private property and that I had permission to be there. I was raking the money in once again.

After a while I noticed that the florists were driving old vans and the tropical plant firms were driving Range Rovers. Had I found a clue? I decided to investigate further. I went to Standard Life, the landlord, and told them I was unhappy that I'd paid my rent on time but was not invited to join the tenants association. After all, I was a tenant so it didn't seem fair. They arranged for me to join so I went to the next tenants association meeting, wearing my only suit, and had coffee with the other tenants. These were the big merchant banks: Shearson Lehman Brothers, Bache Securities, Bear Stearns and others. As we were chatting I told them the plant companies they were using were taking liberties with their charges, and I could do the job half price. They were hiring soil and the fibreglass containers, which would last a 100 years. I suggested they buy the containers and soil from me and then just hire the plants. Over three years, they'd save a fortune.

They all bought the idea and before long I was hiring out thousands of office plants. The profit I made selling the soil and pot bought the plant, and now I was getting the rent for the plants that they'd bought anyway. Bobby was right – you don't need money, just a good idea and hard work. I rolled out the scheme to the rest of the City. I put a radio phone on the stall with Paula as the telephonist and she was great at telesales. I had to hire extra men to help deliver the plants to the banks. Banks all over London wanted my deal. I advertised in the Yellow Pages and called myself a florist. People had no idea we were working from a stall in Cutlers Gardens.

It wasn't long before I was making enough profit to pay a mortgage, so I purchased a shop in Shoreditch on Great Eastern

Street. McQueens was growing fast and by the end of year one I had a workshop, three outlets, four florists, three vans and six interior landscapers. We had five 5ft arrangements for Shearson Lehman Brothers every Monday morning, and hundreds of other orders.

I would only employ the best florists to fulfil my orders and Paula was also learning fast. I bought the best Sia Parlane vases for the shop so the display shelves looked beautiful. The interior landscaping and flower display contracts were paying all the bills and I was driving a new Daimler. It wasn't just the corporate business that was booming, we were in all the Barclays high street banks as well. My staff had access to go behind the counters, where all the money was kept, as we needed to get water for the plants. It's ironic that I had a fake criminal record for robbing safes. We put up and decorated Christmas trees in most of the banks and large insurance companies throughout the City.

Our flowers were also shoots for fashion magazines. We supplied flowers to *Vanity Fair* magazine but after a few months they stopped paying and said we should supply them for free due to the publicity we were getting. I said no. No payment, no flowers. For me it was a very clear business model. I paid for the flowers so everybody had to pay for the system to work (even though at Christmas I sent a bouquet to every receptionist and purchase manager). *Vanity Fair* stopped using us for six weeks and then came back full of apologies and decided to pay us. I'm sure they thought I grew flowers somewhere for free.

McQueens florist was a fast-growing company gaining new accounts daily. All our landscapers and florists wore uniforms – blue overalls with 'McQueens' written on the back in white. We rented out the best plants money could buy and we only sold Dutch flowers. I was buying flowers from Charlie Gardener, who was the first person at Covent Garden Flower Market to import Dutch flowers, which were bigger and better than anybody else's. More expensive, but you get what you pay for. There was even a documentary about McQueens, made by film maker (now film critic and journalist) John Marriott, with his unmistakable voice narrating how a corporate florist works, and why it differs from a local florist.

One day, I drove my Daimler to the gate of Cutlers, accompanied by three of my vans, and six men, as we were creating an installation of plant displays. To my surprise a day boy from Caterham was in charge of the gate. He was pleased to see me. He looked at my car and said, 'You're doing well.' I felt my eyes turn black and extreme pain washed through my body as the whole lot came flooding back in a flash. He'd triggered me. I ignored him and drove on. I parked, got a coffee and realised I was shaking. Maybe I needed some counselling. I couldn't believe that I'd been so rude. My poor treatment at Caterham was nothing to do with him. I must not let them bring me down to their level. I hurried back to the gate only to find he'd gone.

 I wish I'd had the chance to apologise. I felt I'd really let myself down; I really shocked myself. I told my mum what I'd done and she said it showed that I was human. She told me to come to her pub and when I did she gave me a poster of Rudyard Kipling's poem *If*. It's all about the need to stay calm, focused and controlled in the face of adversity. She'd put the word gentle before the last words of the poem so it read:

*If you can fill the unforgiving minute.*
*With sixty seconds' worth of distance run,*
*Yours is the Earth and everything that's in it,*
*And – which is more – you'll be a GENTLE Man my son.*

I hung the poster in my bathroom and read it most days. It gave me a lot of power. I'd recommend anyone to read it if they were finding life difficult, and had lost touch with God like I had, and needed another form of faith.

I took a call to say the Lord Mayor of London wanted to talk to me. I thought someone from the pub was winding me up but the Lord Mayor had chosen McQueens to win the Worshipful Company of Gardeners' Flower in the City Award 1986, for having the best window box display. I couldn't believe it. I'd won an award. Lo and behold I received an official letter from the Lord Mayor of London and went to dine with him and collect my trophy from Mansion House. It was brilliant. Until my landscaper, who was with me, held the top and bottom of the cup and the middle pinged across the dining table, nearly hitting a guest. Yes, the trophy was dented. I had to return it the next year with our mark on it forever.

My customers had no problem spending money and it was enlightening that people spent other people's money easier than they spend their own. My customers had the best flowers on their reception desks. My grandad was right: if you go, go first class. My flowers and plants were the best money could buy. The Gardener family was good to me, giving me credit all the time while the company was growing. It's like an interest free loan and I never let them down, they always got paid. I never burn bridges. I might need to go back to the people who've helped me in the past. The best thing about McQueens was it made my mother proud.

It didn't always run smoothly. One morning, I arrived at Covent Garden as usual at 4am and went around the market buying, getting my orders and stock, called for Ian, my porter, then went to the cafe. Ian brought me the keys and off to the City I went to cut and stand the flowers in buckets of water. When I opened the van I realised someone had made a mistake with the load. I had a complete van load of stock I hadn't bought. I couldn't contact anyone to find out what had gone wrong, because they'd all gone home, and it was too late to travel back to the market as the traffic wouldn't allow it. It was a Friday and the van was full of the best roses, lilies, anthuriums and other expensive flowers, and by the next day they wouldn't be worth nearly as much so I decided to sell them cheap to move the stock. I had Cutlers Gardens, Shoreditch and the Sedgwick Centre florists, and many other contract arrangements to fulfil. It went reasonably well and I managed to get rid of all the perishable stock.

That night, I received a phone call from someone at Covent Garden to tell me I'd stolen flowers belonging to Buster Edwards, one of the Great Train Robbers who had robbed the Royal Mail Train in 1963, stealing £2.6million. They also informed me that Buster's friends had got hold of my porter, Ian, who they thought had made the mistake, got my name and had gone to the City to find me. As luck would have it, they went to the wrong person at the back of Liverpool Street Station. They smashed his stall up only to find out he didn't work for me. He then informed me that when they got hold of me they were going to hold me down and suck my eyes out. Now I've heard a lot of different threats, but this sounded horrific. I was in big trouble.

The next morning I set out early to the market. I was going to South London which was their area, so I needed to be careful. As soon as I crossed the Thames I needed to be ready for the worst. I'd upset the London Mafia. They don't like losing anything, especially their reputation. I walked into the market bold as brass, head high, without fear, trying to make out I was tough. I found the wholesaler who had loaded my van by mistake and then went up to the managing director and told them that the train robbers were going to suck out my eyes because of their mistake, and whatever they do to me, my brothers are going to do to them. He agreed to put it all right and he did, which was a relief. It was a close one, although mind you it was a deal you couldn't refuse. It had a silver lining (and by the way I don't have any brothers) because I became good friends with Buster and we laughed about it. He introduced me to Bruce Reynolds, the brains behind the Great Train Robbery, and I found it a very interesting week.

I needed a break after that so me, Paula and Carly, who was now at primary school, went to the Canaries for a couple of weeks. I needed to de-stress, and it was nice to be able to enjoy some of the money I was making. When I returned, I made sure I always checked my load more carefully.

Once, a customer came in and informed us that we had a branch in Station Road, Sidcup in Kent. We did not so I asked my friend Eric to visit and take pictures and try to get to the bottom of it. Eric was 6ft 3, rather well built and had the deepest Cockney accent you've ever heard. He was also a professional actor and worked for The Ugly Agency, which supplied actors as gangsters, doormen and thugs for TV and films. I actually took it as a great compliment as the owner had replicated our shop just because it was so beautiful. They'd even called it McQueens. I instructed TV Edwards Solicitors to send the owner a letter, and then they renamed their shop.

My little cousin, Lee McQueen, would pass our shop every day on his way to Saint Martins college where he was studying fashion. He'd half break his neck on the bus trying to keep my shop in view for as long as possible. He loved seeing the name McQueen in lights (we started with an apostrophe in the shop name, then phased it out). I always told my mum I'd have my name in lights so it was a family joke. I'd made a big deal getting the name lit up in blue letters on a white background and brass shaded lights, and it did look good in the dark. Lee, who's better known as the fashion designer Alexander McQueen, told me later that it's what inspired him to go for it. He used to dream of McQueen on his fashion line. We all need inspiration and I loved him telling me that. As I've said before, Gianni Russo and Bobby Sulkin inspired me to work hard to fulfil my dreams, so it was nice that I could do the same for someone else.

I was working on the tropical plant displays at Shearson Lehman Brothers when the news about Black Monday broke. It was 1987, the markets had crashed, banking had gone into free fall, but they were breaking open bottles of champagne? It was like a scene from *The Wolf of Wall Street* as they'd made a fortune off someone else's misfortune. My loans went from 4 per cent to 18 per cent interest overnight and the banks started to send back plant displays and cancel flower orders. I soon realised we were over-reliant on the banking industry.

I made enquiries with my many friends in the City and they told me to sell everything, so I put McQueens up for sale and sold it without delay. It was a shame, it was a great business, servicing great companies including many high street and merchant banks, insurance companies, TV shows such as *The Jonathan Ross Show*, and fashion magazines. We also had four bases: Cutlers Gardens, The Sedgwick Centre, Marlow Workshops, where we'd train the interior landscapers, and a wonderful shop in Great Eastern Street. McQueens was, and still is, a great company.

Because of the situation we'd had in Sidcup, when a shop was being passed off as McQueens, our solicitors TV Edwards conducted the sale. They knew the franchise ability of McQueens, so they cut the sale up in pieces. First was a contract for the sale of the premises and second, the goodwill when it comes to corporate contracts. I gave the new owners a signed contract for the Shoreditch shop which allowed them to use the name McQueens and I promised not to open another McQueens for three years or within three miles. I sold the business to a couple who went on to sell the business to the people who own it today. And today McQueens graces the floor of Claridge's Hotel in Mayfair. Mrs Claridge would be pleased.

# CHAPTER 12

# On Cloud Nine

With McQueens sold, it was time to chase my dreams. I was still having trouble with my dad. He said he wasn't a fan of Paula's, but I know it was me he had issues with. I'd had enough, especially with the economic situation looking so bleak. I got Pickfords to pack up everything we owned, put it in a container and ship it to California. I told Pickfords we'd give them a delivery address as soon as we'd found somewhere to live. I was amazed at how Pickfords did their job – they taped up the full drawers and took them, took the pictures from the walls and even packed our clothes. My friends had assured me that California wasn't experiencing a financial crash and I'd do well there. Within two weeks, the three of us were on the plane and on our way. It was January 1988. The American dream, here we come.

I'd been to Las Vegas and California before but this time I had my two girls with me and nowhere to live so it was daunting to say the least. However, I needed to come across as confident so the girls didn't have a panic attack about the unknown, or the change in culture. Our plane landed at Los Angeles Airport and this time I walked past the board of hotels – I wasn't going to make that mistake again. I went straight to the car rental, sorted the car out then we headed off to Santa Monica. I needed to think about where Paula would be happy living. I knew Santa Monica had a couple of English pubs – Ye Olde King's Head and one nearby called The New Scotland Yard pub in Canoga Park in the valley. Not that Paula drank, but we could meet other ex-pats there. I'd been to the King's Head on my last trip for British fish and chips – it's been there since the '70s and is still going strong. They even serve an English breakfast. I thought it was a good place to start. It was a bold move for Paula uprooting and moving to Los Angeles, and she was scared. Until this point, she'd only been on package holidays where they look after you the whole time, unlike me where no adventure was too big. We checked into a Holiday Inn by Santa Monica Pier. We all needed to sleep, so I tucked Carly in and we collapsed in the next bed. It was late at night and we had jet lag to contend with.

I woke up the next day to find them missing. I assumed they'd gone for a walk, and it wasn't long before the door swung open and their arms were full of McDonald's. Paula was visibly shaken. She said she'd had problems with a mentally ill person in McDonald's, and she didn't like it here. I could see things were not going to be easy. I also found that downtown Santa Monica was not that safe. We went out to look for a bank and straight away two aggressive beggars approached me demanding money. I pretended that I was deaf and couldn't speak, mimicking the old park keeper I used to know. They didn't know how to respond and we moved around them and moved on. We found the bank and changed our money to dollars.

When we were in the bank the teller noticed Carly was wearing coloured laces in her trainers and told Paula that they were gang colours, and that we could get attacked. This really wasn't helping. The teller could see Paula was distressed and she produced a book with houses for sale in the suburbs of Los Angeles. They looked too good to be true, and so cheap, so off we went to look at them. On the way, we decided to buy a car so as not to waste money on a rental. The teller was right – it was dangerous for us, especially if people knew we were tourists. We went to look for a car dealership and found one on the 405 highway. While looking at the never-ending rows of cars, our daughter slammed a car door shut on her fingers and was trapped, screaming. I ran to her, shouting at her not to panic. Paula was horrified, as it looked as though Carly had severed her fingers. I then started to scream for help from the garage staff and they came running and released her fingers from the door. Thankfully, they were fine because of the thick rubber inlay. It was scary though – I thought her piano-playing days were over.

I'm not sure if the dealership thought they'd narrowly missed an expensive lawsuit, but they gave me a big discount on a two-year-old Pontiac Sedan family car. We had to return the hired car downtown, so Paula drove the rental car while I drove our new car with Carly in the back. I told Paula to chew gum and look tough because downtown was dangerous. I looked over at her a couple of times in the traffic, and what a great actress as she looked hard as nails.

We booked into a small motel on the edge of Sun City near San Diego. After a few days of relaxation, enjoying the pool and the great takeaways that America has to offer, it was time to get our life in order. We went to the Department of Motor Vehicles (DMV) to take our driving tests but we couldn't get a licence until we had a permanent address, so it was back to Sun City to look for a house.

I bought a tract home for cash, on a new development built on an orange grove named Moonridge Drive, on a complex called Hill Pointe. The houses were built of ticky tacky (low-cost building materials) but were lovely and new, and being the first person in a home was exciting. Our house was a one-storey family home, with two bedrooms, two bathrooms, and a guest toilet situated in a lovely cul-de-sac. The Americans can't believe we sometimes live with one bathroom, no matter how many bedrooms we have. They also think we drink warm beer and can't see through the London fog. Time and time again I had to explain that these were myths. Yes, London used to be famed for its peasouper fog – not to mention the Great Smog of London in 1952 – but this was due to coal fires and we haven't seen anything like that since the '50s.

Our furniture was delayed for some reason and so I purchased a beautiful set of garden furniture, table, chairs and sun beds, which I put inside the house to use until our container arrived. It would have been stupid to waste money on more furniture. The neighbours looked through our windows thinking we were strange. It was like glamping, but we didn't mind as we knew our furniture would arrive at some point. I bought a huge TV with the Showtime and HBO hook up, plus a Nintendo console. Back in England they still only had three stations on the TV and no cable or Nintendo, so this was great fun.

Now we'd purchased a house and a car, we needed to book our driving tests. We walked into the DMV and immediately we were told to fill in some paperwork, then we had our photos taken and we had to take a written test. In England it takes months to get a test. We were told to take a seat, and then a woman called Paula, asked if she had a car and when she said yes, the woman said, 'Come on then' and she got into the passenger seat and Paula got into the driving seat. Paula said she hadn't really driven in California before, and as they began to drive off, I shouted, 'Don't smash the car up.' They returned after about 30 minutes and I was relieved to see the car seemed fine. I stood by the open car window and heard the examiner tell Paula she'd passed. Then she turned to me and said, 'Now Mr McQueen, it's your turn.'

I got in the car and she got in next to me and we drove off. I was pretty confident because I'd driven a lot but the examiner took me to a cross street where there was a dip to help with rain drainage. I was going too fast and went into the dip, then up and launched the car into the air, only just managing to keep control. Paula was waiting for us when we returned after just 15 minutes – obviously the examiner couldn't take anymore – and she came rushing over just in time to hear the examiner say, 'Well Mr McQueen, you have failed.' Paula jumped for joy, punched the air and shouted 'Yes!' It was a Friday afternoon and I couldn't retake the test until the Monday. What a weekend I had – Paula drove all weekend and if I dared even comment on her driving she'd say, 'I've passed my test.' Thankfully, on Monday I passed.

The town we lived in consisted of young families and retired people. It was less expensive than LA or a seaside property. Sun City was less dangerous, which made it easier for the girls to settle in. We got Carly enrolled in a school, and the school bus picked her up outside our door. It was low desert so the temperature ranged from 65 degrees fahrenheit (18 celsius) in winter, to more than 100 degrees (38 celsius) in the height of summer. The gated community had a communal swimming pool and an area for hill walking on site, and the scent of oranges filled the air. I had a large heated jacuzzi installed in our back yard. I could hear strange noises coming from it so I looked underneath and found a tortoise. I assumed it must have escaped from a neighbour, so I thought this was a good opportunity to introduce myself while doing a good turn and returning their pet.

I picked up the tortoise but it was aggressive and kept on trying to bite me. I went to the house on my left and knocked but the guy opened the door, took one look at what I was trying to give him, and slammed it in my face, which I thought was rude. I went to the house on the other side and the neighbour came to the door and explained that it wasn't a tortoise, it was a wild aggressive snapping turtle, indigenous to the desert. It was also a protected species. The man couldn't stop laughing. He told me I should put it back in the desert otherwise I might get arrested. I took it straight to the hill and let it roam wild.

I purchased a second-hand soft-top four-wheel white Wrangler Jeep, which was another part of my dream. I kept it in my garage, and it was my pride and joy. It didn't do a lot for your hair do, but to drive along and feel the warm breeze on your face was great. The first time I tried to put petrol in it, I was at the gas station for ages as I couldn't find the petrol cap. I felt silly when someone had to tell me that it was behind the number plate. I'd drive it out to the surrounding hills and desert – you had to keep an eye out for mountain lions – and it could climb all the mountains and then automatically climb back down on its own. Once I went four wheeling in the rain, and the mud that caked up the Jeep took a week to clean. Never again.

On my birthday Paula bought me a few flying lessons, knowing it was something I wanted to do. I took the lessons at the small local airfield and one day as we pulled the Jeep out of the drive with Paula driving, I shouted 'Stop the car.' I'd seen a spider on her shoulder with a big red spot on its back and I flicked it off her. It went into the road and scurried away. Now Paula hates any kind of insect but this was a deadly black widow spider with a very painful bite. It's one of many deadly insects in the low desert. The hazards of paradise – spiders would get into the car from the garage.

I'd made friends with some neighbours and we'd take their guns – uzis and handguns – out into the desert for target practice. Usually we'd find a dumped stolen car and practise on that. One spray with the uzi would cost $20 in bullets, but what fun. I'd always liked guns since my days on the range at Caterham, and now I was learning how to use more sophisticated weapons.

Paula was having more trouble settling in than me so I bought her some magazines aimed at black and multi-racial women to cheer her up. We were surprised to see adverts for 'fanny slimming' and 'fanny trimming' and thought it was odd that this went on in America, but then we found out a fanny in America is your bottom. How funny. These magazines had lots of great hairstyles so Paula went to a hairdressers that specialised in black hair, to get the one she liked. She looked terrific. She'd told them her hair was natural – it wasn't, it had been dyed and relaxed – and so they permed it. After two days her hair started to fall out, bit by bit until there was hardly any left. She was so upset but it was a true test of my love because I loved her, hair or no hair. It grew back eventually.

The town was so laidback, some people used golf carts to get around, instead of cars. We began to settle in. Our daughter was eight and went straight into school without any problems. The style of teaching was different to England in that they seemed to use the lesson to set work for the evening, so I did a lot of homework with her. It wasn't long before she had a strong American accent and 'Mum' had changed to 'Mom'. She desperately wanted to fit in. We bought her a bike so she could ride around the estate with other kids, and she made lots of friends. When they argued, they threatened to sue each other instead of fight it out, which is what used to happen in England – to me anyway. Carly would go swimming most days with her friends in the pool and once a week we'd go bowling opposite the house. It was a great life and she loved it. Pickfords finally delivered the furniture – it had gone to Singapore by mistake – and we put the garden furniture in the garden. Our life had begun in the wonderful Californian sunshine.

Our friend Peter Conteh, brother of world champion boxer John Conteh, came to stay, and while he was there we had a problem with a rattlesnake in the drive, so I killed it, skinned it, cut out the rattle and gave it to Carly as a present. It was the fashion to go to school with a rattle from a snake to play with, and she was happy shaking the rattle in her hand. Peter was a bit squeamish but helped nevertheless. I pinned the skin to a board and placed it in a sunny spot to tan. Once it was dried I cut some of the skin and wrapped it around a Clipper lighter, glued it in place and varnished it. Now I had a snakeskin lighter, and I put it in pride of place on my coffee table. I thought the neighbours would be impressed but when they came in for coffee, some screamed and one said, 'Vermin on the table!' Another said, 'It's like us coming to London and making a rat lighter. You gotta get rid of that.' So I did.

The Americans were very welcoming and loved our English accents. We were never short of friends or opportunities. The first Christmas we invited my Swedish flight instructor Hendrick for Christmas dinner. He didn't show up so we had it without him, as we also had guests over from London. That night at about 8pm Hendrick showed up. I asked what had happened and he said it was dinner and dinner is at 8pm. I had to explain that yes, that's correct except Christmas dinner is at 3pm in England. So many things get lost in translation. Paula asked him if he wanted champagne, but struggled to get the cork out so I said she should bring it to us. As she walked across the open-plan kitchen to the dining table, the cork went off, hit her directly under the chin and she dropped to the floor smashing the bottle. It was the funniest Christmas ever.

Every Christmas after that, we'd drive to Chino, which is a town where almost every house is lit up with Christmas lights. The houses are in competition and the best one wins the prize – driving through Chino at Christmas is truly magical.

The first year we had a great New Year's Eve party on the *Queen Mary* ship, which docked at Long Beach. We rented a stretch limo and pulled up at the ship, told the security we were invited and they stood aside. It's amazing how doors open when you have a stretch limo and a British accent. Before long we were doing the conga and drinking champagne – it was a great night. The next few New Years' Eves were spent at Venice Beach with the new friends we'd made. We'd watch fireworks on the beach and people would fire their guns in the air. I always wondered, 'If you shoot them up they have to come down. Where did the bullets go?'

We were living near Lake Elsinore, which was a great place to spend a day. A freshwater lake of 3,000 acres, it is the mouth of the San Jacinto River. It was lovely to hang out and watch the boats and jet skis in action. I got a job in sales – knowing how to sell meant I've always got a living. It doesn't really matter what I'm selling but it helps if you've got something people want, and you're selling at a fair price. I started selling pairs of latex gloves, which was a hot commodity because the AIDS virus had reared its ugly head and there was a supply shortage. Hospitals, dentists, care homes, even hairdressers, anyone who worked with the public wanted them. Of course I was no usual salesman, I had a trick. To prove the strength of my latex gloves, I'd put one over my head and blow it up with my nose, so I looked like a chicken. The customer would laugh and then buy 10 cases. I sold so many. As there was a shortage, I'd sourced container loads from the Bank of China. I'd go out and get purchase orders then arrange the deliveries – at least it was paying the bills.

In my spare time I continued my flying lessons at the local airfield until I was sure that I was capable, and knew that I actually wanted to train to become a pilot. I was realistic about my abilities. I knew I had a touch of dyslexia as vowels seemed to float around. I also knew I had slight emotional problems due to my tortured upbringing. I decided that if I wanted to succeed as a pilot, I'd need to hide this part of my life – which was after all what I'd always done. The irony was I found the learning and even the academic side of it quite easy. I was retaining the information, which was something I couldn't do as a child. Maybe it was because it was something I wanted to learn, so I could.

This was the beginning of the best years of my life. When I actually caught the dreams I'd been chasing. Because I'd had it rough in life, I recognised when things were going smoothly and I had to pinch myself to check it was really happening. I was even thankful that I'd had it tough, because I never took the good times for granted and I was enjoying life so much.

On Sundays it became a ritual for us to go for brunch. We went to Bob's Big Boy restaurant in Sun City, or we'd shoot over to Rancho California for all-you-can-eat Sizzler a 10 minute drive away. The food all over was delicious and different to what was available in England: Denny's, Chuck E. Cheese, Wendy's, Red Lobster – it was never ending for food lovers. We noticed we were getting chubby.

By now Paula was bored being at home and she'd found a sales job for both of us in Riverside County. The job came out of the local paper, the *Pennysaver*. The advert said it was a charitable company, working for Vietnam War veterans. Paula really wanted to do something for a charity – she'd do telesales and I would deliver the products. It sounded good to me so off we went for the interview.

We arrived at the address, a warehouse in an industrial site, early but they still let us in. There were people sleeping under the desks in the sales room. I should have twigged then, but we carried on and had the interview. They were only too pleased to employ us, and Paula was happy she had something to get her teeth into. They informed us that they stayed in an area for three years until the area was saturated with their products. When it went quiet they'd move to the next town and go again.

The company was called The Vietnam Veteran Crips, and the company colour was blue. We started straight away. One half of the office was selling for the Vietnam vets and the other half was selling for the blind. Paula would cold call all day selling bin bags, doormats, herbal gardens and all sorts of products. They were expensive but it was for a good cause and people bought because they wanted to help the war vets and the blind people. I would then deliver the goods and collect the money on the doorstep. Paula was doing really well and it wasn't long before she was the top sales person in the office.

One day my neighbour asked where we were working. I explained that we were working for a charitable cause – the Crips. My neighbour's jaw dropped. He explained that the Crips was a huge 30,000-strong gang in California – one of the two biggest in the area – involved in drug dealing, murder and robbery. Most of the gang were military trained and a large number were still in the army. They were the enemies of the Bloods, and if they saw one another they just started blasting their guns. The penny dropped and I realised why they all had blue shoelaces – blue was the gang colour.

We didn't go back. We thought it was best to leave but we still had some commission due, especially Paula, so she called them and told them to give it to Charlie, the genuine Vietnam vet she sat next to. He was so pleased he came to the phone and thanked her. While I have to say that they were really nice to us, we quit while we were ahead and I wouldn't have liked to see it go bad.

This job made me realise that I wanted to quit sales and become a commercial pilot – a career I had put out of my head as I assumed it'd be out of my reach. Not now. Now I was going to reach for the clouds and give it all I'd got.

# CHAPTER 13

# The Power of Love

I shopped about for the best training, not the cheapest, because I'd already flown in some dodgy planes. I also know you get what you pay for. I found an advert for a company called Sussex Aviation at Van Nuys Airport, San Fernando Valley, Los Angeles. Sussex Aviation had a guaranteed course, which means that no matter how long it takes, they guarantee you'll pass the course and get your pilot's licence. As you gain more hours flying, you also become an instructor for a while. In order for me to become a commercial pilot I'd have to move the family closer to Los Angeles. Paula was very supportive and by now Carly was due to leave Menifee Valley Elementary School and go to a junior high school, and it was just the right time to move.

Paula found us a beautiful house in a gated community in Woodland Hills in the San Fernando Valley, not too far from Van Nuys Airport, one of the busiest domestic airports in America and where a number of flight schools are based. We put our house up for sale and within a few months we were packed up and ready to move. To help move everything, we hired a U-haul trailer, which we towed behind the Pontiac, which was already full. I drove the car with the trailer and Paula drove the Jeep. We stopped overnight in a motel and then we arrived in Woodland Hills, which was beautiful. We drove up to our new home, 6169 Periwinkle Way, The Summit, Woodland Hills, and approached the gates where we received our keys from the security officer. He explained that if we had visitors, security would call us first to see if we were expecting them, and if not they'd be turned away.

The house was fabulous: two bedrooms – both with walk-in dressing rooms and ensuites – two further bathrooms, an open plan downstairs and a barbecue at the front. The Summit had tennis courts, gyms, saunas, swimming pools, a party house and many other amenities. We were all so excited.

I called Sussex Aviation and Barat Patel, who had a London accent and seemed nice on the phone, asked me to come in for an interview the following day. I went in prepared but he told me that as I had no academic qualifications – no O Levels, let alone a degree – there was no way he'd take me on a guaranteed course. I drove home utterly deflated, wondering how I was going to explain this to Paula. After all, we'd moved our whole lives here. I knew that if this flight school said this, all the others would as well.

Paula could tell something was wrong as soon as I opened the door. 'What's wrong babe?' she said. 'Are you alright?' I explained that I'd made a big mistake thinking I could become a commercial pilot after not having finished school, let alone going to university.

'Right, let's go,' she said with a look of fury on her face. She told Carly to get in the car. 'And you,' she said pointing at me.

Before I knew what was happening we were at Van Nuys Airport and she was asking for Barat Patel. I didn't know what to do. Was she going to embarrass herself, and me? He came out and she explained to him that even though I was young and had a young family to look after, I'd worked very hard to get the money to pay for his guaranteed course and she had a proposition for him. I would pay for the course in full, upfront, and if at any time he thought that I wasn't bright enough or couldn't cope with the flying, or the academic side, he could expel me and keep the money. Wow! I didn't expect that (nor did he by the look on his face).

He agreed and shook Paula's hand, and then mine. I couldn't believe my ears – he'd accepted me on the guaranteed course and it was now up to me to prove myself. It was going to be four years hard training but oh boy I love that girl! She's a tough cookie sometimes. She gave him the credit card and the deal was done.

I was thrown into the deep end and loved every minute of it. I was like a duck to water. The first technical question is what makes a plane fly? Answer: money. If you learn to fly hourly they will train you as slowly as possible so they can make as much money as possible. It's called 'being hosed down'. The guaranteed course is the opposite – they'll push the student through as fast as possible to save money on plane rental and training.

The school was based at the executive FBO (fixed base operator), a large building in the middle of the airport. Half the building accommodated jet rental pilots, such as Learjet, Cessna and Citation. They could access the aviation fuel avgas, parking, cleaning services, and incoming planes could use the service to load cargo or just to exit the airport. Later I'd learn that when the larger planes were loaded with cargo and heavy, they created wake. If you got behind them in your smaller, lighter plane, they could roll you so you had to be careful.

The other half of the building was my flight school. Barat would stand at the main desk checking his fleet of planes in and out with the dozen or so flying instructors dressed in white shirts, black tie and black trousers. Bob drove the fuel truck and could be contacted by radio to go and refuel aircraft. Henry washed planes most of the time and Barat would give him airtime as payment.

Our classrooms were at the back and started at 9am sharp. My first week was in the classroom, learning how to preflight an aircraft (walk round the plane checking for any defects, check fuel and gas and go through a checklist), the aviation language, drag (the force that opposes the movement of the plane), yaw (the side-to-side movement of the plane), and the principles of flight. Now, funnily enough, I had learnt a bit in the Air Training Corps at school, and it was coming back to me.

My classmates were from all over the world – Sweden, Belize, Saudi Arabia, Afghanistan, Australia and lots of Americans from all states. It was an interesting group and none of them had done anything except school. At 11am, the roach coach would arrive, which was the nickname for the Mexican food truck. The food was different and delicious – quesadillas, chilli bowls with cheese on top, breakfast burritos, which was a full English breakfast rolled up in a tortilla, and great coffee. I was always happy to see the truck.

It was nothing like the schooling I'd ever experienced. I was really enjoying it and soon enough I was up in the air flying all over the wonderful Californian state. I found everything easy, which surprised me. I just couldn't believe I was doing better than people with university degrees. At 26, I was two years older than the rest of the class, but felt as though I'd caught up with society while they were in university. I'd been to the university of life and I was finally back on track. I was getting 90 per cent or more on the written exams, when the pass rate was 70 per cent. I was more shocked than anyone else but, hey, I wasn't going to complain.

There was never a dull moment at the FBO. One day the place was surrounded by secret agents in black suits and Ray-Bans. I could see they had guns under their jackets and I'm not sure if they were Immigration or FBI, but I could feel they were dangerous. Then a big black car pulled up and the President of America Ronald Reagan stepped out. I was really shocked. He smiled at us all, walked over to a jet and flew off. It was all over in 10 minutes. He was one of the many stars that passed through the FBO. One day Sly Stallone went through and my mate Tony shouted, 'Hi Arnie.' Stallone gave him a stare and then smiled. He was lovely. I have to say it made my day.

In order to get up in the air you need to get a private pilot's licence using visual flight rules (VFR). This enables you to fly on a clear day. You would think every day is clear in California but that's not the case because there's a lot of smog and pollution. On those days, it's like flying in nicotine – a dirty yellow haze. Visibility is poor and that can be dangerous flying over LA because of the high density of air traffic. The mountains trap the smog over LA with no place for it to go, but by lunchtime it's mostly burnt off and you can see clearer. But still you need to be very alert because you're in the highest density of air traffic in the world. You need 40–80 hours of airtime to pass your private pilot test, as well as passing all your academic work.

When planes are heading towards each other at 250–500 miles an hour, a dot in the distance turns into a big plane in seconds. It reminded me of home in the East End – no second chances. Most trainee pilots start flying in a two or four-seater aircraft. A Piper low wing or a Cessna high wing plane – both are American manufactured so it's cost effective to fly them in America. Once you get on the runway, you're lined up, slowly increasing to full power, keeping the nose wheel on the centre line. Once you reach the appropriate speed the plane will want to fly on its own, a little tug on the yoke and up you go. Children are known to fly – it's not that difficult as long as everything's working. It's finding the time and money to do it.

Like most things, practice makes perfect but I had a lot of trouble learning to land perfectly, and my problems went on for some weeks. I started to doubt if I was ever going to be able to land properly, and landing is the most important part. I even lost sleep over it because I was the worst at landing in my class. It's very much multi-tasking bringing the plane into land, doing lots of jobs at the same time. Smaller planes come in slow so you have more time to prepare and adjust the plane for landing. Then one day it came together – a bit like riding a bike, I could just do it. In fact I could do it very well. I was now the best in the class. They knew I could put the plane down on a sixpence anywhere. It was the most fulfilling achievement I had flying and today landing is still my forte. I can put a plane down anywhere as long as it's within the limits. So it goes to show that perseverance conquers all.

I performed my first solo flying around the traffic pattern (a rectangular pattern consisting of an upwind, crosswind, downwind and final approach) while talking out loud as if my instructor was still sitting next to me. I must have looked nuts talking to myself but it worked and I was signed off to fly solo. It took about five weeks to get to take the practical test and I passed with flying colours. The examiner turned out to be a cool guy and even showed me how to land on the numbers (land and stop on 20 feet of runway). I had it – the private pilot's licence, visual flight rules.

Paula was so proud and we went for a meal to celebrate, but I still had a long way to go to achieve my goal. After achieving my single-engine VFR I passed my single engine IFR (instrument flight rules), which means flying the plane without looking outside, just reading the flight instruments to maintain a safe flight. Then it was VOR beacons (VOR stands for VHF omnidirectional range), which means navigating your way via radio signals transmitted from beacons on the ground. It's like a sat nav and a touch more complicated than today. Then it was time to take my multi-engine VFR, and then IFR, and after passing my multi-engine practical and written exams, it was time for my commercial VFR and IFR licences.

There's a lot of reading involved in learning to fly and I used videos and tapes to help me. I even went to sleep with them playing in my headphones. It's called subliminal learning. Paula would make the tapes for me by reading every single book into a Dictaphone – I think she knows as much about aviation as I do. I'm sure a mixture of all these techniques helped me get through it. The more you fly the easier it all becomes.

I had some fun in the air. If I had a passenger I'd pull negative Gs (G-Force), which means you create weightlessness in the cockpit. I'd put Maltesers or Tic-Tacs on the dashboard and dive down, then pull the plane up creating the G force, and the Maltesers or Tic Tacs would float across the cockpit and I'd grab them with my mouth and eat them. My friends loved it.

I passed my written commercial licence with flying colours. The Federal Aviation Authority have negative marking, which means if you get a question wrong they deduct points, so it's not in your interest to guess. To pass you needed to get 70 per cent and I got 92 per cent. I guess all that subliminal learning really worked.

Cross-country flying builds up your hours, so it's important to keep it interesting. There's no problem keeping it interesting in California but I would always prefer to fly to Las Vegas Nevada because there's fun to be had there. The annoying thing is that Edwards Air Force Base is between California and Las Vegas and for military reasons it's controlled air space so you'd have to circumnavigate it, which put 25 minutes on the trip. One day, while flying a twin-engine Seneca I decided I'd fly straight through the controlled air space. I clicked my radio and said, 'Edwards tower, this is Seneca Gulf Sierra 164, I'm picking up icing on my wings, need to fly direct to Las Vegas.' Edwards replied: 'Gulf Sierra, that's not a problem. We are nuclear testing and that ice will soon burn off.' Agh! I winged it over, did a U turn, got straight out of their air space and went the long way round.

Sometimes it did pay to be cheeky, like when I was evading landing fees. International airports can be expensive to land at so I'd find a company on the airfield, knowing they'd have a deal with the airport with all take-offs and landings covered. 'San

Francisco tower, Seneca inbound for runway ABC, going to radio company XYZ.' They'd allow my landing and then, when I was on the ground, direct me to the company's parking. I'd go to the company and ask how much replacement VORs were, then leave but leave my plane there parked, have some lunch then fly off with nothing to pay. I'd sometimes fly low over the *MASH* TV set at Malibu Creek State Park, where they made 250 episodes of the hit series. It was like flying over Vietnam with all the tents and trucks on set. Twentieth Century Fox nearly stopped filming after the first series due to a lack of interest, but the second series boomed and it became history.

When we were in our planes, we student commercial pilots would tap our intercoms to make them sound like machine guns while dog fighting one another. Still little boys at heart. We'd come down low and race cars on the freeway, on our way to Santa Barbara, which was my favourite place for lunch. We'd fly out past Carpinteria and out to sea, making sure we were within the glide distance back to land, in case we got engine failure. I'd fly over the oil rigs then land at Santa Barbara Airport. The White Elephant restaurant has great food and service and it was my favourite place to visit. There were beautiful houses to fly over and I'm sure Meghan and Harry are more than happy there.

After lunch I'd head on to a plane graveyard – a landing strip in the desert, a place to store and strip parts of older planes and a fun place to visit, with no landing fees. One day landing in Phoenix, Arizona, I landed next to a prison plane and they unloaded the prisoners in orange jumpsuits all shackled and under armed guard. Con air. It was very frightening because the guards were in anti-escape mode, looking suspiciously at everyone. It reminded me of my time in Boggo Road Gaol.

Flight manoeuvres are important as they teach you how to control the plane in the changing winds, and after a lot of wrestling with the ups and downs of it, it's like riding a bike. You can just fly. Women find flying much easier than men because flying involves multitasking and females are brought up to multitask. Flying lazy eights puts you into every attitude possible with a wind blowing one way. As you fly the figure eight, the plane has to be compensated to stay in that pattern. There are spins and even reverse spins (which means putting the aircraft into a spin upside down). While many of the manoeuvres are for the tests, some are for fun. My favourite is the hammerhead. You fly directly up at full power until the plane runs out of power and, as it loses bite in the air, it just sits there for a moment. Then you do a 180 degree turn and point the plane at the ground and dive towards it. It's a rush! Wing overs, rolls, loops – it all helps making the plane an extension of your body. To fly upside down for a prolonged period you need an inverted oil and fuel system, with injection. If not the engine can cease and that's a problem to say the least.

Under the pilot's seat is a two inch pin which helps move the seat back and forward. One morning on take-off, just as the nose of the plane started to pick up, the pin snapped. My seat slammed back and, because I was holding on to the yoke, I sent the plane straight up vertical, with seconds to spare before the loss of lift and a crash. I managed to pull myself forward by grabbing the passenger seat and pulling myself back into position, pushing the nose down to a normal attitude. I did a go around, and landed. That was me for the day. Phew!

Once Pele, a Swedish pilot mate, was sitting next to me on a night flight and we were practising our night landings when we started to laugh uncontrollably. I was pilot in command and requested permission to land from the tower and I got it. Unfortunately, it was Pele giving me the permission and the tower went mental and were shouting at us. We soon realised we were somehow being gassed in the cockpit and we were buzzing and giggling uncontrollably. Thankfully, Pele thought to open the windows and our heads started to clear. We headed back to Van Nuys still giggling and with huge headaches. We then noticed the compass had broken and leaked fluid all over the cockpit. I always thought it was water inside making the globe float but it isn't, it's kerosene and it had gassed us.

Paula was on a hand-held radio waiting to pick me up from Van Nuys and didn't find it amusing. She'd been scared listening to our strange chatter on the plane. That was another close one. My headache lasted ages. The next day I was preparing for training in the twin engine. I'd been instructed by Tony in the twin until now but I was assigned a different instructor for this particular trip. He took me and another pilot out to the practice area. The other student was from Afghanistan, a pleasant man who told me stories of how they were repelling the Russians from his country. He said that when the Mujahideen captured a Russian, they'd use him as target practice, sometimes betting on his fate, and whoever killed him would lose. He explained that the Russians couldn't stop the flow of weapons coming across the border from Pakistan, and how British Special Forces were helping train the Afghans. Britain's support for the Afghan resistance turned out to be Whitehall's most extensive covert operation since the Second World War.

At first I sat in the back and let the Afghan fly us out. I was going to swap seats at half time and practise some manoeuvres. I was surprised to see the instructor's method of teaching – every time the Afghan touched the wrong button or lever he'd slap the offending hand with a wooden ruler, and say 'No!' After the sixth slap the Afghan went mental, shut off both engines and began shouting in his language. The instructor took control as we were going down, but he struggled to restart the engines, and it took what felt like a very long time for this to work. As you know he fired it up again otherwise I wouldn't be writing this. He demanded that we trainees swap seats and I did the rest of the flying. The instructor said we were lucky we had so much altitude otherwise we wouldn't have had the same outcome – older engines like these don't always restart. I never flew with either of them again. Fuck that.

As you get more licences, the aircraft you can fly become more complex. Wheels retract, propellers become variable and feather, the planes become faster and less forgiving and it all remains very exciting. I even did aerobatics in a Pitts SB2 Special and needed a parachute just in case. The Pitts is sparse to keep its weight down, it has only a couple of instruments and a stick instead of the yoke. I must say I've never jumped from an aircraft, as the training is to glide the plane to a safe landing in a calm fashion.

After 250 hours of flight training I took the practical commercial test, then instrument rating, mountain training, aerobatics, and then finally the commercial multi-engine instrument practical test. This was done over Long Beach Airport at night.

It was 10pm and I was lined up on the runway, the examiner sitting next to me in the twin Piper Seneca. This isn't a cheap plane to rent – it was about $1,000 for a couple of hours. I needed to pass the final test so brakes on, power slowly to full and off I went, up and into the crosswind and climbed steadily leaving Long Beach behind me. Once at the practice area out at sea, I was put through the manoeuvres with no problems. Now I'm very calm in the plane, even when things are not going well. I don't have any fear so I check myself. But on this night my left hand, which holds the yoke, was dripping with sweat and I had to keep wiping it.

It was pitch black out at sea and I was almost at the end of the test with only the final, most dangerous bit, to go. The examiner placed the hood over my head so I couldn't see out of the aircraft. I could only see my flight instruments. It's like playing a video game, only your body gives a false reading to your attitude which you must ignore. Just trust your instruments with your life. I was directed by radio to enter the ILS (instrument landing system). I corrected my air speed and altitude and was starting to bring the plane down to the runway when BANG!, the examiner killed one of my engines. The plane tried to roll out of control. DEAD FOOT DEAD ENGINE. Recover, emergency checklist, feather the engine and keep on the ILS. 'Well done,' shouted the examiner. 'You have passed. Now you're a real pilot.' Then he pulled the hood off my head.

The twinkling lights of Long Beach were the prettiest sight ever. It felt like Christmas and I'd just got the best present. But I didn't buy it, I had to earn it, which made it much more valuable to me. A dream had come true.

Paula threw a big party at the party house on the Summit to celebrate. All the pilots came, as well as all the local Brits we'd become friends with. The entertainment was great as Paula hired the world champion female wrestler Queen Kong, and her daughter Princess Kong. Everyone enjoyed themselves and what a fantastic way to celebrate my achievement.

With the commercial licences in the bag, I had to pass my instructor's licence. In order for me to become an instructor I had to do a teaching programme and I needed to get a California teacher's licence. That's when the penny dropped. I was trained that in order for my pupil to learn, he or she must have their five basic human needs met, otherwise they wouldn't be able to retain the information given to them. These basic human needs are as follows: shelter, food, water, warmth and last, but most importantly, they need to be giving and receiving love. Learning that was like a bomb going off in my head. It's no wonder everything seemed so easy to me. I was giving and receiving love so I could retain anything. And no wonder I had such problems retaining information as a child. The day boys at school were always better at academia than the boarders and now I know why.

When you're teaching a new pilot, you have dual pedals, just like a driving instructor, because steering the plane on the ground (which is called taxiing) is done with pedals, and you use your feet to steer and brake. Most new students I flew didn't know the steering was done with pedals and I'd jokingly tell them to steer for a moment. They'd grab the yoke and use it like a steering wheel and go into shock when they felt the loss of control. Really, I was in control with my feet but they thought it was broken. Funny.

I took up one young man for the first flight after he paid Sussex Aviation a huge amount of money. I couldn't believe he'd paid without even trying it first. They do say you need the right stuff to fly – you've got to be bright enough to learn and stupid enough to try. After five minutes we were over Los Angeles and he got very sick. I told him to be sick out the window because the floor of the aircraft is sealed and the sick would slosh up and down. Then I knew I'd be sick too. He opened the window and puked heavily, and the wind sucked off his Ray-Ban sunglasses. I took him directly back to Van Nuys Airport and he demanded his money back. I often thought of the people in Los Angeles who were being sick on and wondering what type of bird throws up like this and wears Ray-Bans?

I was awarded my instructor's licence. Barat Patel, the man who had doubted me, was in disbelief. In all I'd obtained seven licences. On top of that, I was doing better than the university graduates.

Once you can fly in the LA air space you can fly anywhere in the world.

My favourite place is Santa Catalina Island, with the airport in the sky, as it's perched on a tabletop mountain 20 miles off the coast of Los Angeles. It's the closest you can get to landing on an aircraft carrier. The first time going there it's recommended you have an instructor on board. It's a tricky steep landing but really exciting, and an adrenaline rush. I'd fly out to Catalina Island just because I loved it. The clouds were always beneath the runway so instead of climbing from the runway on take-off you'd fly off the end of the runway and dive down into the clouds and pick up incredible speed. It was better than any rollercoaster, with your body screaming that it's all wrong. What a buzz.

Charlie Chaplin's half-brother Sid Chaplin was the founder of Chaplin Airlines, one of the first airlines in America, and he went back and forth to Catalina Island, which was bought by the Wrigley (chewing gum) family in 1919. After Pearl Harbor, when the Americans entered the Second World War, the runway was obstructed with rubble to stop the enemy using it. After the war they started to make it into the wonderful place it is today.

After landing at the airport you can catch a minibus into town. You can visit the beautiful botanical gardens, go hiking, kayaking, ride in golf carts round the island, stay in hotels or cabins, or camp in tents on the gorgeous beaches. Catalina has something for everyone. From beautiful beaches to top restaurants. It really is one of the wonders of the world, a tranquil place and just a 30-minute jaunt from the madness of LA. I tell my friends to rent a plane and pilot for a great day out. If you do rent a plane you only pay for the air time, so you can book a hotel or cabin and stay overnight, and it's not too expensive. It's a wonderful experience.

I decided to open an air service taxi called Entertainment Air Tours. I gave out leaflets outside the Chinese Theatre, Hollywood – which has all the film stars' hands and footprints in cement on the forecourt – offering to show people 'the homes of the rich and famous by air'. I'd take any work going just to stay airborne. I'd fly over Michael Jackson's house, which was the first house after leaving the runway at Van Nuys Airport. Then on to Madonna's house and I'd say, 'There she is' and the customers would start clicking their cameras. I couldn't really see her. Then I'd fly on to

Malibu to see the movie stars' million-dollar homes. If I ran out of chat I'd sing 'Hollywood la la la Hollywood' and that would get me a smile. My pilot mate Bob even took a guy up to throw his dad's ashes out over LA – unfortunately the ashes all blew back into the cockpit and they were covered in the dad. Best laid plans often go wrong.

I could write about flying forever but this is not what this story is about, so back to the saga.

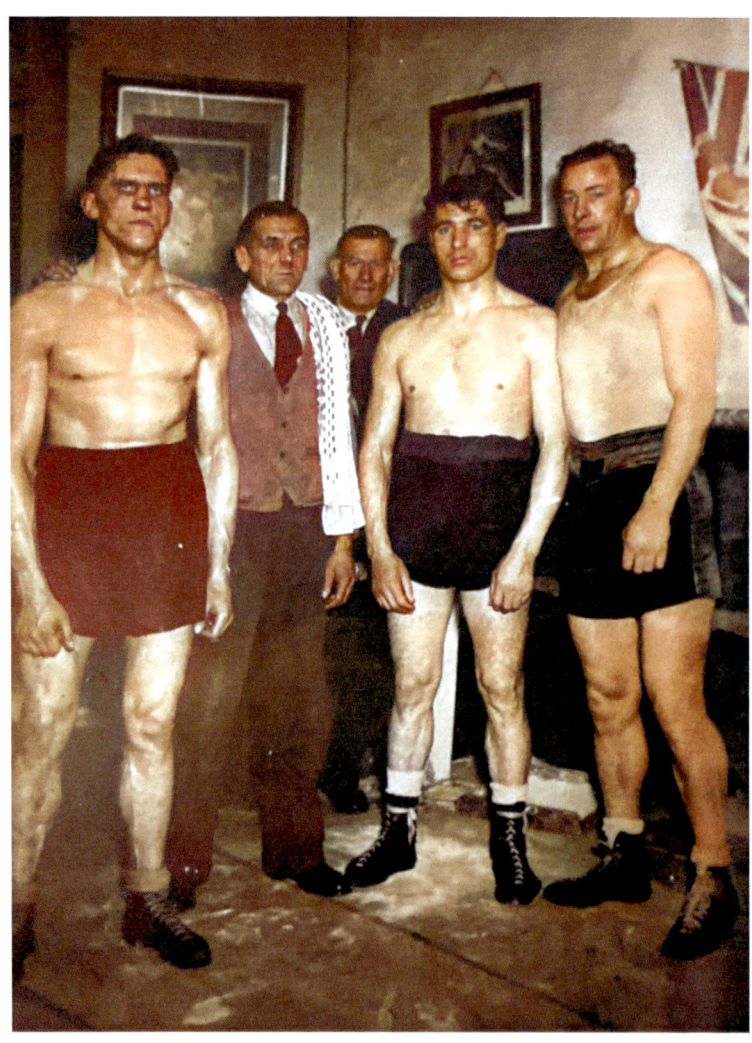

My grandad George Last far right, 1939

My Nan and grandad Maggie and George Last

A small group from Mottrams. I'm third from the left, second row from the top

Caterham hockey team. I'm first left, front row with the leg pads

I'm second on the left front row, with the prep school rugby team

Me aged 15 years old just before I was thrown onto the streets of Soho

Me flypitching in a market aged around 15

Tony from the punk shop and me

Me with the flat cap with some mates hanging out down Petticoat lane
aged 16

Me on the left with Graham (and a life-size cardboard cutout
of Ian Botham), who gave me the gift of the gab

Me going to Caterham in my dad's taxi

Me aged 17 at a show in Las Vegas with Jeff, Jodie and a friend

Me and Danny squashed into the motorhome with all our programmes
on the way to the 1982 Commonwealth Games in Brisbane, Australia

Jamie, me and Paul at the Commonwealth Games just before our arrest

My pitch in Petticoat Lane (the one with the extra X), with Paula and Chrissy

McQueens shop

One of the McQueens vans at the flower market

The Lord Mayor of London
Sir Allan Davies, GBE,DSC
Mansion House 1986 Flower in the City Award
First Prize Window Box Display

McQueens wins the Flower in the City Award for the best window box
display, 1986

Paula, me and Carly going on our holidays after the Buster Edwards saga

Peter Conteh, brother of world heavyweight boxing champion John Conteh, and me skinning a rattlesnake in California

Me with the old twin-engine Seneca learning to fly

Flying tourists over the houses of the rich and famous with my
Entertainment Air Tours business

My business card

My celebration party after passing my commercial pilot's licence, which means I'm now a real pilot. I'm far left, second row with my thumb up

Paula and I saying I do... Saying I do, in front of the Rev Jim Hamilton, the vicar in the film, *Honeymoon in Vegas*. The king of I dos

Marrying Paula at the Little Church of the West in Las Vegas in 1990,
with Kim's grandaughter as the flower girl

Kim Krantz, far left, who gave Paula away, pictured with her mother, daughter and grandaughter

Carole McQueen Florists (named after my mum), specialist wreath makers

My innovative flower machine

Me on the news being interviewed about the vending machine

The birth of McQueens Flowers, Cutlers Gardens

HE USED TO BE AN EAST END FLORIST UNTIL HE MADE A KILLING ON THE KRAY FUNERAL."

The *Daily Mirror* cartoon of me by Charles Griffin after I provided the flowers for Ronnie Kray's funeral. This picture is the original, which I bought

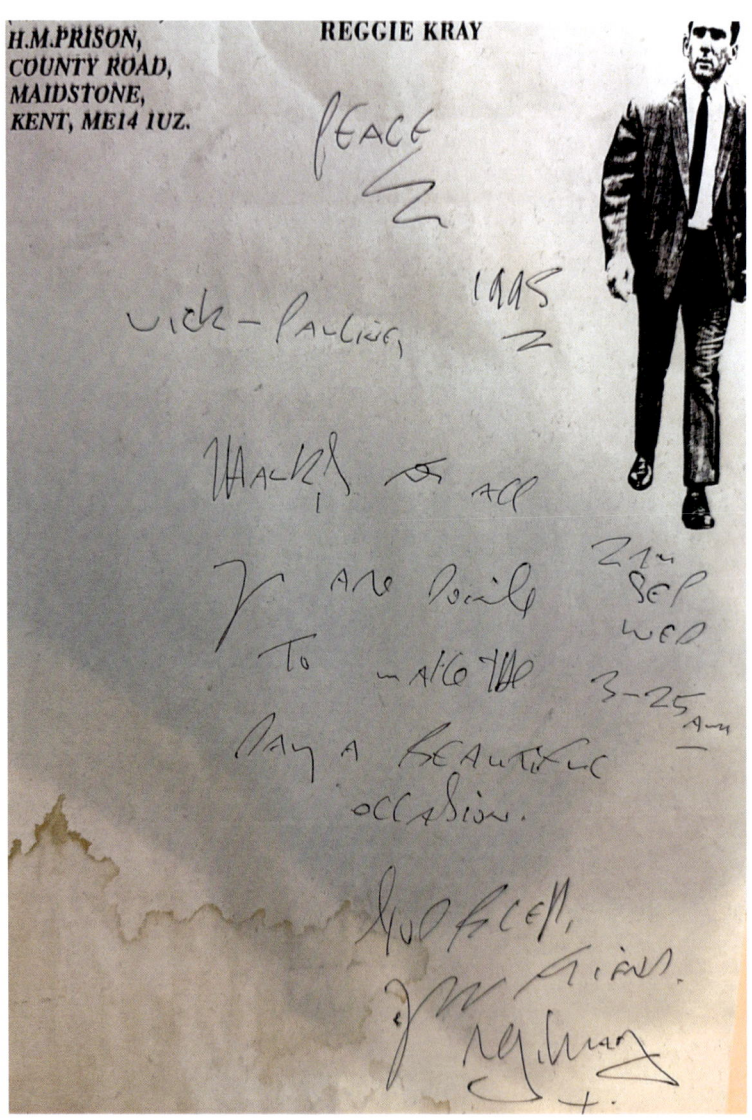

A thank you note from Reg Kray for providing all the wreaths for
Ronnie's funeral, 1995

# BULBWORLD™

*Plant The Planet – Save The World*

**Created by Carole McQueen Florists**

Written by Jill Truman    Illustrations by Brian Norwood    Lyrics by Cody & Green

My BulbWorld book from 1999. It was way ahead of its time

The cast of BulbWorld the musical at Harlow Playhouse, before going to the Royal London Palladium

Paula and Amy working on the cross for Reg Kray's coffin

*In loving memory of*

LEE ALEXANDER McQUEEN

(1969 – 2010)

The order of service card given to me at my cousin Lee's funeral

Me at Caterham, standing next to a statue of Rev Townsend, after returning to ask for an apology. The police were in the room to the left

Me and my good friend Gianni Russo at Beautique restaurant in New York

Pauline and Nicholas McQueen representing UKIP in 2014

# CHAPTER 14

# The Limey

California is a great place. It offers something for everyone, including a blast of sunshine for breakfast with your coffee. California is the most populated state in America with 12 per cent of all Americans living there. It's such a cool place – you can surf in the morning, fly up to Big Bear Mountain in 30 minutes, go skiing in the snow for the afternoon, then home with the family in the evening. There's never a dull moment. Some weekends we'd drive up to Big Bear, rent a cabin, go shopping in the town then to the ski hire shop and off to the slopes. Skiing fun all weekend.

We'd also drive up to Hollywood some Saturday nights and watch the parade of lowrider dancing cars. Young men would compete to see whose car could dance the best. Their music would play loudly as the hydraulics of their cars would bounce up and down to the beat. It was great fun to watch.

California's food was crazy: Sizzler for all you can eat, Denny's for breakfast or snow crab legs at Red Lobster in the evening. I became an expert at barbecuing, and learnt to baste the ribs with sauce. Outside cooking became a big part of our life, and I loved to cook because I was good at it, thanks to Gianni Russo and the guys showing me real men cook. We'd go to the Red Onion nightclub, Hollywood's jazz or blues clubs or party on the *Queen Mary* which was permanently docked in Long Beach. Every day was exciting. The theme parks were close by – my favourite was Six Flags Magic Mountain and Universal, which were aimed more at adults. Our daughter loved Disneyland. We really were living the dream.

I took up tennis and was absolutely useless. I liked to play tennis with the girls – at least I had a chance with them. I was playing one day when a young guy shouted out, 'Where you from mate?' in a Cockney accent. 'East End,' I replied. 'And me,' he said with a big smile. After a chat and checking that he wasn't a plastic Cockney (a mockney, a made up Cockney), we admitted that it truly is a small world. His name was Narve, and we're still friends today. I invited him to Sunday lunch, as Paula would always cook the traditional Sunday lunch – roast beef, Yorkshire pudding and all the trimmings – a comfort food for any Brit away from home. Narve loved it and soon we ended up with a houseful of Brits every Sunday. It was a perfect end to the week, and of course we'd help each other if need be.

One day I received a phone call from a friend saying that Narve had had a heart attack and didn't have insurance. They took him to the county hospital, which was really for poor people and where they were only legally obliged to stabilise the patient. When Paula and I arrived with a carrier bag of fruit we asked for him at the desk. We were told we'd have to pay $5 to be told which ward he was in. I paid it and we went up to his ward. I was gobsmacked by the amount of people on trolleys in the corridors with gunshot wounds. It took a few days for his mum to get over so Paula made sure he was looked after until then, and before long he headed back to London. I got the best health insurance for the family after that. You live and learn.

Life goes on and Paula was doing well too, she was now head nurse of a medical clinic, and she was getting a great salary. Paula had trained as a nurse when she was younger but had given it up to join the employment agency. The wages were twice what we'd get in Britain and as it was cheaper to live, there was much more money for fun and leisure. We were getting lots of visitors from London and while I loved seeing them, I didn't think I'd ever live there again. Too many damp memories.

The only blot on the landscape was that Paula was having trouble falling pregnant. We'd been trying for a while so she wanted to look for help. It was some years after the success of the first test tube babies – in vitro fertilisation (IVF) – and one of the original team had opened a clinic in Encino, California. We went to see what could be done.

The doctor's name was Jeffery Steinberg. He had done his initial training at Bourn Hall Fertility Clinic in Cambridge England – the world's first IVF clinic – and had worked with Dr Patrick Steptoe and Dr Robert Edwards, the original pioneers of IVF. We made an appointment, and after he examined both of us and took samples, he told us IVF was possible. It was very expensive but we had the money, so we went ahead.

The nurses taught me how to inject a liquid called Lupron into Paula's bottom every day. They showed me how to squeeze an orange that simulated a buttock, tap the needle to remove air bubbles then inject. When I could do that correctly, I could inject Paula. Lupron prevents ovulation, and improves the quality and quantity of eggs available for fertilisation. The first time I did it, I was standing with the needle in my hand and said, 'Medication time', like they did in *One Flew Over the Cuckoo's Nest*. Paula wasn't amused and decided to inject herself after that. Lupron had physical side effects, such as aching bones, and mental side effects, including feelings of aggression. Wanting a baby was emotional enough, without having to deal with these side effects.

After three months of self-injecting, Paula was ready for egg retrieval. We went to Century City Hospital and met Dr Hill, a partner of Jeffrey Steinberg. It was much nicer than the county hospital but as they were taking Paula to surgery the anaesthetist came running up to us and said he'd not been paid. I had to write a cheque there and then, using Paula's belly to rest it on. The eggs were retrieved from Paula, placed in a Petri dish, injected with my sperm and after a few weeks, when they developed into embryos, four were implanted in Paula. We were told to expect a multiple birth, which would not have been a problem. In fact, it would have been a blessing. Then we waited.

Some weeks later we were told something had gone wrong and Paula had miscarried the babies. They said they were going to do it again but this time for free (bar the stay in hospital and the anaesthetist). We started with the Lupon injections again, but Paula was not in a good place mentally, as she was trying to come to terms with the loss of the embryos. The Lupon didn't help. Three months later we went back to Dr Hill and this time they brought in an Oriental specialist to drill the eggs for free, which we thought was a bit strange. They had great success and made 11 embryos, implanted four and froze the other seven. While

Paula was recovering I went for a smoke outside the hospital, and Richard Mulligan, an actor who played Burt Campbell in the TV show *Soap*, was also having a smoke and we had a chat. You meet the best characters smoking.

Some weeks later, the Encino Clinic called to explain that it had gone wrong once again but they didn't know why. Paula was now an emotional wreck and I was 30 grand out of pocket. They still had the embryos in the freezer and told me they'd be kept indefinitely until Paula was able to cope with another attempt, and I'd only have to pay a fraction of what I'd already paid to just have the implant surgery.

It was a sad time for us and it took us a long time to recover. To be honest I don't think we ever have. They kept the embryos frozen at Century City – they were labelled 'Caucasian pilot, multi-racial nurse'. Dr Steinberg asked if we wanted to sell them and I told him that even if I was broke that would be inappropriate, and he explained that it would be helping a childless couple. I was very firm and told him no way.

I'd go aerobatic flying to clear my head. Flying was good for me because it stopped me thinking about my problems. I wouldn't even have the urge for a cigarette for up to five hours in the air, yet as soon as I was on the ground, I'd chainsmoke. Maybe looking down at the planet made my problems seem small and insignificant.

Carly was now 13 and a proper valley girl. She was going to Parkman Junior High School in Woodland Hills and loving it. She swam in the pool after school, spent weekends at Disney or Universal Studios, went to concerts and basically lived the Californian Dream. It was totally different from my childhood, and Paula and I believed that filling her life with love and happiness was more important than her academic qualifications. She didn't have a trace of a British accent left, whereas I'd hung on to mine. It was my identity and it had seen me through some tough times. It gave me a feeling of belonging and I would never let it soften – I was Cockney and proud.

There was no class system in the States. You either had money or you didn't, unlike Britain where you're pigeonholed by class, no matter how much money you have. Everybody has a chance in America. I was being called the 'limey' at work and didn't know whether or not to be offended, so I checked it out, but to my surprise it meant very little, which cheered me up somewhat. It came from the fact the first British seaman arriving in the Americas used to eat limes on board ships to stop getting scurvy. The limey Cockney was OK with me. Another difference between Britain and America was the clothes sizes. Paula loved going shopping because whereas she was an English 12, the American equivalent was an 8, which made her feel slim.

My favourite breakfast – aside from Catalina Island – was at Venice Beach. The cafe served the best grand slam in town – buttermilk pancakes, link sausages, bacon, eggs and hash brown with maple syrup on top. When I first saw someone eat it I thought it looked disgusting. When I tried it, I was hooked. Venice Beach was buzzing with various characters and sellers there – a great place to people watch. I loved looking at the muscle men pumping iron on the beach.

Not only was every day like a holiday in the sunshine, but the vacations were also great – visiting Danny and Kim in Vegas, going down to La Jolla in San Diego, or up to Big Bear for a weekend in the snow. All really cool trips. It was just everyday stuff for our daughter, but I felt very privileged and special. I would have been happy with a caravan on the beach, like Jim Rockford in *The Rockford Files* so living well was very nice.

One weekend, we went to visit Danny and Kim in Las Vegas for a short break when, out of the blue, they said we'd been living in sin long enough, and we should get married. We hadn't discussed getting married and Paula had changed her name to McQueen by deed poll years earlier. However, the next thing we knew, we were being swept along with Kim's plans.

She said we needed a wedding fit for film stars so she booked the Little Church of the West, the oldest freestanding wedding chapel on the Strip, which features in the Elvis Presley film *Viva Las Vegas*. Built in 1942, it's moved around Vegas but is now on the east side of the Strip. Superstars who have tied the knot there include Zsa Zsa Gabor (1949), Dinah Washington (1965), Judy Garland (1965), as well as modern celebrities – Bob Geldof (1986), Billie Piper and Chris Evans (2000), and now Nicholas McQueen.

We booked into the honeymoon suite of the Flamingo, where Danny had been the manager. It's where Bugsy Siegel started and is real Vegas history. The whole Krantz family turned up, even the grandkids were throwing rose petals up and down the aisle. Kim gave Paula away and a mate of mine was best man. We had the works – white stretch limo, big wedding cake and endless champagne. It was truly a beautiful wedding – March 18th 1990 is a day I'll never forget. The minister, Rev Jim Hamilton, had a dodgy leg and I discovered he was the minister in the Nicolas Cage film, *Honeymoon in Vegas*. I'll never forget that he said, 'Love means all things. Love is all things'. It really resonated with me. The power of love is amazing. We enjoyed it so much we stayed an extra week in the honeymoon suite.

Despite the lights, Vegas back then could be a cold place, as it attracted people from all over, and no-one seemed to have any history there. When I asked anyone where they were from it was always somewhere else. Today it's different as vast amounts of people are born in Vegas. I always loved visiting because we knew Danny and Kim so I could have the fun of the casinos and also get involved with their family life, which was priceless.

It took four hours to drive back to LA. It's a drive through the remote desert of Death Valley, and half way there is a town called Barstow where we stopped for lunch . I'd been there many times before, delivering aeroplane propellers to the Barstow Airfield, so I knew it well. I would usually fly on to Vegas to make my trip fun while they fixed the load I'd delivered. The tumbleweed rolling across the highway and dust devils swirling like mini tornadoes used to amaze me. The more remote we got the more tumbleweed there was.

Back in the City of Angels, Paula went back to managing her medical clinic in Encino, and I was back in the air for the next cargo delivery. Paula was very happy being a newlywed after so many years together. Her friends thought a surprise wedding was so romantic. I told them it was the best day of my life – and I wasn't lying.

With all my flying experience I now had the opportunity to work all over the world. I'd speak to international employers and I realised their requirements were always different. One guy said if I could fly I had the job, but that made me wonder how good were the people who maintained their planes and managed their mechanics. I'd already had problems with planes. I'd also learnt that the area immediately around any airport is dangerous. The properties are cheap because of the noise, and that attracts some dodgy people, so living or even staying anywhere near an airport is not advised. It's prudent to base yourself at least 30 minutes away.

I wanted to see a bit more of the world so I went for a job in Costa Rica, which is between Panama and Nicaragua. But then we were hit with a problem. We found out that Carly was being bullied at school but hadn't told us. Every day she used to walk to school with a friend and on this particular day the friend brought her grandmother's 9mm automatic handgun with her, and they both played with it on the way to school. Once in the playground, the friend held it to the bully's head and said, 'If you hurt her anymore, I'll blow your fucking head off', while our daughter stood at her side. The teachers ordered everyone in the playground to hit the floor as they moved in and apprehended her. The girl was arrested and taken to juvenile hall, which is a youth detention centre. We never saw her again.

The whole situation left Paula and I deeply disturbed. I had enough knowledge of weapons to know how bad things could have been. There was another problem – my mother was sick in London and, in all honesty, I was a bit tired of living out of a small suitcase flying around north, south and central America. I thought it was time for pie and mash back in London. I felt the need to quit while we were ahead.

# CHAPTER 15

# George's

We arrived back in the UK and sorted out the usual – somewhere to live, Carly's school, and then how to earn some money. I'd heard the nightclub business was doing well in the West End so, after some discussion with a friend, we started to look for a venue in the East End. We planned to open a club in Shoreditch. This area was pretty much deserted in the evenings, which would allow us to stay open through the night without disturbing anyone. As long as the fire regulations were adhered to we wouldn't have too many problems with the authorities. Licensed or not.

Shoreditch was a lucky place for me. I'd worked there a lot in my life and it was where we bought the first property for McQueens florist. I did well in Shoreditch. I contacted James Gough, who founded Stirling Ackroyd estate agents. I'd given him credit on the plants for his first office where he slept under his desk, and when he started as an estate agent he worked for Jeremy Scott who unfortunately died of cancer. James then took over. I knew James was a public schoolboy who didn't have a good word to say about his school days, so we had a connection. He was a self-made millionaire who was now buying up warehouses in Shoreditch for £5 a square metre, and selling them for £20 a square metre. He supplied me with the derelict warehouse for our club.

My partner and I opened Shoreditch's first nightclub at 5 Christina Street and we called it George's, as it was both our middle names. We didn't bother with a licence as we were going to stay open all night anyway. If anyone asked what was happening we said it was a private party and completely legal. It was a perfect place because nobody lived there so we weren't bothering anyone.

Growing up in a pub had given me many skills in the hospitality business. I worked as head barman and my partner took care of the food side of things. Narve, my mate from California, who was living back in London, worked as door security. In reflection I think it was more of an ego boost for me. I must have been mad. George's stayed open till 10am, so it was a nightclub and a breakfast club. It could hold 700 people and over time we hired it out for blues, raves, garage, techno and even a Rastafarian Christmas. I like lovers rock, which is calming music, so you can imagine this loud music nearly killed me after 10 hours. I always wore cotton wool in my ears.

On the nights when we hadn't hired the space out we played garage. We had a group of regulars from the local area who enjoyed the different themed nights we held. Whoever rented the club would decorate it in their style so it always looked different – laser lights ,spinning disco balls, projectors screening films or psychedelic images on the walls. One night someone brought a dwarf lady, a pretty girl no more than 3ft tall, in mini skirt, stockings and suspenders, and she danced on the bar all night, tip-toeing around peoples' drinks, as she swung her arms up and down and wiggled her tush. Everyone thought she was brilliant and bought her drinks all night. When Paula turned up and saw her, she went crazy as she thought I'd hired her. I had to explain that it was nothing to do with me.

The hirers rented the door, meaning they would sell their tickets and I would keep the profits from the bar, cloakroom and food. We also provided the security, and took offensive items off the partygoers. The weapons some people carried were unbelievable, and it wasn't as though they were tough guys – just ordinary people afraid of what others might do. I found it shocking and offensive if they carried a squirter of ammonia or acid. I'd ask them what they thought they were going to do with that in my club. We'd also confiscate any food or drink they tried to smuggle in themselves. We'd say, 'You're not coming to a picnic you know.' Obviously we made our money from the food and drink – even the cloakroom was worth hundreds of pounds per night.

The Rastafarian Christmas Day 7th January rave proved interesting. I didn't even know they celebrated Christmas on a date other than December 25th. I also didn't know they didn't drink alcohol. All they bought at the bar was soft drinks and curried goat, rice and peas. They were the easiest and nicest group we ever had there. Coxsone Sounds were playing the tunes – they were brought in from Brixton – they played reggae music while the Rastafarians chanted and jumped up and down like it was religious. I used to chat to the Rastafarians at the bar who explained that while some guys had their hair in locks for fashion, real Rastafarians have locks for religious reasons. Real Rastas are peaceful. All so calm and placid, it was like a breath of fresh air considering what we usually had to put up with .

One night we had trouble with a group of 10 men who stole my gold Longines watch. It was on my wrist one minute, then it was gone. The men were with the DJ, and his crew, and were the only people left in the club aside from my partner, the barman and me. It started with an argument over their wages – they'd drunk twice the agreed wages and owed me money. They tried to tell me the drinks were free. I had to explain I only give the first drink for free. I locked the club down and my partner, the barman and I told them they weren't getting out until I had my watch back. It didn't take long for the watch to appear on the bar but I was feeling very stressed.

Another night I rented the club to a crowd from Oxford. They paid me a lot of money to rent the door and they had the biggest, most expensive, sound system I'd ever seen. I thought it might blow the roof off it was so loud. They completed the set up by 4pm and informed me that they'd sold out of tickets and to expect a busy night. I told them we close when they stop buying drinks and if there were a few left in the morning it might be possible to stay open for £100 an hour. About 6pm they started to arrive in campervans – there must have been 100 hippy-like vans. They turned out to be a group of New Age Travellers called Spiral Tribe who lived permanently in their vans, and they'd organised it like a flashmob. They filled the club to breaking point then started to get rowdy. Some of them were outside removing anything that wasn't bolted down, smashing car windows and stealing the radios – just being a nuisance. The police closed the road with riot police both ends of Christina Street and the police commander came to the door with the fire brigade and tried to close us down due to fire regulations. We allowed the commander to walk around the club to inspect the fire exits and the fire extinguishers but they couldn't close us down because we had it organised. Then one of their leaders, a New Age Traveller, about 6ft 6 with a head like a basketball, who was paralytic after drinking at the bar all night, said. 'I've had a great night drinking and now I'm gonna fight that gaffer', meaning the police commander. 'No,' I said. 'No!' This was all I needed. I had to do some fast thinking and I said to him: 'What needs to happen is you can work for me on my security team. All you have to do is stand and guard the bar and you can have free drinks. You've got to keep the rest of your gang calm so there won't be any trouble.' Thankfully he agreed.

We had the worst night at the club and got away with it by the skin of our teeth. We took a lot of money but honestly money is not everything. This was when I knew I'd had enough. If I continued it would kill me. I couldn't stand the music and had cotton wool in my ears, I couldn't stand the drug taking and I couldn't stand the stress when we had trouble, plus I only saw daylight when I made my way home. I ended up hating it. Surely there was an easier way to make money. I needed to go back to flying. Living out of a small suitcase didn't seem so bad at this point.

What I hadn't realised was that I'd started the biggest party area of London since the West End, and it's still going strong. Today they come from all over the world to enjoy themselves in Shoreditch. I still go there on occasion. I visit the Troy Bar in Hoxton Street, which has the best Caribbean food in London. The owner Edward is a friend of mine. I like to hear the live music in his club, especially the saxophone on jazz nights.

I bought Carly a wire haired fox terrier, just like my grandad had bought me. Chippy had given me so much pleasure as a child. Terriers are dogs fit for royalty – King Edward VII, who reigned 1901–1910, owned a fox terrier and took it all over the world. The dog's name was Caesar of Notts (1898–1914) and he slept on a chair next to the King's bed.

A statue of Caesar is on the King and Queen's joint grave at St George's Chapel, Windsor Castle with an inscription written by Queen Alexandra that reads: 'Our beloved Caesar who was the King's faithful and constant companion until death and my greatest comforter in my loneliness and sorrow for four years'. If it's good enough for the King and Queen, then it's good enough for us.

My daughter loved her dog – a best friend for an only child. She named him Chippy.

# CHAPTER 16

# Florist to the Firm

Much as I wanted to look for a job as a pilot, my mum had been diagnosed with pancreatic cancer so no way could I leave London, and Paula and Carly wanted to stay. My mum had private medical insurance so she had the best treatment. She was fitted with a morphine machine with a line which gave her mobility for a long time while this ugly disease took its hold. It was all about the quality of life as her cancer was incurable. I found it difficult to accept, as she was only 50.

I bought a derelict shop in Roman Road, Bow, Mile End. I was going to name the shop after her as she was very ill. I wanted to move back into floristry but I didn't want a corporate florist this time, I wanted a local florist and I wanted it to specialise in wreath making. I'd researched the history of wreath making which fascinated me as wreaths have always been the custom at burials. Historically, the wreathmaker in the village was always treated with respect because if not, you wouldn't have flowers at your funeral. We purchased a pillar-box red Fleur de Lys van; this was a replica of a Roaring Twenties van, with huge brass headlamps and a big step to climb up into the cab. Not only was it distinctive, it was great for advertising and helped us launch with a bang. It was also big enough to carry two van loads worth of stock. We had the colour changed to racing green and my mum's name – Carole McQueen – hand painted on the side by Dave, a coach painter who operated out of a garage in Ellesmere Road. His trade had been handed down from father to son using a thick gooey paint which had a strange dirty smell. The finished van made my mum smile. I told her she was going to be famous. 'More like infamous,' she said. She wasn't wrong.

Carole McQueen Florist opened at 409 Roman Rd. On the old maps Roman Road started at the Aldgate end of the Roman Wall of the City of London and stretched to Colchester. One mile from Aldgate a hamlet sprung up, which was called Mile End. This is where we chose to go to work, in the heart of the East End. The council had recently changed the name of the East End to Tower Hamlets, instead of using the hamlets' names of Stepney, Poplar, Wapping etc,. For me the East End will always be the East End.

Our shop needed major renovations, structural as well as cosmetic. We chose a British racing green colour for the interior too. It was similar to the shade used by Harrods, which is one of the most expensive shops in London. We wanted it to ooze luxury because the flowers we were going to sell were the more expensive types, but we were selling them at lower prices, so it wouldn't be in anyone's interests to copy us. I knew no-one would be able to undercut us.

I was the first florist to bring Dutch flowers to the City of London and now I was the first to bring them to the East End. I'd arranged a line of credit with Gardeners wholesale flower importers and told them I'd clear their stand at the end of the week. This meant I would buy whatever they had left on their stand just before their new delivery, at a discount of around half price, regardless of what it was. I suggested this for two reasons: one was that Roman Road was also a street market where you could sell bargains, and two because we were going to hit the wreath-making side of the business. Wreaths need open flowers instead of buds, and open flowers are slightly older. The Dutch quality would outlast the cheaper flowers and still be beautiful and fresh in peoples' vases long after the cheaper versions had died. I stuck to my grandad's instructions to go first class. It's a winning formula. As well as flowers, we also sold helium balloons, cards and handmade chocolates.

The shop all went to plan – it was a needed service – but the wreath-making side of the business exploded. We were continually employing and training staff to keep up with the demand and we were at full capacity when our storage facility was completely full. Our customers came from all over London, even East Enders that had moved out to the suburbs would come for our wreaths. It wasn't unusual to send lorry loads of wreaths to Kent, Essex and even the suburbs of West London. Our craft ranged from the usual ring wreaths, which we'd make in various styles, to crafting wreaths shaped in things the deceased had owned or loved – dogs, caravans, slippers, Rizla packets. You name it. There wasn't anything we couldn't model out of flowers. The stranger the request the more interesting the challenge, and the staff loved it.

The traditional way to build a wreath was to shape with wet moss then wire in the flowers as the moss gave the blooms longer life. But we were working with Magic Moss, a company in Canning Town who made a dry version, which was more suitable for creating different shapes. You had to give the blooms a good drink before you cut and used them, and then match and blend the colours to create great effects. It's an art form, and it's what I liked about the job. The style with which we mixed our flowers set us apart from the rest of the florists, and floristry colleges sent their students to us to get experience from our shop and to learn the old traditional techniques we used, and the modern ones we also implemented. We'd also teach the local girls to arrange flowers so they always had a skill to use if they wanted to – whether it was to gain money, self-worth or happiness. I enjoyed this more than flying a plane. Sharing my time with the people I love is worth more than all the tea in China.

I created a hot air balloon flower arrangement, which became one of our best creations. It was 5ft tall, with a giant netted helium coloured balloon floating over a flower arrangement in a basket. When we delivered one of these it usually brought the recipient to tears because of the sheer size of it. I suppose they thought it measured love. I can't count the number of times the lady I delivered it to gave me a hug. She'd be shocked, speechless and emotional. I'd usually have to navigate it into the house. One was sent to Paula Yates at the Big Breakfast studios, which was around the corner from our shop. She rang and thanked us. Carole McQueen Florist soon became a magnet to the rich and famous, and it was my privilege to meet a lot of interesting people.

We all need to send wreaths and apologies or send flowers to the one we love. It's certainly not the easiest way to make money

– I was in Covent Garden in the early hours of the morning, every morning, and working with flowers is hard, hard work. But it's a lifestyle, and for me it was all about the pursuit of happiness. To me, my customers and all my staff were like a big family of happy people.

The shop had a basement office and all sorts of people came to chat, have a cup of tea and take a rest from shopping up and down Roman Road. I welcomed them in as long as we didn't have a big job on. People interest me and I always make time to get to know interesting people. I like to listen and most people like to talk, and I hold a lot of personal secrets which will stay secret. I got to know who has mistresses, who needs to apologise, who's fallen in love and been struck by the elusive lightning bolt, who dies and who cries. I used to think it was like being a priest as they trusted me and I was to be trusted. If I was the cause of gossip it would ruin me.

On March 17th 1995, I got a phone call from Laurie O'Leary, who I knew through my dad. He told me Ronnie Kray had died after collapsing at Broadmoor Hospital for the criminally insane and Reggie Kray wanted to speak to me. Laurie informed me that Reg, who was in Maidstone Prison, would be in touch with me by phone tomorrow lunchtime. He said Reg was trying to come to terms with the death of his twin and if I showed the appropriate respect I'd be fine. He said Reg always announces himself so when I answer the phone and a voice says, 'Reg Kray speaking', it's not a joke, it's him.

I knew Laurie as he'd lived opposite my dad for years. Not only was he manager of the world-famous clairvoyant Doris Stokes, he managed various bands and even organised tours for Marvin Gaye. He also looked after Ronnie Kray's affairs on the outside, and he'd once ordered a wreath for Buster Edwards on behalf of Reg. I hadn't heard Buster had died and checked it out, just in case I was getting involved in an argument. Unfortunately it was true.

Laurie had been working with the Krays on a business level since the 1960s at the Krays' nightclub, Esmeralda's Barn in Wilton Place, Knightsbridge, where Laurie was manager. I had a lot to think about that night. It didn't take a genius to work out what was coming. The next day I got a phone call. 'Reg Kray speaking,' said a soft voice, and I'd hear that greeting many times in the coming years as this was the first call of many.

The Kray twins were Britain's most high-profile gangsters and the closest we came to having our own mafia. Born and raised in the East End, the identical twins came into the world on October 24th 1933, with Reggie 10 minutes older than Ronnie. They ran organised crime in London for nearly 20 years with their gang called the Firm, and were involved in murder, armed robbery, arson, protection rackets and long firms (which is when they place lots of small orders with a business, pay promptly, be considered trustworthy and then place bigger orders they never pay for). If you upset them they'd maim you or kill you without a second thought. You didn't swim with the fishes in London, you were placed under a flyover sucking up concrete. They were the only criminals monitored by military intelligence at the time because they were a threat to national security. Despite this, many people loved them for their Hollywood gangster image. They were criminal showbiz, rubbing shoulders with the rich and famous, even Hollywood A listers.

They killed a lot of people and a lot of people went missing, but they were finally arrested in 1968, and a year later convicted and given life sentences (with a minimum of 30 years) for the murder of Jack 'The Hat' McVitie, a minor member of their gang. Ronnie was also convicted of the public execution of George Cornell in the Blind Beggar pub, to which Reggie was an accessory. The trial at the Old Bailey was the longest and most expensive at the time.

I was caught between the devil and the deep blue sea. If I refused, anything could happen, and if I did it wrong I'd also get in trouble. It didn't matter that Ron was dead and Reg was inside. They had many contacts walking the streets who would do their work for them. I decided to bite the bullet. I'm not in the business of vetting customers – it's not my job to ask where their money comes from. I'm just the florist, so I decided to do my job.

'Hello Reg,' I said. 'I'm sorry for your loss.' My heart rate increased. 'Thank you,' he replied. 'You know why I'm ringing, I've been told you're the best man for the job.' 'No problem Reg,' I replied. He went on to tell me that he wanted the very best flowers, absolutely no expense spared, and Laurie would sort out the bill.

He then said, 'I've been told to call you Nicky, is that right?' 'That's right Reg.' He went on to tell me he'd made me an appointment at Maidstone Prison. I didn't need a visiting order, they'd be expecting me. This was so he could decide which flower arrangements he wanted. I told him I'd bring photo albums for him to look at so he could get an idea of what he wanted. The appointment was at 2pm the following day and two guys would be at my shop at noon to escort me to the meeting. 'Is that alright?' he asked. 'Of course,' I said. 'I'll see you then,' he replied, and hung up. My hand that held the phone was now sweaty. I hadn't experienced this since the early days holding the yoke of a plane.

The girls in the shop prepared the albums and I dressed smartly in a suit and tie instead of the usual work jeans. I'd arranged with my friend Danny Williams to drive us as I felt that was better than getting into a car with two guys I didn't know, especially when they were friends of the Krays. I remembered what happened to Gianni Russo's character in *The Godfather*. Fuck that – start as you mean to go on. Danny was excited about meeting Reggie Kray, whereas I was more anxious. On Laurie's advice I'd taken off my watch and made sure I wasn't wearing any rings. Apparently Reg would say, 'That's a lovely watch or ring' and 50 per cent of the time you'd leave without them and he'd sell them to a prison guard.

Reg's friends turned up at 11.30am and after a brief introduction we were off. We chatted all the way and before I knew it we were outside Maidstone Prison. It brought back memories of Boggo Road – some things you can never forget.

H.M.P Maidstone, built in 1819, is one of the oldest penal institutions in Britain. A category C prison holding 600 inmates, it's where Reg married his second and last wife, Roberta Jones. Today Maidstone Prison is used to hold foreign nationals. I went inside and told the guard we were here to see Mr Kray. 'This way,' he replied and took us to the visiting room where the four of us sat down. There were four other people in there waiting to see him, and we sat on two tables of four. It wasn't long before Reg came to the other side of the large visiting room, walked to an empty table in the middle and stood there. He spoke to a guard who came to me and said Reg wanted to see me first. It was like he was holding court and this was the queue.

The first thing I noticed as I approached the table was his Harley Davidson belt buckle. He was much shorter than I'd imagined – only about 5ft 7 – and he smiled and seemed pleased to see me, which I suppose was a good sign. He made no attempt to shake my hand so nor did I try. He sat down and put his elbows on the table clasping his hands and said: 'I go to bed at 8 o'clock. I sleep on the floor. Red Indians sleep on the floor.' I was speechless. I thought, 'Is this what happens to you when you spend 30 years in a cell?'

I was used to all forms of strange behaviour. The death of a loved one affects us all differently: some are angry, broken, numb, and others are over the top and hysterical. But I needed to be more careful than usual when it came to responding to him. This was a gangster of epic proportions who had lost his closest relative, and he still had a large following and a lot of power outside the prison walls. He was now the undisputed Godfather of the British mafia. He may have been in prison but his suits were made in Savile Row and his shirts were bespoke and made by the shirt maker to Prince Charles. He said the Firm told him he needed me to do this job for Ronnie. He told me he wanted the closest thing to a state funeral. This was a big deal.

After a while he started to relax, and I got the impression he could show himself without playing me. I opened the albums containing the photographs of all the possible wreaths available and he went through each page slowly, stopping briefly at the wreaths that interested him. I could see his eyes glazing as the emotions kicked in. Then he closed the albums and said, 'Nicky, this is what I want you to do.' He leant forward and said, 'Get your pen.' I pulled out my pen from my inside pocket and wrote down his exact instructions. 'We will speak soon,' he said when I'd finished. 'Send those two over on your way out' and he pointed to the guys I'd come with. He was nice. I warmed to him.

He rang the next day: 'Reg Kray speaking.' He adjusted his order as he'd changed his requirements slightly, and he told me more about what was going to happen on the day. The press had got wind of our involvement and were trying to get information from us at the shop. I'd had a meeting with my staff and told them there were to be no loose lips. Narve and Micky Goldtooth took turns in providing security at the shop to keep the press away so the girls could do their job.

Reg had insisted that anyone ordering Ronnie's flowers should only use me, as he didn't want any second-rate flowers turning up. That was easier said than done. The phone didn't stop ringing with orders but I pulled the plug on the 100th wreath as my staff were working flat out and it was too much. Rule number one: don't be greedy. The calls were coming in from all over the world, from stars of stage and screen as well as mob guys from New York, Los Angeles and Glasgow, all wanting to place orders to pay their respects. They were ordering wreaths in the shape of boxing gloves and boxing rings because of the Krays' successful boxing careers. Money was no object to these guys. The names on the cards were breathtaking.

Reggie and I spoke on the phone most days, and we got on well. He also sent me lots of letters and he used his 1960s headed note paper, which bore a picture of him when he was young. One letter was dated and the time given was 3.30am. It made me feel a touch uneasy to think he was thinking about me in the middle of the night. He was arranging a huge funeral for Ronnie, knowing it was going to bring parts of London to a standstill. His personal wreath read 'TO THE OTHER HALF OF ME' in large letters made of pure white chrysanthemums.

We made all 100 wreaths with special requirements. One read 'THE COLONEL' – which was Ronnie's nickname as he was the one who gave the orders to the gang; he was the driving force and the killer – in large floral letters. Laurie came in the shop and gave me ten grand to pay their part of the bill. We were still selling bouquets but no more wreaths. The press were still trying to get a glimpse of what was happening inside the shop and we were dubbed 'Florist to the Firm'. The staff worked seven days and three nights leading up to the funeral. It was the biggest funeral London had ever seen for someone who wasn't a royal or a politician.

On the day of the funeral we had police escorts to get the flowers to the undertakers: W. English & Sons in Bethnal Green, and we had blue flashing lights for at least six trips in our Roaring Twenties van, with its huge brass headlamps shining bright. Paula and my friend Chris were taking it in turns to deliver the flowers and put them carefully in position, and I would personally check each wreath before it left. The last van load of flowers was accompanied by my florists, who not only wanted to see the event, but were also on hand to help move the more delicate arrangements. The funeral cortege were told not to move until they had all the flowers on board.

Traffic was at a standstill and the pavements were full of people for miles, with menacing-looking security everywhere. Reg had also ordered flowers in the shape of a broken heart for the grave of his first wife Frances who took her own life aged 23. He'd also bought fresh flowers for his mum Violet's grave. There were bouquets of red Bukhara scented roses on board our van for Reg (who was allowed out of prison to attend) with plenty to throw into the grave. The most important wreath was the cross for the coffin, a 5ft long, tightly packed cross consisting of Bianca white scented roses, with the spray in the middle of the cross created out of Bukhara red roses. As the cross was moved it left a trail of the sweetest scent.

The world's press were all over taking photographs of our wreaths and the police were also out in force, both on the ground and hovering above in helicopters. More than 10 cars were in the procession and once Reg was in his car, the horse and carriage hearse pulled away to make its way to St Matthew's Church in Bethnal Green, near Brick Lane. Nobody stopped at the traffic lights. The police asked us to put our van last so they knew where the cortege ended. On one side of the carriage was the wreath 'TO THE OTHER HALF OF ME' and on the other side hung 'RON', a wreath made with pink gin chrysanthemums – which are actually lilac in colour – with orchid sprays on the side. One of my favourites.

After the church service the army of gangsters got back into the cars while the well-wishers climbed up on walls and roofs of buildings to get a look at them. Some even shimmied up the street lamps. Then it was on to Chingford Mount Cemetery where the Krays bury their dead. It was a long road leading up to the cemetery gates. Crowds still lined the street and there were people everywhere: well-wishers, mourners and people just wanting a glimpse of Reggie. Ronnie was laid to rest and Reggie laid flowers on his loved ones' graves, and then it was back to prison. It wasn't the last time I'd hear from him.

The wake took place at Lenny McLean's pub The Guvnors. I was so tired as we'd worked through the night and I was pleased the job had gone well. The Firm was there and so were the police, filming everybody from the rooftop opposite. The Firm left guards to monitor the grave for days afterwards as the press coverage continued.

Reggie thought my team had done a great job and his letters of thanks were never ending. He asked if there was anything he could do for me and if so I shouldn't be shy. Just ask. Hmm.

The day after the funeral, Carole McQueen Florist was blasted across the global press, and the *Daily Mirror* even put a cartoon of me in the newspaper. It was a picture of me drinking champagne and smoking a cigar on a beach with a couple of beauties and the wreath 'RON' in the surrounding trees. It read: 'He used to be an East End florist until he made a killing on the Kray funeral.' I loved it and bought the original from the cartoonist Charles Griffin for £70, after visiting his office in the *Daily Mirror*. It still hangs on my wall today. Robert Maxwell, Ghislaine Maxwell's father, had previously owned the *Mirror* and had stolen millions from the employees' pensions. When he was owner, he noticed in one edition that Griffin's cartoon had 'Fuck Maxwell', written on a wall in the background of the cartoon, disguised as graffiti. Maxwell went crazy but Griffin defended himself by saying someone had added that once he'd finished the cartoon.

The shop was now infamous so my mum was right. She'd look at me shaking her head and smiling.

The majority of our fresh stock was bought at the big markets, such as New Covent Garden flower market at Vauxhall, but when we only needed a small amount of flowers, we'd go to the local flower market New Spitalfields. Paula liked to go there because we didn't need to get up early but I didn't like it as there were too many pigeons, so I'd meet her at the shop. One particular morning I went out to the van to unload and saw a pigeon splattered across the radiator. It had been hit with force and was a real mess. I asked Paula if she'd had an accident. She said she hadn't so I showed her the mess the van was in. Some months earlier I'd gone to New Spitalfields in a suit and tie because I had a meeting later in the day. I was standing writing out a cheque inside the building when all of a sudden wallop, I was covered in pigeon shit, and I mean covered from head to toe. It was as though a flock of birds had done a synchronised shit on me and the stench made me want to vomit. The market had nets above to catch the bird poops, but the netting had got so heavy that it collapsed, just when I happened to be under it.

The market authorities took me to their offices so I could have a shower and they gave me a paper suit – like the forensic teams have – to put on. I had to walk across the whole market looking like I was sniffing out a dead body, as the porters from one end to the other were shouting 'Shithead!' and crying with laughter. It was so embarrassing and it ruined my day. I'd asked the market authority insurers to pay for the ruined Boss suit I was wearing but all I got from them were tears of laughter and they told me they'd put my letter of claim on their office wall to cheer the staff up. So that's why I get up early and go to New Covent Garden where there are no pigeons. At least Paula got one – but the bloody thing took ages to get off the van. Every so often Paula would go to Covent Garden for me. She didn't mind the early start because that meant she could go home earlier in the afternoon. One day after Paula had been to Covent Garden a customer came into our shop. He said he was only there to buy his wife flowers because he'd never laughed so much earlier that day. I asked him what he meant and he said that he was a lorry driver and he'd been waiting in the traffic at London Bridge to go through the police check. Our van with a lady driver was right next to him. He said she yawned and stretched, with her hand outside the window not realising she had a lit cigarette in her hand, she screamed in pain as her hand hit something. Then he heard voice say, 'Stupid bitch', which came from a cyclist with a big bindi in the middle of his forehead where her cigarette had hit him. The lorry driver said he hadn't laughed so much in years. Paula had said nothing about it to me or the girls, but I suppose it got a sale.

Fairground owners – showmen – would often use the shop and their traditions were similar to the Cockney funerals. All of them send huge wreaths, with each family member trying to send a bigger wreath than the next. One day a showman came in and asked for a door key in his Irish country accent. Carly sent him up the road to the hardware shop where keys were cut. Ten minutes later he was back and said in his Irish accent, 'No lady, I want the darkie! The best wreath maker in London. My mum has died.' He meant Paula. We sat him down and he made a huge order while having a cup of tea. He ordered wreaths in the shape of his mum's caravan, her television, her music player and pretty much all her favourite possessions. Four days later he came back to pick them up, and filled two lorries with wreaths.

In 1996, a year after Ronnie Kray's funeral, it was his memorial. Reggie ordered a huge wreath which said, 'TOGETHER IN SPIRIT WE WALK AS ONE' with clasped hands in the centre. It was so big we had to move it in a lorry so as not to damage the flowers. He also organised a flypast while the gravestone was being laid. The prison wouldn't let Reggie out for it but he asked me and Paula to attend to keep his older brother Charlie company. The press were there as usual and Paula and I were on the national news once again.

Reggie didn't pay in full this time and still wanted to order from my staff and add to his credit account. He was sending all manner of gifts and wreaths to people. He even sent the girls in our shop to the toy shop to buy Lance presents. Lance was a boy who'd run alongside Ronnie's hearse for miles during the funeral. They were told to put it on his tab. The bill was now £4,000 and I stopped it and called Laurie to demand payment. He apologised but told me he'd warned me, and that he was only in charge of Ronnie's money. Reggie told me on the phone that I'd had loads of free advertising and I should be thankful. He'd long firmed me, which is what he was famous for. I was upset and spoke to a couple of people in the same prison who had accounts in the shop and were on the same wing as Reg. They both asked him for my money and a couple of days later I got a message back saying I'd be getting paid. Now that can mean one of two things: I'm getting my money or they were going to put a hit on me. Someone did come in with the cash but it was only £500. I never saw any more money and Reg stopped phoning.

We did all the Krays' funerals. Gary Kray was Charlie's only son and he died young, which was sad. Charlie was a gentleman and was in my shop a lot drinking tea, and burying your child is the very worst thing you can do, but I'm running a business so he had to pay up front. Charlie would reminisce about his childhood, and how he and the twins and cousin Billy would nick a wooden beer barrel from Truman's Brewery, put one of them inside, then roll them down Brick Lane. When they got out of the barrel they couldn't stand up.

Lenny 'The Guv'nor' McLean would pop in the shop to make sure we were all OK. Lenny liked chatting to the girls and he was quite famous at the time as he'd appeared in the film *Lock, Stock and Two Smoking Barrels* alongside Jason Statham and Vinnie Jones. This particular day he was shaping up like a boxer in front of the shop, saying to Paula, 'Hit me. Hit me.' He was always asking her to punch him, so this day she did. She punched him with a belter, straight to the solar plexus. His eyes widened as he fell to the ground with a crash. He couldn't breathe. He was a huge man and he really wasn't expecting that. I had to help him up and make him some tea. I'm sure he liked the girls' sympathy. Unfortunately, it wasn't long before he became a customer, as he died in 1998. He was another person who wanted to go first class.

The shop welcomed a never-ending procession of gangsters and stars wanting the best flowers money could buy. Most of them had become friendly with us while we were burying someone they loved, and they nearly always came back for a cup of tea to talk about the person we'd buried. It was strange psychology because a lot of the time we didn't know them that well, we just provided the flowers, so the staff were under orders to treat them nicely – it was like we were counsellors.

One day, the phone rang and a soft voice said 'Reg Kray speaking.' I'd already been told he was very ill and was expected to die. I never thought for a second he'd want me to make his own funeral flowers, let alone order them himself. He wanted the same flowers as his brother, exactly the same. I knew we were going to be busy so I cancelled all my appointments. He ordered the flowers five days before he died of cancer. It was the first and last time I experienced that. Reggie even sent me tickets for the funeral. He still owed me money, so his wife Roberta had to pay up front for all that he ordered. It was another huge gangster funeral, dealing once again with the most vicious men in the country and trying very hard not to get anything wrong. Fortunately, everyone seemed pleased.

Off we went once again to St Matthew's Church. The streets were a log jam of people and we had to push our way through the crowds. Heavyset gangsters acted like doormen on the gate and admitted us with our tickets. On entering the church I could see that all the chairs had names on, and our names were at the back – the worst seats there. Thanks Reg.

Now I'd already had a phone call to say that Freddie Foreman, Tony and Chris Lambrianou and the rest of the old guard from the Firm had boycotted the whole event due to being told that Reggie wanted young gay men to carry his coffin and not them. So the Firm were not coming, yet I could see their names on the chairs at the front of the church. On the best seats. As my grandad always told me to go first class, off I went and sat at the front in the empty chairs with my company. Maureen Flanagan was the only one sitting on a chair in the row, she was a friend of mine and was famous for being one of the first Page 3 girls. She was good friends with the Krays, and still a very attractive woman. There were film stars and famous people dotted about, and the church was full of TV cameras, which meant it was unlike any church service I'd ever seen before – and I'd seen a few.

As we settled down we noticed the Rest in Peace sign that rested on top of the cross of white Bianca roses was screwed into a ball. Reg had purposely ordered them because they were the same roses Ronnie had on his coffin, and their scent filled the church. I told Paula to get up and fix it as the world would be viewing our work when Reggie's coffin left the church. It certainly never left our workshop like that. Someone had screwed it up. As Paula got up and walked towards the coffin, the security edged forward in protection mode before realising she was correcting the damaged wreath. All was now well, and the service started.

After the service the cortege left to go to Chingford Mount Cemetery to bury Reggie with Ronnie. The streets were lined with people like this was a hero going to his grave, all very similar to Ronnie's funeral.

After the graveyard burial it was back to the Horn of Plenty pub in the East End for the wake. This was Solly's pub, and I knew him well as the East End is a small place. Solly was a small guy full of character, very chatty with big round spectacles. On arrival he came up to me and whispered that they were going to kill me. Now I took this to mean they were upset, not that they were literally going to kill me. He went on to explain that the chairs I sat in at the church were supposed to remain empty, to make a statement. 'It was for the world to see and you ruined it,' he hissed in my ear. I took a deep breath and carried on, not telling the rest of my party as to not frighten them. As for a message to the world, I've just done that for them in writing – I hope that this puts things right.

# CHAPTER 17

# The Green Man

As well as funerals, TV work was piling in from the Three Mills Studios in Stratford, London. We were working on shows including *Bad Girls,* which was set in a women's prison. I had a contract with Shed Productions to install and maintain the jail garden and I needed to spend at least one day a week on set, in a fake prison. It reminded me of Boggo Road and the threat of solitary confinement in the black hole, eating only bread and water. It was something I could never forget. The fibreglass TV prison was a replica of Oxford Prison – which is a hotel today – and even up close you couldn't tell it wasn't made of stone.

One day the production company told me they needed a summer greenhouse in winter, which we made. These were the sort of challenges we'd get. Every day we faced different demands on different jobs in different locations. After finishing the summer greenhouse, one of the production team rang Paula and asked if I watched *Bad Girls.* She told them I didn't so they insisted I watch it that evening because my greenhouse, which I'd worked so hard to produce, was going to have a starring role. That evening Paula and I sat down in front of the TV just in time to see my beautiful greenhouse get blown up in a prison break. Paula laughed, but for the life of me I couldn't find it funny.

We also worked on *Footballers' Wives, London Bridge, London's Burning, EastEnders, The Jonathan Ross Show* and *Later...With Jools Holland,* and we had movie work all over the country. I was known as the green man on set. Anything plant or floral was my department.

One film (the name of which I can't recall but it was about ghosts) asked me to create a fake Walthamstow Market flower stall, which the two ghosts would buy flowers from. They had to use me in the film as they couldn't find an extra who could wrap the flowers right. When they'd finished filming they told me to throw the flowers away. Of course I didn't, I sold them cheap. They shot it all but it was too dark so they had to do it again (each shoot cost £3,000, but they said they were insured for this kind of thing). So I had to set up another fake stall, appear as an extra again and once again, I sold the flowers off cheap. I was also paid for my acting. What a great job.

My staff really enjoyed the variety, never knowing what was coming next. We used to get invited to a lot of the wrap parties, and they were also offered roles as extras. Paula and two of my staff were in *Footballers' Wives*. There was a christening and Paula and the girls delivered the flowers on camera. Paula was actually offered a bigger role as one of the prisoners in *Bad Girls*. I had to tell them to stop poaching my wife, and my staff, and to get their actors from the agency like they were supposed to.

Once, while we were working on *EastEnders*, we were told they needed a wreath made of white silk carnations to read 'FRANK' in 20 inch letters with lilac sprays. I ran to the bookies to place a £20 bet on Frank in *EastEnders* dying. I got great odds and all the girls in the shop followed suit, placing smaller bets. We thought we were going to make some money. We waited a few weeks and, sure enough, Peggy flew out to Spain for Frank's funeral. But it was an insurance con and Frank was very much alive. Oh well, that taught us a lesson. We lost our money.

I've always enjoyed a project. If I have an idea, I like to get it out of my system by giving it a go. I always prefer to regret what I did do rather than what I didn't. The flower game is flawed when you're trying to grow a business. This is because the stock is perishable and it allows staff to steal and say the flowers were no good so they threw them away (yeah, right). So I had an idea.

I decided to invent a fresh-flower vending machine with a carousel system. By doing so I'd eliminate staff costs and rule out pilfering. I built my first machine at Allen Jones' chair frame factory ALS in Hainault, Essex. Allen was very good to me and gave me and my friends the run of his factory. It went well and I paid a small fortune for the design copyright and intellectual property paperwork to prove that this was my invention, and to prevent anyone else from copying it. We designed it to look like an old Victorian stall and set it up in front of the Royal London Hospital on Whitechapel Road. It sold bouquets and had to be stocked morning, afternoon and night. It was there for three years but we did have some problems with people breaking into the machine to try and steal the technology. They were trying to find out the widget that was keeping the flowers fresh when, in reality, it was just fresh flowers, and a pair of ladies' tights holding it together because the fan belt kept slipping. In hindsight, we should have had it chain driven.

The flower vending machine made great headlines in local and national papers. The TV soon had me on the news with reporters saying it would be big, and comparing it to the jukebox. I was interviewed by all the news channels, ITV, BBC, SKY News and many others, and received huge orders for the machines from all over the world, especially hot countries because the machine was chilled. One of the orders was from Israel, for 50 machines, but I couldn't find the right manufacturer, and a foreign company stole the idea and the concept. The carousel system is still used today to vend various products.

The shop was really busy with famous funerals coming in the whole time. It always starts with a phone call, just as it did when Ian Dury, the singer and frontman of Ian Dury and the Blockheads (famed for songs including *Hit Me With Your Rhythm Stick*) died. The call from New York wasn't unusual but the order was. The caller proceeded to order a giant wreath which said 'DUREX'. I explained that in Britain, Durex was a well-known brand of condoms and he thanked me but said it meant exactly the same in the United States. He told me that when Ian organised his US tour he tried to get Durex to sponsor him, and told them it was because he was going to use plenty of their product. We fulfilled the order and it was placed in pride of place on top of his hearse. I think Ian Dury would have had a laugh at that.

Christmas put a lot of pressure on us, as we were selling more than 200 Christmas trees on top of the normal work, as well as Christmas wreaths for graves. Winter is the time when people give in and die, so it was one of our busiest times. It's ironic that Christmas time, traditionally the happiest, most magical time of year, is the dying season. We trained scores of young girls to be fast and professional at floristry. The teacher training licence I'd obtained in California, in order to teach trainee pilots, gave me an understanding of how to get the best out of our students.

When they came from college, they were very slow at making the arrangements, taking an hour to make one piece. Paula needed to train them to work at the speed I wanted, which was 12 minutes per piece, and it had to be perfect. Time is money and we sold time. They could make a living from flowers if they were fast, perfectionist, and not scared of hard work. It was the only way to be successful in the flower game. Because floristry is hard work – moving buckets full of dirty water, sacks of discarded old flowers, cutting and standing the new flowers in fresh water. Trainee florists didn't realise what the job involved – it's not always playing with pretty flowers. Some couldn't stand the pace or last the course but I'm proud to say that many of our employees, both male and female, have their own businesses in London now and are doing very well.

My mum died. It was a blessing really, after the long battle she'd had with cancer. She only weighed about 5 stone towards the end. Enough said. I found it difficult as most of us do, but she had a beautiful send off. I missed her terribly and stayed at home for a few months after her death, moping and lacking in motivation. The shop ran without me so I didn't really have to bother.

To make matters worse, Paula wasn't feeling too good. She was behaving out of character and I felt she was angry, miserable and just not herself. I thought it must be hormones or something so in order to cheer her up, I bought an all-inclusive holiday to the Canary Islands thinking she'd appreciate the change of scene and much-needed rest. While we were on the plane she started screaming in pain and throwing up green vomit. The pilot organised an ambulance to be waiting at Gran Canaria Airport and when we landed she was taken straight to hospital. They discovered her kidney had grown four times its size and needed lancing and draining to give temporary pain relief. She was full of poison.

She was put into a medically-induced coma for over a week, while I slept in a chair next to her. I was told the kidney needed to be removed. The hospital had undoubtedly saved her life but when she came round, she said she wanted the surgery in England. When we arrived back at Gatwick, our medical insurance company BUPA had an ambulance waiting on the runway and took her straight to hospital. The kidney surgeon told us that she needed two weeks complete rest before he'd remove the kidney, and then she had it removed. This was a serious operation taking away a major organ and I cannot thank the people looking after her enough. Professor Frank Chinegwundoh and the staff of The London Independent Hospital gave her the very best care. They explained that it had taken 15 years for her kidney to get in this state and this was the reason she'd had problems getting pregnant. They told me Jeffrey Steinberg really should have run some kidney tests during IVF as it's the first thing any doctor looks for when fertility problems arise.

Once Paula had recovered, she wanted to retrieve her embryos from the freezer in LA as it wasn't too late for us to have children. We contacted the clinic, which was now in Las Vegas, and were told they'd lost them, which we found hard to believe. More like they'd been sold on to childless couples. We couldn't get to speak to Jeffrey Steinberg, even though he'd taken our money. They refused to tell us where our seven embryos – our potential children – were. We took legal advice to try and locate them, only to be told that America has a thing called statute of limitations, which meant that after seven years they were no longer legally liable. As it had been 10 years, we didn't have a leg to stand on. We don't have this in Britain so it was all the more upsetting for us to think we might have children in the world and we don't know them, or even know if there were ever children. And if our kids were out there, we couldn't even pass on important medical information to them.

# CHAPTER 18

# Alexander McQueen

My little cousin Lee, better known as the globally renowned fashion designer Alexander McQueen (Alexander is his middle name), rang me in a panic as his set director had messed the catwalk up and he needed my help. I pulled my staff off the TV set they were working on and we went to Christchurch in Spitalfields to see how we could correct the problem. He said the models had to walk through a dirty fire escape and did we have any plants or something to make it look better? I'd helped him before when he needed flowers and I wouldn't charge him. Now it was 1996 and although he was well known at this point, having launched his own fashion label four years earlier, he still didn't have any money and I believe he was making all the clothes by hand. Plus, he was family, and his big brother Tony was my babysitter when I was a kid and was the best fun. Not many people wanted to look after me as I was a handful so I've got a lot of affection for them. Some of my family would turn out their lights when they saw me approaching their house and pretend they weren't in so they didn't have to look after me. But good old Tony was always there for me.

My Aunt Renee (who was also Lee's aunt) funded the fashion house Alexander McQueen because Lee's dad, my Uncle Ronnie, had refused to, for whatever reason. He probably regretted that as Lee was a breath of fresh air in the fashion industry and made a huge impact right from the beginning. Lee went to Saint Martins college, and the fashion editor and nurturer of young talent, Isabella Blow, bought his entire first collection and backed him financially. She'd visit me at my shop and have a cup of tea on occasion. Her husband Detmar Blow also supported Lee and attended his shows, which went from strength to strength.

When Lee invented bumsters – trousers that didn't quite cover the bum – he was dubbed the 'bad boy of fashion'. During his apprenticeship in Savile Row making suits, he became infamous for chalking penises in Prince Charles' suit linings. He even made suits for Mikhail Gorbachev. I wonder what he put inside his linings? Lee was a great tailor – his men's suits were made to perfection.

We got to Christchurch in the heart of the East End to repair the catwalk entrance, which was dirty old plasterboard and unsightly. I'd designed an arch made from more than 300 of the deepest red, almost black, Baccara roses. I wanted it to be subtle so as not to overpower the clothes, and the scent was amazing. Lee reckoned the smell would boost the models' confidence as they entered the catwalk, which was in the shape of a crucifix, to the sound of organ music and gunfire.

We nailed pins in every inch, which took hours, and people walked past sniggering,  wondering what we were doing. After three hours of pinning, we weaved contorted willow around the arch and added Hypericum with variegated ivy, soft Ruscus foliage and white Stephanotis then we added the roses. The arch was beautiful, and all of a sudden the sneering audience began a round of applause. The entrance for the models was now spectacular and it put a smile on Lee's face. You'd never have known it was a plasterboard doorway.

The show looked amazing and I also made two thank you bouquets, one for Lee and one for his mum Joyce, which were presented at the end of the show. Afterwards, I was invited backstage to drink champagne with Lee, Kate Moss and other models (Paula and the girls were tired out and went home). We passed the Cristal champagne bottle to each other, taking huge swigs out of the bottle to get the bubbly lift. Kate was nice and down to earth, and now we've seen her help Johnny Depp you've just got to love her.

Lee was starting to come down from the stress, knowing he'd created another winner. He just needed to wait to hear what the press would say. He invited me to the after party at a leather bar in Soho so I caught a black Hackney cab – the best taxis in London and part of the reason London is a great city. We stopped outside a bar, which had a big sign that said IRONMAN. Two 6ft 6 gay guys, with arms the size of my legs, rippling with muscle and wearing leather waistcoats, were on the door so I tried to act tough. I entered and everyone was so very nice to me. I was ushered to the VIP area and then I got introduced as Alexander McQueen's cousin, the florist. Gay men flocked around me asking me if I was a designer too. 'No,' I replied in my deepest Cockney voice, 'I'm a florist.' I didn't get drunk, that's for sure. Lee was a hero to the gay community.

The next day the press gave a sullied report on the flowers saying Lee had put his mother's flower shop in the frame and that couldn't have been further from the truth. My company was Carole McQueen Florist, which was named after my mum not his. It was too late for him to put me in the credits of the programme so he'd asked me to put my business card on all the chairs. I really didn't need more customers, as we'd already peaked as a company, I only did it to comply with his wishes as he was racing around getting ready for the opening. It only takes one idiot to mess up a live show and I didn't want that to be me, while he was putting the final touches to his genius. The press inferred he was greedy by using his mother to do the floristry and it upset him.

Needless to say the show, Dante, has since been heralded as the greatest fashion show on Earth and a turning point in his fortunes. Not long after this he became head designer for Givenchy in Paris. Lee not only conquered the world of fashion, he changed the way people thought about fashion and to do that is truly wonderful – an East End thing. A gay icon, Lee was awarded British Designer of the Year by the British Fashion Council four times between 1996 and 2001 and a CBE (Commander of the most Excellent Order of the British Empire) in 2003. I'm very proud of my little cousin.

# CHAPTER 19

# BulbWorld

I started to have strange dreams and one was about a story called *BulbWorld*. I knew what it meant. It meant that I should pass on some of my horticultural knowledge to adults, and especially to children.

Children would come into my shop and buy a fully grown daffodil in a pot, take it to school and pretend they'd grown it themselves. It was supposed to be their science homework. I always thought it was a shame that they were missing out on the pleasure of actually growing a daffodil. That's when I thought I could write a story and make flowers and plants more interesting for them. They may think planting trees is boring but it's the answer to global warming and offsetting pollution.

I knew about pollution only too well, not only from flying in the Los Angeles smog, but by the lead deposits left on the petals of flowers displayed outside the flower shop. The blooms only had to be outside for a couple of hours and they'd be completely covered with little black dots, making them worthless. If this was happening to flowers, what was happening to humans, young and old, who breathe in polluted air? The scientists had warned the world but governments and corporations took little notice due to the financial impact of making the appropriate changes. This was the late 1990s and we weren't as educated about the planet as we are now.

The only way I could see how to change things was to educate children about how reforestation can help the planet and slow down global warming. About how planting fir trees tactically, in areas prone to flooding, can enable them to suck up the water like a sponge, and how trees can shade walkways and so on. The plan for *BulbWorld* was to get them interested in planting at a young age.

I put a team together to produce a children's book that came with a pack of bulbs. Jill Truman wrote the book to make it suitable for five year olds, and Brian Norwood drew the characters and all the illustrations. The Bulbs would come to life when the children were at school, or asleep, and have magical adventures in the garden. Paula opened McQueen Publishers to produce the book and I started to think of ways to promote the book and its concept. How to get the message out: 'Plant the planet, save the world.'

I decided to turn *BulbWorld* the book into a musical and the project went from a few costumes to a full musical with a 35-strong cast and 15 production staff. My friend Jerry Cody and his Welsh band helped in a huge way. Then I was introduced to the music production company Joe & Co from Soho, who owned the studios where Frank Sinatra – who taught my good friend Gianni Russo to sing – recorded his music. Joe & Co consisted of Justine Campbell, Paul Cartledge, aka PC, and Phil Jewson. Phil and PC did a great job writing most of the songs and their studio skills were second to none. They work together like a pair of slippers, and their creativity together is extraordinary. They're behind the music for *The Big Breakfast*, *Only Fools and Horses*, and the *Go Compare* adverts. They even arranged the production of *Bolero* for Torvill and Dean when they reproduced their Olympic-winning ice-skating performance on *Dancing on Ice*. They're still going strong today, working on Dean Street, Soho, and making music with stars including Adele and Take That, winning awards on the way. So you can imagine how great the *BulbWorld* music was. They also knew the importance of getting the message out about global warming.

We organised an open audition for the actors and advertised in *The Stage* newspaper. Jerry and I sorted through the sack loads of applications. We had a lot of roles to fill and there was no shortage of talent coming forward. I told Paula to get us a fringe theatre, or maybe Stratford. She made the appointments and off to the theatres I'd go. After landing Harlow Playhouse in Essex, we then secured the London Palladium, one of the biggest and most famous theatres in London. I couldn't believe it.

I was frantically busy with the auditions which were being held in South London. Jerry and I auditioned the actors, kids and adults, and after the final auditions we had our winning cast. It all went well but Jerry and I handled it very differently. He was joking all the way while I was stressed out. The star of the show was the American-born British singer Sinitta, as well as Michael Lewis, aka Saracen from the TV show *Gladiators*. After the roles were filled we used the dance space at the bottom of Ellesmere Road in Bow, close to our shop, for rehearsals three times a week. We opened McQueen Productions and employed a choreographer, voice coach and acting coach. I was producer and director.

Our production meetings took place at the Tardis. The Tardis was a door in the wall by Farringdon train station, which had no signs or anything to indicate that it was there. Once you entered, it opened up forever with lots of space to hold meetings with the 15 production staff. Bruce Reynolds, whom I'd got to know via Buster Edwards, provided me with the Tardis free of charge, and even gave us food and drink. He thought our project was a great idea and much needed. I also got to meet his son Nick Reynolds, the sculptor famed for making bronze death masks of famous people. He went on to join the band Alabama 3, in which he still plays the harmonica. Alabama 3 are famous for writing the theme tune for *The Sopranos* which starts: 'You woke up this morning, got yourself a gun.'

*BulbWorld the Magical Musical* opened in 1999, highlighting the problem of global warming, the need for clean air and the large number of people getting cancer in the inner cities. The message was modern but the production was based on the nineteenth-century variety shows that were held in the music halls of the East End. Our musical had a variety of acts, including circus skills and a variety of music, including pop and opera, some of which I wrote, having sat through so much opera when I was at Caterham. The child actors used to run around between rehearsals singing the pop songs from the show, only to end up mimicking the opera singer and loving the opera songs the best.

The entire cast sang the opening number, *Plant the Planet, Save the World,* which was the first of 24 songs. The encore was *The Pie and Mash Song,* an uplifting Cockney number that I wrote after it came to me in another dream. The cast voted it their favourite and people said it was like a number from Lionel Bart, who wrote the musical *Oliver!* He'd done what many had said was impossible by turning Dickens into a musical, so that was a great compliment. If he could turn Dickens into a musical then we knew we could turn *BulbWorld* into one.

We advertised on enormous posters on the side of number 8 buses which said, 'Plant the Planet, Save the World: *BulbWorld the Magical Musical*. The buses travelled from Bow in the East End down Oxford Street to the West End, so we knew we were getting the word out around London. *BulbWorld the Magical Musical* started in the fringe theatres doing two shows a day and, believe me, it's hard work making sure a full cast is ready and able twice a day, when so many are involved. As we were swinging a girl high up across the stage, there were numerous health and safety issues that needed to be arranged and complied with. Scaffolders were required and everyone involved had to be professional, and I had to trust them. If one person turned up drunk, or didn't turn up at all, or there was an accident we'd be in trouble, so it was nerve racking.

We had a lot of near catastrophes but the show always went on and it worked well. The last show before the Palladium was at the Harlow Playhouse and then we were ready for our West End debut. The set was taken down by our scaffolder friends, Pat Sweet and Martin Fox, and moved to the London Palladium, where we'd sold 2,000 tickets.

The cast were extremely excited to be performing at the London Palladium. Built in 1910 and located in Argyll St, Soho, the Palladium is renowned for its Royal Variety performances and its royal box. The stars who have graced its stage are too many to mention, but here are a few: Frank Sinatra, Bing Crosby, Judy Garland, Danny Kaye, Sammy Davis Jr, Peggy Lee, Liza Minnelli, Ella Fitzgerald and even The Beatles. Now it's *BulbWorld the Magical Musical* from the East End.

Everything was set, and the cast were ready, doing their singing exercises and milling around the dressing rooms where the very best entertainers had been before us. The atmosphere was electrifying and we hadn't even set foot on the stage. I rushed round the theatre for my last final check – lights, sound, special effects, stage manager and props – and then we were ready for one of the greatest nights of our lives. On stage at the London Palladium.

The lights dimmed, the curtain rose and 35 singers burst into the first song. It was a big sound, it was a big show and the audience loved it. No-one walked out at the interval, which was the first test. The entire two-hour show went without a glitch. We had as many encores and standing ovations as *Oliver!*, and I could hear people singing *The Pie and Mash Song* as they left the theatre, which is the second test to see if a show has legs. I was over the moon. We had a winner! The after party was upstairs at the London Palladium with lots of stars.

We sent the material to the BBC to try and get a TV show made, believing it was in the world's interest. But we were informed by the BBC children's department that *BulbWorld* was too political for children's entertainment. Now, more than 20 years later, we see the world flooding and fires burning, and we think how *BulbWorld* could have educated more children – who are today's adults – on the climate. We're proud that we managed to put 10,000 books out into the world, people put the show on up and down the country, and schools planted *BulbWorld* gardens with their pupils. All of these things got children talking about global warming. But more could have been done. We didn't charge any fees for using our material as planting the planet was our priority.

Children visited our *BulbWorld* – which was in our shop – from as far away as Manchester because they wanted to save the world. As part of our promotion, our publishing department sent the book to famous people with children, and this paid dividends and *BulbWorld* became a bestseller in WHSmith. Then I got two letters that surprised me. One was from Prime Minister Tony Blair who said '*BulbWorld* was good for children of all ages', adding that his kids liked the book and, in his opinion, it should go to the Frankfurt Book Fair. I didn't know anything about Frankfurt. Then I opened the second letter which informed me that I was invited to the Frankfurt Book Fair, the biggest book trade exhibition in the world. The government was going to foot the whole bill for McQueen Publishers to go! We were going to represent our country in literature and maybe get some global sales. I found it strange that I – dyslexic and uneducated – had been asked to attend. I did it with the help of my wife. Today, I use my computer's spell check as I punch this story out with one finger.

So off we went to Germany to attend the Frankfurt Book Fair, the oldest book fair in Europe, at more than 500 years old. Now, as you know, I go first class. We flew from City Airport – the East End airport – with British Airways and checked in to Frankfurt's five star Intercontinental Hotel. There were four of us – Paula, Shelly, who was in the cast, our friend Amanda, who was a great sales person, and myself. Aside from us, our entire hotel floor had been taken up by Disney. I couldn't believe my characters were standing alongside the world's greatest talent. What a rush. I was hoping Disney would buy it (we can dream). I felt hugely privileged to be representing Britain in literature. At breakfast I wore a *BulbWorld* T Shirt with Stingy the Weed on it. He's the bad guy in the story and his motto is, 'I always come back.' We had such a laugh.

I didn't really know what to expect at the fair but it was just another street market with stalls full of books – fiction, non-fiction, children's, puzzles, comics, everything you could think of, all trying to get global sales. It was cliquey though, because they all knew each other. Lots of plastic smiles. After one day I had a plan.

I'd brought along some T shirts and promotional items from the musical and I found a couple of children and paid them to wear the T shirts, walk around the fair and linger at the stalls run by American publishers. If asked, they were told to say it was their favourite book and gush about how much they loved it. After a few hours, we started to get publishers visiting our stall.

Random House were the most aggressive. They demanded global rights and made me promise not to sell to anyone while they organised the paperwork. They said we had a hot tamale (something very attractive). Ronald Palmer was dealing with us, and he was a professional at his job. I liked him.

We celebrated all the way home and got back to Britain feeling great having secured a global rights deal. But after a few months, it fizzled to nothing. I didn't get the signed deal I was promised and I shouldn't have taken the book off the market without a written contract. I'm a man of my word and stupidly believed a verbal contract was good enough. Maybe it serves me right, as I had employed some Cockney trickery to hook them in. Ron did make me laugh with the ending to his emails: TTFN. I had to look it up. Ta ta for now. I hadn't heard it before. How funny.

# CHAPTER 20

# Too Young to Die

I started to suffer badly from indigestion. I was too busy to address it, and would usually drink a small brandy to clear the pain, which did work. When I finally did go to the doctor, I was given some indigestion medication. But then I collapsed and was taken to Homerton Hospital in Hackney where they kept me in, saying I needed emergency open heart surgery because the spells of indigestion I'd been experiencing had actually been heart attacks – more than 50 of them. The excessive damage had changed the shape of my heart from round to oval. It was very serious and it was possible I might not survive. I was kept at Homerton Hospital for six weeks while they prepared me for the op and then I was moved to St Bartholomew's Hospital (Barts), Smithfield, where they performed a quadruple heart bypass.

My notes had me down as Catholic and so I got a visit from the priest. I was in a private side room with my family, saying goodbye, as they thought I might not survive the operation. When the priest arrived, he said he'd come to give me the last rites, which are the final prayers given to a Catholic shortly before they pass away. I told him I didn't believe in God. How could there be a God when I'm dying so young? I was only 40. I told him the God story was a load of rubbish, and he responded in a broad Irish accent: 'Now Nicholas, you have to look at it like an insurance policy. I'm not even going to charge you for the policy but if you get to the pearly gates and you don't have it, you will feel very foolish and I have travelled all the way from the East End to give this to you. Now come on.' I laughed so much and I hadn't laughed for ages, so I let him go ahead. I took the last rites and was cleansed of my sins. He then gave me Communion, Confession and anointed me with the holy oil. I couldn't believe it was happening to me, but it was. I was being prepared for death. He left telling me he'd pray for me.

After that the nurse came back, gave me a razor and told me to shave my legs and chest because they were going to take the veins out of my legs and put them in my chest. I shaved ready for the operation, which was the following morning.

Apparently the operation didn't go too well at first. It took eight hours to complete and at some point I died and went somewhere in the afterlife. I was with my mum and four others, and we spoke telepathically, making a pentagram of thought with our minds. I was free of pain, and feeling warm and at home. I didn't want to leave but they told me telepathically that I had to return. I'm not sure if it was the drugs or not but when I came round, I believed in God once again. Now that doesn't mean I need a priest, imam or rabbi as a middle man. I just go direct to God. Yes, I saw the light. It was crimson light, not white. It was a light grey rocky area of the afterlife, and the light was like a magnet to me. They sent me back as I had unfinished business.

I wasn't out of the woods yet as now I was infected with the superbug MRSA. The medics thought it may have been caused by my body being open so long. It's known to be caught by dirty surgical instruments and I could see deep inside myself through the hole in my chest, where it was eating my flesh. Having got through the operation, the doctors thought this might be the end of me, and after two weeks on intravenous antibiotics I was sent home so I couldn't infect anyone else in the hospital. The nurses would care for me at home. It's scary to be too sick for the hospital. I knew MRSA had killed a lot of people.

Thankfully, I beat it, although it's had a lifelong impact on me. Not only did the operation leave me with Type 2 diabetes, but the damage I sustained means I now live with heart failure. I lost my first class medical to fly planes, and hard work now had to be a thing of the past. I can't walk far without getting breathless and having chest pains. My legs and ankles swell, I have chronic indigestion and I'm often exhausted. But at least I'm alive. Only around 50 per cent of people with chronic heart failure survive five years and 30 per cent survive 10 years. I'm way past that! I did hear that the surgeon was fired for taking too long to do the bypass, the nurses had complained that they'd worked four hours overtime and the NHS could have saved two people with that many hours' work and the money it had cost. When I heard that it felt as though my life was seen as a waste of resources and the staff thought he should have let me die. It took me a long time to recover to even a fraction of what I was before.

My dad rang me and told me of Lee's death. Lee Alexander McQueen CBE 1969–2010. My cousin Michael, Lee's brother, had taken the news to Uncle Ronnie, who is my dad's older brother. Lee had hanged himself with his favourite brown belt in his wardrobe. Uncle Ronnie didn't cry. He just kept saying, 'Why have you done this to me, my poor boy Lee?' Lee had left a suicide note to look after his dogs, and an apology.

We were already dealing with the death of my Aunt Joyce (Lee's mum) a few days earlier and Lee had killed himself on the eve of her funeral. Her death had hit him very hard. I'd been in contact with Aunt Joyce quite a lot leading up to her death because she was the genealogist of the family. We both had a huge interest in the McQueen clan, an ancient clan of the Scottish Highlands based on the Isle of Skye, and our name derives from Gaelic. (Bally MacQueen – the town of MacQueen/McQueen – was in Skye.) The last clan chief was McQueen of Corrybrough, but today we have no chief, which makes our clan armigerous (which means we have, or are entitled to have, a coat of arms). Our McQueen clan motto is 'Constant and Faithful' and our plant badge is a sprig of boxwood or whortleberry worn in our beret to identify us in battle.

Aunt Joyce had written a book on the subject in 1992 – *McQueen the History of a Clan*. McQueens have kinship with the High Kings of Ireland, and are known as Clan Revan supporters of the MacDonalds. They're known to be fierce and they guarded the daughter of the chief MacDonald who married a chief of Clan MacKintosh. The McQueens are the royal guard. A McQueen was called to a meeting with the Laird of MacKintosh in 1743 because a black wolf had eaten two children in Morayshire. The McQueen was late for the meeting, which upset the chief, until the McQueen produced the black wolf's head from under his cloak. The killer wolf had already been dealt with. That is the reason our clan was awarded three wolves' heads on its coats of arms.

I'd travelled to the Isle of Skye with Paula after my mum's funeral to find some peace and ease my pain. I'd told Paula Mc means 'son of', so I must be related to the royal family. Son of Queen. Paula and I went to the MacDonalds' castle where we met a genealogist and she told us more about the McQueens. They were the Island army and after the war of the Jacobite rising – the Battle of Culloden – the McQueens led the Scottish charge at the King's army, with grapeshot being fired at them from cannons. They were the best fighters the MacDonalds had.

They were retired to Skye after Culloden, to fish and farm to pay the MacDonalds' rent. When the MacDonalds came to collect the rent, the McQueens fought them off and kept the land. 'Typical,' said Paula. 'Royalty my foot.' Today, we're all friends. It wasn't the story I wanted to hear but it's wonderful to learn that my genes go back so far. I can't thank Aunt Joyce enough for her hard work in finding out more about our family's history. The McQueens are the Queen's guard, and the bad boys of Scotland.


Despite the shock announcement of Lee's death, Aunt Joyce's funeral went well and Uncle Ronnie was remarkably strong. Losing one loved one is bad enough but two is unthinkable. No-one is prepared for that, especially as Lee was only 40 and had taken his own life. The family had so many emotions: sadness, anger and bewilderment. Lee had everything you could wish for and everything to live for. But he'd had a troubled past. Like me, he'd been sexually abused as a child (by his older sister Janet's then-husband Terence Hulyer), and like me he chose to throw himself into work and projects. Lee had created a global empire.

Lee was the second of my cousins to hang himself. My cousin John Thompson had hanged himself a couple of years earlier. As children, John and I were very close and we'd often play together so his death was very painful for me. When it happened my father lectured me about suicide. He'd lectured me on this subject many times before, so I gather he knew more than he was letting on. It was starting to worry me – was there something in our genes? So many people kill themselves from temporary despair. I saw so much of it in my flower shops. We have to remember that things will be better tomorrow and if not, then the day after tomorrow. For sure you're going to feel better one day soon. I had fought to live, so no way would I do something like that. I wouldn't give my enemies the pleasure.

In the run up to Lee's funeral, Uncle Ronnie's house was surrounded by security provided by Lee's business partner, the global fashion house Gucci, who owned 51 per cent of his company. The family didn't organise the funeral, it was done by the executors of the will and their trustees, as a trust had been set up for this.

I received an invitation to the funeral as though it was a ticketed event, and I knew it wouldn't be like Aunt Joyce's funeral. His untimely death had rocked the fashion world and we knew this would be a big deal. He was buried in his McQueen kilt, with black sporran and white tassels, which he was famous for wearing at funerals. He'd worn it at Isabella Blow's funeral in 2007, after she also killed herself. She was his good friend and mentor, and her death really hurt Lee. He used to go to her castle some weekends to escape the madness of London.

Lee's funeral was at St Paul's Anglican Church, Wilton Place, Knightsbridge. It was a Victorian church built in 1840 and a beautiful building. I met my cousins Mason McQueen and Dean Jacobs outside the church. Mason is a black cab driver who became famous for teaming up with Sir Terry Wogan to drive him round the country for their TV show, *Terry and Mason's Great Food Trip*. He went on to appear in a number of TV programmes where he showed that London cab drivers are the best in the world by driving a tuk-tuk in Mumbai, India, an ice cab in Alaska and so on. I loved those shows and he was a big hit with viewers. My funniest time with Mason was in Costa Rica when we were walking through a surfer town called Tamarindo on the Pacific side of the country.

'Nick, look,' he said as he bent down. 'A child has dropped their toy. As he picked it up, it came to life in his hand and everybody in the street started to run. When the locals run you run. It was a langosta, a flying lobster with a waxy green crab-like shell and barbed claws, five inches long. When they land on you they hook in and tear your skin off. They come in a swarm twice a year, migrating from Brazil and flying down to Mexico then back again. That's life in the tropics.

Together, we entered the church. We'd been told only family flowers would be accepted, so the staff in my shop made me a spectacular wreath. The outside of the church was full of famous people from the fashion world: Naomi Campbell, Kate Moss, Daphne Guinness, Stella McCartney etc., and as we entered the security took our mobile phones and placed them in an envelope with our names on. It took ages to get inside the church and I already felt as though we were being bossed around by outsiders.

Funerals are always sad but to see my Uncle Ronnie and my cousins, Lee's siblings, bury their youngest isn't what's supposed to happen. The service was over before I knew it and the four pallbearers took Lee's coffin back to the hearse. Once it was inside the hearse the flowers were placed on board with a wreath saying LEE in big white letters. This was placed at the back of the coffin and that was my last sight of my cousin.

The wake was at Claridge's Hotel, and was also organised by Gucci. It just goes to show what a small world we live in – McQueens florist was soon to open in Claridge's. The waiting staff were very attentive, giving us champagne like it was going out of fashion and serving us with canapés, but I found it difficult to find something to eat due to my diabetes. Many of Lee's fashion friends, such as the hatmaker Philip Treacy, were there and Gucci big wigs were floating about with many lovely people. It was more like the opening of an art show than a funeral. It was nothing like the way we bury our dead in the East End. I spoke to the vicar who'd given the sermon, and most of the conversation was about Lee taking his life. We spoke about suicide and what a waste of a very talented young man.

I spent a lot of time outside smoking, and while outside I noticed Stella McCartney counselling one of my cousin's sons who was close to Lee and was visibly upset. Stella was really lovely, which surprised me, with her being so famous. Her dad Paul had done a good job as she seemed like a really beautiful person. It was a long day without much to eat so after a while I left to get some food alone. It was truly a sad day.

It is said that my family took Lee's ashes to Skye and scattered them at Kilmuir, among the spirits of our ancestors of the McQueen Clan, on May 29th 2010.

My cousins suffered a lot of pain trying to recover Lee's personal possessions, and after a year were still not even allowed into his flat. They took legal action to get his stuff back but by then it was moth-eaten and not in a good condition. Total disrespect towards my family.

Lee was suffering from anxiety and depression. I knew this after the fact because he left 100 grand to the Buddhist Centre in Bethnal Green to help with their work on anxiety and depression. I also discovered that Lee had written a lot of suicide letters before hanging himself in his wardrobe. I go to the Buddhist Centre on other business so I know them very well. They do a great job helping the community with their project Breathing Space, which promotes mindfulness-based cognitive therapy. Focusing on depression is the most effective way of stopping it from coming back.

Twelve months after the funeral, a remembrance ceremony was held at St Paul's Cathedral. It could be held there because Lee had been awarded a CBE. Again, it was full of the fashion world including Dame Anna Wintour the long-time editor of *American Vogue*, and the actress Sarah Jessica Parker, who was a good friend of Lee's and an avid wearer of McQueen. A dozen pipers stood on the steps in full Scottish dress, drowning out the traffic with their music. Inside the cathedral, Bjork sang. She was another friend who wore McQueen on her album *Homogenic*. His clothes were on display everywhere.

Today, there is a McQueen store in every major city in the world and his designs have been the subject of numerous exhibitions worldwide, and is the most visited exhibition at the Victoria and Albert Museum in London.

The company still thrives, dressing stars such as Lady Gaga and even providing the royal wedding dress for Catherine (Kate) Middleton when she married Prince William in 2011. Sarah Burton OBE led the design team until 2023, putting femininity and a lightness into the designs, while being flanked by my cousins, Lee's sisters. Sarah's successor is Seán McGirr.

# CHAPTER 21

# On the Political Rollercoaster

And this is where my story began. It is 2014 and I am standing as Mayor of Tower Hamlets for UKIP, the United Kingdom Independence Party, which was founded in 1993 and since then had campaigned to take Britain out of the European Union (EU). By 2014, this decision – exiting from Britain, otherwise known as Brexit – now looked more likely.

As noted earlier, my political career started in the bowels of a gentleman's club where three men and a woman were waiting for me: Wayne, Andrew, Mark and Wayne's wife Diane. During a two-hour long meeting to see if it was possible to field a UKIP candidate against the seemingly corrupt current mayor, Lutfur Rahman, we agreed on our political position and decided which roles we would take on and what monies we would add to the fundraising pot.

We also discussed how we were going to procure 20 more councillors to oppose Tower Hamlets First, the independent party headed by Rahman, plus the two main parties Labour (Democrat) and Conservative (Republican) who seemed to be defeated by Rahman's underhand tactics. I was told that Diane was going to be a paper candidate for the mayoral role. I had no idea what that meant and was told she would go down on paper but had no intention of actually doing the job. I saw this as an insult to the working-class people of Tower Hamlets. The working class were going to be asked to push through the crowds of Rahman's men blocking the way to the polling stations only to vote for a ghost. I was totally against that so I said I would become the mayoral candidate, and if successful, I would do the job to the best of my ability for my community.

They agreed and I was told that I'd need to be interviewed at UKIP head office, behind Claridge's Hotel. I arrived with my heart fluttering, and not just because I'd had a quadruple bypass. I knew that I had to disclose all my skeletons, whether I had a graveyard full or not. I couldn't let the tabloid press, or my opponents, drag anything out of my past to bring me and my fellow politicians down. I explained that as a child I'd been framed by Surrey Police for a crime I'd not committed. I also let them know about some other run-ins with the Metropolitan Police.

I also mentioned the twists and turns of my career and, after many questions, I was told I'd passed the interview and been approved as the mayoral candidate for Tower Hamlets. I was relieved it was over. Over the years, I'd turned down so many opportunities because I couldn't face an interview, knowing that if I did reveal a caution for theft, I'd be known as a criminal, and if I didn't reveal it, I'd be known as a liar. There's nothing worse for someone aspiring to be a gentleman to be known as a thief or a liar.

The moment my name was released, the press were interested in me, not least because of my relationship to Lee. It was clear that my main opponents were Lutfur Rahman, and the Labour candidate John Biggs, and I was looking forward to doing battle with them at the hustings, which is where candidates debate each other and field questions from the public. I knew I'd talk common sense as it's the only language I know, and they wouldn't beat me in debate as my argument was far too strong. But trying to win over the Labour votes could prove difficult as the working classes of East London had been voting Labour for generations, regardless of the candidate.

I personally felt the Labour Party was now full of extremists, communists, socialists and anti-semitics, and the working class were no longer represented by them. I truly believed it was in my country's best interest to free us from Lutfur Rahman (who had been thrown out of the Labour Party), and from Europe. I wasn't doing this for money or for my ego. I felt I was doing the right thing for Tower Hamlets and Britain. I felt I could survive the other candidates as well as the twisted political system, and maybe make things better. I'm Machiavellian by nurture and libertarian at heart.

My first meeting was with the Electoral Commission (an independent commission that reports to the UK Parliament), Scotland Yard, the Metropolitan Police, and the opposing political candidates. This was to set out the rules. We needed to build confidence and trust in the electorate due to allegations and complaints about fraud taking place in the 2010 elections and by-elections. Integrity had been lost. I raised the point that 30 people had voted from a one-bedroom flat only to be told by the police and Tower Hamlets council that this was not illegal! Votes had been counted from empty blocks of flats. It amazed me that the penalties for cheating and breaking the electoral laws were next to nothing, even though there were millions of pounds involved. You'd be punished more for shoplifting. You can run for office even if you're a known criminal. It didn't make sense.

The incumbent mayor Lutfur Rahman did not attend this meeting, and this became commonplace throughout the election process. He only attended his own political rallies.

Now it was time for the first hustings, which was held in a Christian church. My CV reads like I'm a posh boy: Caterham School, commercial pilot etc., so people were surprised at my strong Cockney accent and some even laughed at me, as though I shouldn't be engaging in politics.

I'd not debated since I was a schoolboy, and while I understood the principles, I was a bit slow at first. I tried to use flash cards to help me answer the public's questions, but it proved to be too stilted and awkward so I changed tack and just dealt with all questions off the cuff, which was more efficient and effective. It also made me appear to be genuine – because I am. The flash cards, and my inability to read them quickly, made it look like I was faking it and reading off a script. I also decided to use oneliners to engage my opponents. One to shock, two so they all remembered me and three so they knew what I stood for. After listening to what I had to say, I started to gain support and we assembled enough councillor candidates to field a full team.

The hate mail came quickly: death threats, pictures of the male anatomy, letters detailing their disgust at me not wanting Brussels and the EU to run our country etc., all dropping through my home letter box. I wasn't worried. People were just letting off steam and I was obviously having an impact, which was a good thing. People were engaging and we were gaining support despite all the naysayers predicting it wouldn't happen. Paula was less relaxed so I'd get up early to pick up the mail before she could see it.

My dad was convinced that someone would try to assassinate me. He was obsessed with terrorist attacks and would remind me of the July 7th bombings in London in 2005, and the 2001 attack on the Twin Towers. I had to explain to him that I'm a Cockney and I had my wits about me. I knew not to go to a party in a skyscraper or let someone sit behind me in a car. I'm an eye-for-an-eye Christian and am not one to turn the other cheek. If the world wants to go blind it's the world's choice. I was going to be fine. I was not going to be bullied, terrorised or give up my freedom of speech at any cost.

I'd never believed that it was possible to win the election – UKIP was too small a party for that. What I did know was that I was going to get a platform to share with the community the benefits of leaving the EU and what was really going on with corruption in Tower Hamlets Council, which seemed to be affecting the most vulnerable in our community.

Tower Hamlets spans the East End, which is one of the poorest areas in London. It didn't seem right that in such a wealthy country children should need foodbanks, survive on soup and live in tracksuits as they had no spare clothes. There were no kids' clubs any more, which was the very thing that had kept me stable in my childhood.

All the candidates, other than the Conservative Christopher Wilford, were left wing or Islamist and John Biggs was desperately trying to get the Islamic vote as, at that time, 34 per cent of Tower Hamlets was Muslim. I said to the audience, 'Would you really vote for Biggs? It'd be like giving a lighter back to an arsonist' because John had previously been leader of Tower Hamlets Council. He went so red he nearly burst a blood vessel. He took it well though. People roared with laughter.

This was my technique for years to come. Some dubbed me the bad boy of East End politics, just like Alexander McQueen was the bad boy of fashion. On occasion, organisers of the hustings would ask me if I was going to be well behaved. Some people liked my style and would come to the boring political hustings just to see if I was going to stir things up. I was told many times that they wouldn't vote for UKIP but they would always come to see me if I was debating.

There were rumours of Muslim extremists using our public buildings for hate speeches as well as all manner of illegal practices being used to win the election. The Electoral Commission really was not fit for purpose, allowing democracy to be stolen by electoral fraud. The BBC current affairs programme *Panorama* made allegations that Rahman had given £3.6million of public funds (and had taken money from popular charities) to give to Islamic charities in order to get votes. After that, Eric Pickles, the Secretary of State for Communities and Local Government, ordered an investigation into the misuse of public money. The investigators set up an office inside the council building and their findings were not clear to me. What was clear was that institutions like to keep quiet about wrongdoing in order to try and keep public confidence up and maintain their good reputation.

I was on the lookout for any breaking of electoral law and as Paula and I were driving home from Sainsbury's in Whitechapel, I passed a poster for 'Lutfur for Mayor' hanging on a council building. It was the size of a truck. I'd already had enough of seeing his face all over council building sites, the free council newspaper and dustbin vans, all giving him an unfair advantage as none of this advertising was going on his personal election bill. I flipped. I told Paula to pull over and keep the car running, then I opened the back door of the car, went up to the sign, ripped it down, put it under my arm and ran. Instantly six Bangladeshi men started shouting, 'You bloody bastard' and started chasing me. I dived into the car with seconds to spare and Paula drove off like a rocket with the door still open. I thought I was going to have a heart attack – they nearly got me! I managed to pull the door shut. Paula said, 'And now what?' I replied 'It's illegal. Take me to Mark's house.'

Mark Webber was the secretary of UKIP Tower Hamlets at the time, and a friend of mine. When I told him what I'd done, he went crazy. 'That's theft,' he said. 'You're making me an accomplice.' I told him it was flapping about in the wind causing a public nuisance and could have injured someone, so I did the right thing and removed it. I explained that I was taking it to Louise Stamp at the council's Electoral Commission.

The next day Paula and I picked up the sign from Mark who'd folded it neatly and managed to squeeze it into a rather small box. We went to the council building, where I was already a regular visitor, and took it up to Louise's office. We explained what had happened and she wasn't too pleased at my have-a-go-hero behaviour and said: 'Next time you need to inform us, and we will go and remove any illegal signs.' She asked me to get the sign out and as we unwrapped it, it kept opening and opening, getting bigger and bigger. It stretched from one side of her office to the other with no room to spare, and her room sat 24 people. She couldn't believe her eyes. It was massive and must have cost a fortune to have made. It was in full colour and Lutfur's face was enormous, accompanied by both Bangladeshi and English writing.

I was now in a jolly mood as I knew I wasn't going to be arrested, so we left her office and proceeded to leave the building. As I got in the lift, there was a man in there who I recognised from another meeting with the Electoral Commission. I asked him what party he was with. 'Liberal Democrat', he replied proudly. 'I'm with the Green Party,' I said and he went ballistic. 'No you're not,' he ranted. 'I know who you are, you're UKIP.' He didn't find me amusing, and nor did Paula, but I was laughing so much. I didn't expect to have this much fun. Politics was supposed to be boring.

The hustings continued around the borough, and some we weren't invited to because they were hosted by the extreme left who didn't want to leave the EU. Plus my Jewish wife wasn't wanted. We thought the Labour Party and the Muslims were anti-semitic. We believed that not inviting us to these hustings was rude and racist, not to mention undemocratic. Sometimes we'd attend as part of the audience.

After one of these, Paula, my nephew and I decided to go to Efes restaurant in Commercial Road for a late meal. Efes is a Turkish kebab restaurant with table service. We were halfway through our meal when our table was surrounded by seven Bangladeshi men. They were intimidating us with the way they were standing, and then one of them, with his neck dropped like he was a gangster, said in a Cockney accent: 'The mayor is downstairs and he wants to see you.' I replied: 'Tell the mayor I'm eating', which annoyed him. 'You don't understand,' he said. 'He wants to see you and he wants to see you now.'

I threw my cutlery onto my plate and stood up, only to see none of them were taller than 5ft 2 so now I'm now looking down on them. I was fuming at being harassed at my table while I was with my family, and eating. I told my nephew to stay put while I sorted it out and went with them down the stairs into the basement. In a reflection I could see my nephew hadn't listened as he was behind me. Once in the basement I could see more than 50 Bangladeshis having a party, with all eyes on me. Now I knew my nephew had some martial arts experience – or so he said – and I was prepared for the worst and pretty pleased that he'd followed me down. Suddenly the jeering started. 'Mr UKIP, Mr UKIP,' they shouted. I was smiling now as it was only half intimidation.

I walked over to Lutfur who had his hand out and a cheeky smile on his face. I provided him with a very firm handshake and he told me how well I was doing in very difficult circumstances. All of his councillors were present and I greeted them all individually. Not all were friendly faces and some looked at me as the enemy. Now I knew where they hung out after the council meetings. I hadn't even known this room existed even though I'd eaten here many times. We returned to the table, reassured Paula that all was well, paid the bill and left. She told me I shouldn't have left the table but I said that when we become too civilised, the uncivilised will take over.

There was so much skulduggery going on. All campaign material was given to the Post Office to deliver with the post, and mine wasn't arriving. Then a picture was sent to me showing my leaflets being dumped in the bin by the thousands. It was obviously a postman. The police investigated and found the culprit – a known socialist – but it was too late to reprint so we were at a disadvantage. Nothing was done.

Campaigners were collecting postal votes from people at home and even had the cheek to laugh that they'd already been to the old peoples' care homes first and collected their votes. They had cheated the postal votes. I would not have done something like that. I was beginning to find the unsavoury game-playing very stressful.

The Mayor of Newham, Sir Robin Wales, said we were living under an apartheid system in Tower Hamlets since Lutfur Rahman had taken over with his executive powers. I appeared on three different Bangladeshi satellite TV stations explaining and debating how it was in the interests of Bangladeshi people to vote UKIP for their immigration needs. Even if they didn't vote me in for mayor they needed to vote UKIP in the European election taking place at the same time. One day my team and I were at Chrisp Street in Poplar, answering questions from the public when Lutfur appeared with a large entourage. They swooped on me and all shook my hand smiling and joking around, once again calling me Mr UKIP.

It was around this time that I had a massive heart attack and was rushed to hospital by ambulance. I thought I was finished. I was instantly on the operating table where they put some stents in me, and my pain vanished. What a great feeling. After I'd recovered, it was back to the hustings. Paula thought I must be mad to continue but I knew too many people were relying on me. I started so I will finish.

My campaigning continued. While going around the Isle of Dogs, where Canary Wharf is based, talking to constituents, some European newcomers to Tower Hamlets told me they'd vote for me if I closed the council estates so we could get rid of the riff raff. I had to explain that I'm also riff raff!

It was now three weeks to the election and on my way to a hustings, I received a phone call from my uncle to tell me my dad had died. I was devastated. Worse, he'd hanged himself – the third member of my family to do so. It was like we were having an epidemic of suicide. I'd seen him two weeks earlier and had noticed his face was very swollen, like he was retaining water or something, but who knows? The funeral came a week before the election and there was a large turnout of family and friends. My childhood fishing friend Michael was there to pay his respects; I suppose the nice side of a funeral is getting to see the old faces. I was upset and confused by my dad's decision but just had to keep myself together and get to the finishing post.

Finally it arrived. The day of the mayoral election, local council election and European election all in one. Bangladeshi crowds were outside the polling stations telling people who they should vote for, bullying people and even trying to block their way. Illegal behaviour. When I went to vote I had to push past people and once inside the booth it took me ages to find my own name on the ballot paper. It was listed alphabetically and UKIP was last and appeared underneath a fold on a long piece of paper. At the end of the day the ballot boxes were taken to a council office for storage overnight, then to the Troxy, a large entertainment hall in Stepney, for the count the next day. The Troxy was built by George Coles in 1933, with a revolving stage and Wurlitzer – a one-man-orchestra with piano, drums etc,. It was originally an Art Deco Cinema and now it's a venue for hire, still with a Wurlitzer in place.

We weren't happy about the ballot boxes being kept at the council offices. That's like asking someone who's been accused of robbery to look after your money – especially with all the rumours going around that this was not a level-playing field. But we had no say and now the boxes were arriving at the Troxy. It took ages to get through security and some hours for it to start. Apparently there were 800 people involved in the count – counters, agents, candidates and so on. And there were a quarter-of-a million votes to count. My team and I were examining the seals and complaints were already being made that seals had been tampered with. The count started, and the boxes were opened. It didn't take long to realise that the contest was between Lutfur Rahman and John Biggs, and it was going to be close.

Now I had received lots of complaints from people who said they couldn't get to vote. Some had been blocked at the polling station, others said they'd got in the polling station only to find their vote had already been used. My agents at the polling stations reported that they'd seen people voting twice after changing their clothes, and others had said that some Bangladeshi women were being told how to vote and who to vote for. Elderly people were being carried in by two people. There was also a phone campaign going on where Lutfur's team would call people all day, from 8am to 9pm, asking if they'd been to vote yet, and telling them not to forget to vote for Lutfur. His voters also provided a free taxi service, picking people up and dropping them back home. It seemed that every facet of the election was being rigged in his favour.

I had already been approached by the Labour Party for my second preference votes, which are needed if the winning candidate doesn't achieve at least 50 per cent of the total votes in this first-past-the-post system. In that situation, the second count with the second preference votes would determine the winner. The Labour Party told me that in return for me asking my voters to put Labour down second, they would plough millions into funding the children's clubs that I desperately wanted for the East End. Nevertheless, I refused to give the Labour Party socialists my second preference votes, instead giving them to the Conservative Party. This was despite the fact UKIP head office had advised me to give them to Labour's John Biggs so he could beat Lutfur. In hindsight, I feel that I made a mistake by letting my personal feelings cloud my judgement, but I felt this way because Biggs had been going around mosques giving speeches to get votes and that upset me. I thought that was against the rules.

As I watched the votes coming in, and seeing it was a close-run election, I spoke to Alibor for a while who seemed happy with the progress he was making. Alibor Choudhury was Lutfur's second in command, his agent, and the treasurer of Lutfur's independent party. Many of the Bangladeshi counters were being shouted at in Bengali, which none of the English could understand, so who knows what was really happening and what was being said. What a fiasco. I needed a break so I went up to the balcony where you could get snacks and coffee for free, and looked down at the chaos while getting a caffeine fix. I didn't know then that this was going to be the day to change East End political history for a long time to come.

Outside the venue in Commercial Road, gangs of young Bangladeshi men had lined the street being rowdy and aggressive, and if Lutfur lost it felt like it would kick off. Cars lined the road making traffic jams for miles. I went out to have a cigarette and came face to face with around 1,500 Bangladeshis all of whom hated me. Then the police came, all flashing blue lights and sirens, and things got worse. It was becoming more and more volatile. The crowd was building – it was obviously being organised and more troops were being called for. People must have been coming in from some distance away. I decided my best bet was to go home, after all it was in my interest to get out of there while I had the chance. I had to push past people as they blocked my exit, yelling at them to move.

I managed to get out and heard later that only when the count came in and word spread among the crowd that Lutfur had won thanks to second preference votes, that it dispersed. The police should never have allowed it to get like that because if Lutfur had lost it would have been a very different outcome. I got my deposit back because I'd received more than five per cent of the vote, and that was a success for me.

The counting nonsense went on for days because of the European vote, and because of the complete mess the Electoral Commission had created. There weren't enough staff and people were being prevented from re-entering after a smoke break. There were also complaints that ballot stuffing (when there are more votes cast than people to cast them) had taken place and that there were false declarations on nomination forms. In all there were 84 complaints to Scotland Yard's Specialist Crime and Operations Directorate of Electoral Fraud, yet the police made only eight investigations due to lack of evidence. On June 3rd, a man was arrested for conspiracy to defraud the postal vote. It felt like democracy had been stolen.

After three days the count and recount were over. I may have lost but UKIP candidates across the country had been elected to represent Britain at the European Parliament, so it was a huge success for our team. I went up to the council to collect my envelope from Louise Stamp containing my deposit of £500 which I'd never expected to see again. Paula and I went off to the Ivy restaurant in Soho to celebrate with my team. What a great time we had. We laughed our socks off.

It wasn't long before I was asked to run for Parliament by UKIP's head office who said they'd provide me with media training and then give me a test to see if they thought I was good enough to go ahead and represent them. I was already skilled at dealing with the British press, TV and radio, and knew how not to put my foot in it, and also be economical with the truth if necessary: 'Send me an email and I'll get back to you on that.'

The training took place at UKIP's head office behind Claridge's Hotel. I had to pass all sections of the training before being tested. Lisa instructed me on politics in the general sense, as well as our own policies, which I needed to know back to front. Peter coached me on speeches, and I was also coached on debating and TV and radio interviews. I went through a good few weeks of training before I had the test but when it came I was ready. I felt I was so much better at being a politician now as it had been a rollercoaster of a campaign going up against Lutfur Rahman and John Biggs.

When I arrived for my test there were two people in front of me. It was a two-hour wait and a great opportunity to do some last-minute swotting. I had no idea who was going to test me until I entered the office and it turned out to be Paul who was a very good barrister and a professional at tearing people to pieces in argument. He portrayed himself as an aggressive left-wing journalist trying to get me to say something not politically correct to make me appear racist, and to portray the party in a poor light.

Paul was extremely difficult to out argue, and would use all manner of tricks to bamboozle me. At one point he misinterpreted what I said to make me look bad and I leant forward and gave him as good as he was giving me. Then he smiled and told me I'd passed. I was now a party political candidate (PPC) and able to stand in the general election. Paula, who had also passed her PPC (she'd got into politics after driving me to so many hustings and meetings), was waiting outside and as it was lunchtime I invited Paul for lunch and the three of us went to Oxford Street to eat. It wasn't long before both of us received our PPC cards.

I was given the seat of Limehouse to run for which was a great honour. It had been formerly held by Clement Attlee, who served as prime minister from 1945 to 1951, and whose social reform created the National Health Service (NHS) which cared, and still cares for the nation and is loved by all.

People were upset with the way the count at the Troxy went. Angela Moffat, one of Tower Hamlets' UKIP team, decided to complain to the MP for Limehouse, Labour's Jim Fitzpatrick, and she asked Paula and I to accompany her to the meeting, which was being held in Parliament. We met Jim in the cloisters of Parliament and then on to the tea rooms for a chat. I was surprised that he was adamant he'd pay for the tea because up until now none of the career politicians I'd met had put their hands in their pockets to pay for anything. As Angela made her complaints Jim noticed Paula's UKIP umbrella – he hadn't realised we were UKIP – and his eyes bulged and he went into a Scottish brogue accent. Paula couldn't believe it as she thought he was English. I knew he was Scottish, but thought he'd lost his accent, but there it was loud and not so clear, because none of us three could understand what he was saying. What a funny afternoon that was. We laughed all the way out of Parliament. I like Jim. He'd done a good job for the East End over his 20 years of service in Parliament. I was going up against him in the next election and I knew I'd be opposing him in many hustings over the next few years.

Tower Hamlets activist Andy Erlam approached me to ask for help to take Lutfur to the High Court for cheating in the election. It was going to be a cross-party action and Andy said he'd pay the bill if necessary. I couldn't help because I was going to run for MP, but Angela Moffat did.

The Tower Hamlets four – Andy Erlam, Angela Moffat, Azmal Hussein and Debbi Simone – did take Lutfur to court, and on April 23rd 2015 they won. Lutfur Rahman was found guilty of cheating the election. He had to pay £250,000 court costs and was barred from politics for five years. He was also disbarred as a solicitor. His agent Alibor Choudhury was also found guilty. The Judge, Richard Marry QC, said that Lutfur had run a 'coach and horses' through the election laws, doctoring postal votes, bribing voters with generous grants and getting clerics to tell voters it was their duty to Islam to vote for him. He was dishonest and ruthless. His campaign 'worked glove in hand' to make John Biggs look racist while he used racism and Islamophobia as a stock response to any criticism.

Lutfur took £100,000 from a charity for Alzheimer's and gave it to Muslim lunch clubs when the clubs hadn't even applied for the grants. His party also took postal ballots from people against their will. Peter Golds, the Conservative councillor who had tirelessly opposed Rahman in the council meetings stated the authorities had never taken these problems seriously. With this now all in the open, we now had to repeat the mayoral election.

It was brought to my attention that UKIP's chairman, Wayne Lochner, wanted someone else to run for us as mayor in the re-election, and was using his position to remove me. I didn't like that idea one bit. I'd spent a lot of time and money promoting myself and the party, only to be cheated out of the first election so this was my Ides of March. Wayne was pro-gentrification and I was pro-Cockney and against gentrification, believing that what makes London great is the local people who keep London running. So many properties have been bought by the rich and are left empty while they reside in their second or third homes somewhere else, thus rendering parts of London dead and soulless.

We called for an emergency meeting to do a coup d'état, so we could remove Wayne and take political control over UKIP Tower Hamlets. We made sure we had the majority votes at the planned meeting and would make Mark Webber the chairman, and I would run for mayor again. We hired a room at the back of a pub in Poplar and called for his resignation but he refused to leave so we had a vote of no confidence, which we rigged, and voted him out. He went berserk. Wayne's supporters called us the mafia, which I thought was hilarious.

I was back on the campaign trail once again for mayor. I'd funded the first campaign but this time round I had help. The meetings started with Scotland Yard on how to improve the safety of voters at polling stations. The Electoral Commission also did an investigation into the 2014 election, to ensure we never had a repeat of that. It was decided that police would be at every polling station in Tower Hamlets and the count would be moved to a larger venue to make it more difficult for people to riot outside. Tower Hamlets is the only place in the whole country where we need the police to help us exercise our right to vote.

Lutfur filed for bankruptcy, while his wife held his assets, and my friend Andy Erlam got a bill for £300,000 because he chose to do the right thing for the East End. That is to protect the foundation of our democracy and the right to a fair vote while the Government, Electoral Commission and the police were sleeping. The judge said he had exemplary courage and I agree.

The volatile political situation in Tower Hamlets had intrigued the country so in the 2015 mayoral election I had nearly as much airtime as Nigel Farage, who was leader of UKIP at the time. I was in the public eye continually, in newspapers and on radio and TV, where I held my own thanks to the great training I'd received. I debated at many hustings and TV and radio programmes, some with Jim Fitzpatrick and Wes Streeting, the Labour MP for Ilford, as well as imams, socialists and Christopher Wilford the Conservative candidate. At every one I explained how Britain would be better off leaving the EU.

I received a call from Gawain Towler the UKIP press secretary. He wanted Paula and myself to take part in a political rally about diversity, which was being filmed at Westminster and aired nationally on all channels. We were now a major national party, and a multi-racial group of us turned up and did as instructed. I was introduced to Nigel Farage at a hotel near the old Scotland Yard headquarters and Paula and I had a photo shoot with him.

The left wing had constantly tried to brand us as racist, so by attending the rally we could show the public that there was nothing racist about our party. It turned out to be quite a bizarre day. As we arrived, one side of the street was lined with white demonstrators shouting at us – black, white, Asian and multi-racial members of UKIP – that we are racists. They waved copies of the *Socialist Worker* newspaper at us and some even threw eggs. Once inside the Emmanuel Centre, we mingled with the press, and a photographer asked Paula if he could take some photos of her. He asked her to sit on a chair on stage and as he started to snap her he asked if she'd been on holiday recently. 'No,' replied Paula. 'I'm multi-racial.' He helped her off the stage and as he did, he rubbed her face with his finger and thumb trying to see if her colour would come off. Pretty shocking and upsetting. It's so sad to think people thought UKIP would black people up.

Paula was scheduled to give a speech on diversity, which was being televised on the news, and as she did, she was on stage with me (white) and another woman (black), when two young white middle-class hecklers shouted 'Racists!' Paula responded perfectly. She said, 'There I see two middle-class children with nothing better to do than to call a 60-year-old black Jew a racist.'

We were being abused racially by white socialists. It made the national news the following day.

To cut a long story short I didn't beat the Labour Party candidate, Jim Fitzpatrick, to become MP for Limehouse and I hadn't expected to. I played my game using my rugby skills. If I couldn't get the ball I'd frighten them off the ball and get my message out to the public with my direct oneliners, and explain how leaving Europe could save us money that could pay for social programmes for the less fortunate. Society is assessed on how well we look after the less fortunate, not how well the middle classes live. This pushed the Prime Minister David Cameron to give his famous speech at Chatham House, whose aim is to build a 'sustainably, secure, prosperous and just world' (and where, incidentally, Ed Smith, the chairman of Caterham is the treasurer) on November 10th 2015, giving the British public the right to a referendum to stay in the EU, or leave.

As we all know, at the referendum on June 23rd 2016, we, the British people, chose to leave Europe, to regain our sovereignty and run our own lives. It eventually led to Prime Minister Boris Johnson and the Conservative Party plagiarising a large part of the UKIP manifesto and stealing our policies, and as they were now saying everything I'd been saying for years it left me in a bit of a quandary. Make no mistake, I'm very happy. This was what I wanted, and already it's paid dividends as we were able to get vaccinations very quickly and this saved us from the worst of the Coronavirus. Not only have the British people saved money, we've also saved lives. We've led the world on how to save Ukraine from Putin. Why do you think thousands risk their lives, crossing the English Channel in small dinghies with their children? It's because we are great – we are a great society. We are Great Britain.

In March 2017, the Mayor of London's Officer for Policing and Crime asked Her Majesty's Inspectorate of Constabulary and Fire and Rescue Services (HMICFRS) to investigate the Metropolitan Police Service's operation into the alleged criminal offences arising from the 2014 mayoral elections in Tower Hamlets, which involved the outgoing mayor Lutfur Rahman and the councillors for 20 wards. Concerns had been raised as there were no criminal convictions. On March 20th 2017, the police decided to mount a new operation to review and re-assess the allegations. It was called Operation Lynemouth.

# CHAPTER 22

# Old Friends and Foes

There are still many private gentlemen's clubs in London and once you're a member there are reciprocal clubs around the world that you can use. The most famous and prestigious clubs are Boodle's, White's, The Reform, The In and Out, Buck's, The Garrick, and The East India Club is up with the best of them. They're retreats for gentlemen, a place to mix with men of similar interests. You need two members to nominate you if you'd like to join and there's a strict dress code in place – no tweeds after 6pm and always a shirt and tie. They're a place to reside while you're in London, or you can just drop in to use the restaurant or bar. The unwritten code is 'what goes on in the club stays in the club'.

Each club is slightly different and attracts a different clientele. White's, founded in 1693, is a haven for royals and counts King Charles and Prince William as members. The late Queen also visited twice, with her last visit in 2016. Former prime minister David Cameron resigned his membership because of their men-only policy, even though his father was once the chairman. Boodle's, founded in 1762, is one of the most prestigious in London. It got its name from its head waiter Edward Boodle and is associated with the Conservative Party: its traditional dish being an orange fool. The In and Out Club (1862) was originally for naval and military men but today non-military, and women, can join. I go there for dinner and an evening of cigar smoking with a large group of friends. I find it extremely relaxing to smoke a Vanilla Corona or cherry cigar.

The Reform Club (1836), was started for the benefit of the Radical and Whigs who had pledged support for the Great Reform Act of 1832 to give votes to middle-class men only, and not the working class. You need character, talent and achievement to join and be nominated by two members. Buck's was founded in 1919 and two years later invented the bucks fizz (champagne and orange juice). The Garrick Club is for gentlemen of the arts: writers, poets and actors.

The East India Club (EIC)was founded in 1849. It's situated at 16 St James's Square London. It's one of the less expensive gentlemen's clubs, and to join you must have attended a public school and your headmaster must write you a reference. It's supposed to be a home from home for gentlemen with food, drink, good company and 66 bedrooms to sleep in when the need arises. George IV, then prince regent, was dining there when victory at the Battle of Waterloo was announced. The Duke of Wellington's aide-de-camp presented him with the victory dispatch and he went on the balcony and announced victory to the people. Originally known for accommodating officers from the Army and Navy, it has a long list of famous members including Queen Victoria's husband, Prince Albert, Lord Mountbatten, Denis Thatcher, Sebastian Coe and even Nigel Farage takes the odd pint in there. The rule of thumb is to stay loyal to each other, which is why you don't hear that much negativity. The old boys' club. But then again, around 10 years ago, its treasurer Alfonso Ramirez ran off with £552,000 so you can get gentleman scumbags, just like the one who robbed the safe at Caterham.

Now I'm not allowed to join because of the stitch up I received as a child. Not only was I obviously not going to get a reference from my headmaster but I learnt that in 2014, while I was fighting for the political future of my country, I was being slandered in a speech given in the East India Club by the Canadian Supreme Court Judge The Right Honourable Graeme Mew. The same Graeme Mew who had been head boy at Caterham when I was there, and whose assistant I became when the school produced *Joseph and the Amazing Technicolour Dreamcoat*.

The speech was to mark the retirement of Jim Seymour as housemaster at Caterham School, and it is here in its entirety:

Forty two years was the number of years that the fictional schoolmaster, Chipping – Mr Chips – spent at Brookfield School prior to his retirement. And so it was that 42 years ago, on 1st September 1972 to be precise, that Jim Seymour, freshly graduated from Hull University, took up his post as senior biology teacher and assistant to John Jones in Townsend Boarding House. It was the same year that I entered the main school in the third form, where my cohorts and I were among the first pupils taught by Jim at Caterham. Seen from the perspective of 13 year olds, we were unfazed by the fact that the school's senior biology teacher was just 22 years old.

Jim originally hails from Yorkshire, but his dulcet tones bear the distinct stamp of Cheshire, where he grew up with his parents in Altrincham. He was inevitably, and some might say lamentably, drawn to support Manchester United, an allegiance which must have tested his loyalty of late.

If Jim had not been a teacher, he might well have become a designer of custom holidays, having participated in many trips, both official school ones and with groups of his colleagues at Caterham. These have included Paris and Amsterdam trips and annual visits to the Lake District. True to his enigmatic nature, none of those trips have involved conveyance by aeroplanes, infernal machines from Jim's perspective that he has never desired to travel on. Ever the accomplished hiker, he has never deemed it necessary to acquire a driving licence.

It is not just in the classroom that Jim has excelled. As a housemaster and the Head of Boarding he has been responsible for the pastoral care of generations of Caterhamians. For many years he coached athletics – particularly track. He is also a great thespian and produced *Oliver!* circa 1989, working hard on that endeavour, as on so many others, out of school hours and beyond the call of duty. He also did much backstage work on various productions. I well remember him as the stage manager of Bill Richmond-Pickering's productions of *Twelfth Night* and *Midsummer Night's Dream* in the '70s.

Despite the trips, he has not always enjoyed his excursions away from Caterham. John Jones recalls an occasion when a naughty boy stole pocket money from other boarders in the House and both John and Jim had to go up to a sleazy pub in the East End of London to retrieve it. Jim was somewhat shocked having to go up there!

It is perhaps not surprising therefore that Jim has decided to return to his Yorkshire roots and will be returning to his cottage near Thirsk – between the Dales and the Moors – where he will no doubt be able to indulge his passion for walking. I am sure that there will be many visitors from Caterham.

Jim – a modest man with much to be boastful about: athlete, sportsman, walker, traveller, mentor, collector of antique plates, loyal friend, the most dependable of colleagues, indefatigable worker and, above all, teacher extraordinaire – we salute you. We celebrate everything you have given to our school and those who have passed through it. We lament your imminent departure, but above all we say thank you and wish you a happy, invigorating and long retirement.

Not only was this wrong – even though John Jones says he recalls the occasion he went to London with me, it was actually Jim Seymour and a young policeman – Mew also slanders my wonderful late mother. There was nothing 'sleazy' – a word I tend to connect with immorality and prostitution – about my late mother. She was a real lady, who was known throughout the City of London, and was loved and respected by all who knew her. She gave her time to counsel anyone who had been dealt a cruel blow from life and they would leave her company empowered once again, with a spring in their step. Her friends were many, and they were powerful and important people. When my mother owned the Magpie pub next door to Bishopsgate Police Station, she made it home from home to the officers in the Regional Crime Squad and Serious Fraud Squad. She'd open especially for them after a dangerous mission was completed. So not only do they slay themselves trying to keep the lid on a pack of lies, with this ungentlemanly behaviour they also bring the East India Club into disrepute. I now think John Jones lied because he was supposed to be my guardian. They are far from gentlemen and their recollections are wrong. I can never forget what happened to me.

Now I was going to show these guys how to write. I wasn't looking for revenge, not even justice, as I didn't think any of that would make me feel better. I just wanted to put the record straight, and to show everyone involved in Caterham – the foundation, the trustees, the board and the headmaster – how much pain they can cause with their bad decision-making, and how this can impact on you for life.

When I was writing this book and sent it to people in the publishing world, they told me that not only did I have a story that needed to be told, but that I should contact the police and tell them of the abuse I'd suffered at Caterham. It would be the right thing to do for all the children who are adults now and living with the memories that I have, and all the children currently in the system and those in the future. That way they might think twice before doing something like this to another pupil. My brothers, and now sisters (as Caterham now admits girls), are still sleeping in those dormitories and should have as much protection as possible. If we protect the children, we protect the institution.

I pondered, and continued writing my life story. Then I thought I should contact Gianni Russo to make sure he didn't mind me writing about him. Not only did he not mind, he suggested Paula and I come and visit him in New York, which sounded like a wonderful idea. Our wedding anniversary was coming up and it would be romantic to spend it in New York with Gianni serenading Paula at the table in the intimate setting of the lavish Beautique restaurant.

Paula deserved a treat as, like me, she was suffering from ill health. Around seven years earlier, she'd developed breast cancer BRCA 1, which is very common in women of Ashkenazi Jewish origin like her. She had a mastectomy and breast reconstruction, and went into remission, but around a year ago a tumour was discovered in her bones – one in her femur and two on her spine. They were benign but cause her a lot of pain and she needs regular cortisone injections. She was sent home from hospital with just a bottle of morphine as they could do very little.

After one of her operations a rabbi was at the bottom of her bed when she woke. She thought she'd gone to heaven and was in the wrong place, or was it the morphine? The rabbi proceeded to tell her that she's a very special Jew as BRCA 1 can be traced back to Miriam in the Bible. He offered us a lot of help.

I often think of the embryos in California. How the laws in America are so different to the rest of the world and protecting their identities stops us telling any possible children of the genetic heart disease problems I have and the genetic BRCA 1 cancer gene that has ravished Paula's body. I can't warn anyone and it feels so wrong. Dr Jeffrey Steinberg won't even talk to me.

In March 2017, the same month that the police committed to investigate the fraud surrounding the mayoral elections, we made our way to Gatwick Airport. This was our first time in New York and we were excited. We'd booked three nights at the Ritz Carlton Hotel, Central Park, as it was said to be the best hotel in the city. But when we got to the airport, we discovered we'd been thrown off the flight. We went to the British Airways assistance desk and explained that Paula had bone cancer and I suffer from heart failure, and staying calm is very important to surviving a long trip. We were told all sorts of stories about why we weren't going to travel: they were using a smaller plane; the computer had overbooked by 45 seats and we were among those chosen to be bumped off. I explained that we'd booked a British Airways package with hotel and Broadway show, and reiterated that we both had serious illnesses. Nothing. Then I threatened legal action and after two hours of hanging around we were told we were back on the flight.

We were now both pretty ill with stress. I had tightness of the chest and Paula was sweating, (in fact she was 'cooking', which is one of her symptoms). BA had found 45 volunteers to leave the plane, who were prepared to fly to Newark the next day which is a cheaper option than flying to JFK. It seemed a lot of airlines were doing similar and this was the second time it had happened to me with BA.

We boarded the flight only to find there was no air conditioning, and we were now overheating and dripping with sweat. The captain informed everyone that the air conditioning would work once we were up in the air. It wasn't going well and I couldn't come down from the stress. I stayed awake the whole way and worried about us both.

We arrived at 10pm local time and our excitement kicked in and gave us the uplift we needed to continue. There were no queues at Immigration and we went straight through to the taxi rank and hailed a yellow cab. The driver was a Sikh man with a blue turban who was interested in our London accents. I gave him the name of our hotel and, as we set off, I glanced at the meter which was already on $52. I was shocked thinking it was so expensive and wondering what the end fee was going to be. I was pleasantly surprised to see the meter didn't increase as we flew along the freeway. That was the total price configured by the GPS. I was now starting to relax and enjoy the view out the cab window – it was just like the movies. I was still a bit worried though because when it's relaxed that's when the heart tends to fail. Nevertheless, we were both smiling by the time we got to the Ritz Carlton.

The room was better than expected because it was massive and the large bed was the most comfortable I've ever slept in. The next morning we went to Sarabeth's, the restaurant next door to the Ritz Carlton, which is famous for its American breakfast. You can wait up to two hours for a table. The atmosphere was absolutely buzzing with some 30 waiters rushing around. The menu for me was unusual but I was there to try something different. I chose the short rib hash and I wasn't let down. What a breakfast feast.

Our day consisted of a tour by limo. Our driver, Moniere, did a great job slipping through the traffic jams that plague New York and although it rained continuously, it didn't dampen our excitement. We started by going to the Masonic Temple in Manhattan, which is home to 70 New York lodges, and also houses the Bible George Washington – the first President of America – used in his inauguration. Then we travelled to Hell's Kitchen, Harlem and the Bronx. I didn't think we were going to enjoy it as much as we did. New Yorkers get bad reviews for being rude and not having time for anyone, but we found it the complete opposite. Straight talking they might be but they're friendly, funny and really welcoming to visitors. I love New Yorkers. We visited the Apollo Theatre, famous for launching the careers of Michael Jackson, Richard Pryor and lots of other stars. The best part of our tour was just people watching, seeing the locals going about their everyday business.

The jet lag had kicked in and the travelling had caught up with us so we went back to that beautiful bed for a siesta. We were going out to Bemelmans Bar at the Carlyle Hotel that evening on Gianni's recommendation, so it was a good idea to get some rest. Carlos the doorman escorted us to the hotel's limousine, which was free for guests. Our driver was waiting. We arrived at Bemelmans Bar and took a table by the baby grand piano. It was 5.15pm and the pianist Chris Gillespie was due to start in 15 minutes. We read the menu, which also contained the story of the art on the walls. In 1947, artist Ludwig Bemelmans had painted murals on the walls of the bar in exchange for room and board. He was famous for his picture books *Madeline* and he was also an artist for *The New Yorker*, *Vogue* and *Town and Country* magazines. The whimsical scenes of Central Park, with ice-skating elephants and smoking clothed rabbits transformed the art deco bar and its 24 carat ceiling, which attracts world leaders, politicians, movie stars and socialites.

The waiters were dressed in white tuxedos and kept us supplied with blue point oysters, crab cakes and drinks, and even showed me a place to smoke on Madison which was by a warm blower. Chris played the piano for three hours, singing some of the world's most beautiful songs to perfection. Thanks to Gianni for the recommendation as Bemelmans is now my favourite bar of all time. Woody Allen and a jazz band play there on Mondays. I'd love to see that. Maybe next time.

Back at the Carlton, I had a smoke before going up to our room. I enjoyed watching New York whizz past on 5th Avenue, even if I was standing in the rain. I watched the long line of horse-drawn carriages picking up customers and driving them around Central Park. A line of limos were waiting for the hotel's VIPs. There was even a full team of bodyguards waiting to fly into action, as and when their guests – the Arab prince or his family – came down for air. Smoking outside gets you a show every time. You get to meet and talk to a lot of people that might not talk inside the hotel. The staff were wonderful at the Ritz Carlton. Nothing was too much trouble for them.

When we got to the room a bottle of champagne on ice was waiting for us – a gift from the hotel to celebrate our wedding anniversary. Paula doesn't drink so she was buzzing after one gulp and I had to drink the rest. A perfect end to a great day.

The next morning we left the hotel and started to walk towards Times Square as we needed a few presents for our two grandchildren (Carly had made us grandparents in 2008). Just around the corner we found Frank's Gift and Camera shop run by Franky, Mr Super Salesman who was so funny, a real New Yorker, with more patter than me. We bought some gifts just to get out the shop. We went back to the hotel for lunch as Paula said they made the best steak and fries ever. I finished lunch and went to the bathroom and on the way back two young Orthodox Jewish boys stopped me on the stairs, asked if I was Jewish and explained the importance of Passover, which they were celebrating. They wanted to give me a blessing, believing God had sent them into the hotel to find me.

I took them to our table, introduced them to Paula and said she was Jewish. She told me to let them bless me so they wrapped a leather strap around my arm with a block on it and put a Koppel (Jewish bullcap) and block on my head, and asked me to repeat a Hebrew prayer. They then took some pictures, gave me a dollar and told me to put it in the first charity box I saw when I arrived back in London. This meant we were now on a mission for God and would stay safe.

After lunch we rested our eyes for a couple of hours. Yep, another siesta. We're getting old. That evening we were going to the Beautique restaurant where Gianni was putting on a show. Before leaving, I went downstairs for a smoke and took my normal spot just away from the entrance. I hadn't even lit my cigarette when an African American man I'd given money to the day before came up to me and asked for a dollar. He said he was hungry. 'Look how skinny I am,' he said. I lit my cigarette. 'You don't look skinny,' I countered and told him I'd given him money yesterday. 'It wasn't me,' he said, removing his baseball cap. 'Are you saying all us black guys look alike?' I frowned. 'Don't start all that,' I said and gave him $5. He took the money. 'See you tomorrow,' he said. I laughed until I had tears in my eyes. Cheeky sod. Paula turned up and she laughed all night saying how I, Mr Streetwise from the East End, had been mugged in New York.

That evening we got into our usual limo and headed to Beautique. When we'd looked at the reviews it was described as a millionaire's playground restaurant with a secret room for the rich and famous. Gianni was waiting for us and as soon as I saw him, we started chatting like we'd seen one another yesterday. We spoke about Kim and Danny Krantz and the old days, Gianni's 26-seater dining room table and the family days he hosted in Las Vegas. It was really nice to reminisce about good people that we'd met on our journey through life, especially as Kim had given Paula away at our wedding. Gianni introduced us to some of his friends telling them we'd flown all the way from London to see his show. He looked great. No way did he look or act as though he was 75 years old. He was still the lovely charming man that I knew when I was a kid.

The restaurant was stunning. The decor was inspired by Coco Chanel's home and had walls lined with rose petals and a gold leaf ceiling, with glittering chandeliers and original art on the wall, which was for sale. The maitre d' sat us next to two lovely ladies and the night began.

Gianni burst into song. He was backed by a saxophone player, drummer and a guy on keyboard. He sang some of Frank Sinatra's songs, and really reminded me of Frank. (Not only did Sinatra teach Gianni to sing, Old Blue Eyes was godfather to one of Gianni's sons). Gianni is a great showman, chatting between songs, reminiscing and telling funny stories about the *Godfather* movie and the old neighbourhood when he was a kid. We ate rock oysters but I put too much tabasco on mine and burnt my mouth. I tried to cool my mouth with the wine and every time I finished my glass, the waiter poured me another. Gianni mingled between sets and chatted to the customers. He sang for more than three hours – he has an amazing amount of energy – and it was a great night. While on the mike, he thanked Paula and me for coming from London, and told everybody of our long friendship. The waiters brought me a load of drinks they wouldn't let me pay for. What a night. I'd have loved to go back again but it's now closed.

When we were with Gianni, his friend Anthony 'Tough Tony' Federici told us to come and eat in his restaurant, Parkside, before we got on the plane home. We didn't like to call him Tough Tony because we didn't want to upset the New York Mob (but later we found out everyone called him that). Gianni asked me what Tony had said to me and when I told him he'd invited us to eat in his restaurant, Gianni said in a deep New York accent, 'When Tough Tony tells you to eat in his restaurant you go.' He said it was only 20 minutes from the airport and a good meal at Tony's and a glass of wine would make us sleep the whole way home.

The next day we said our goodbyes at the hotel. I was sad to leave the friends I'd made but that's travelling for you. Moniere, our driver, was waiting in the limo to take us to Tony's restaurant, across the Brooklyn Bridge for the last time into Queens.

When we arrived we asked Moniere if he'd like to come in and eat with us, but he declined. Alfredo, the maitre d' who ran the place when Tony wasn't there, asked one of the pretty girls to seat us at the table that was waiting. We were served all different breads, some I'd never seen before – not even in Italy – as well as cheese and salamis. I ordered some really nice white wine, followed by minestrone soup and mixed shellfish on linguine, Parkside style. Paula had the garlic langoustine. Parkside Restaurant in Queens is one of the best places I've ever eaten. With our bellies full, we slept the whole way home. Gianni Russo was right again. It was a wonderful break and it had given me time to make my mind up. I'd made a decision.

# CHAPTER 23

# The Old Boys' Club

In 2017, I reported my child abuse to the Metropolitan Police. I was told I would be visited by a detective constable (DC) from Tower Hamlets child protection and Chris arrived on my birthday, November 13th. My grandchildren were visiting and had brought me a cake and cards, and Chris and I also had a slice of cake and a cup of tea. He was dressed as a police constable although I found out later that he was a detective constable. I was a little apprehensive, most probably because of how I'd been treated by the police before, and although I warmed to him, my instincts told me something wasn't right. He interviewed me for two hours, and I made a statement which he jotted down in his notebook. I signed every page to legitimise it.

Now remember, if I told one lie, just one exaggeration, not only does it ruin this book but it could put me in prison. The report he wrote then went to his boss at the Metropolitan Police who thought it should be investigated by Surrey Police, as Caterham is in Surrey. I was told they'd be in touch. Around three weeks later, Surrey Police contacted me to do a further interview on the telephone with a policewoman from Guildford. Two further weeks passed and on New Year's Day 2018, a detective from the Reigate child abuse squad emailed me to introduce herself and ask for some more information, which I provided. The investigation had started.

During the officer's questioning I started to analyse things more deeply to see what they had done to me. I knew I suffered from post-traumatic stress disorder (PTSD) and it amazed me that after all these years I'd still not unblocked some memories. It took days for me to remember my torturer's name, which got me thinking even deeper about how this had affected my mind.

It was though her probing had pierced a tiny hole in my memory and now it all came flooding back, including his name – Mr Robinson-Fuller.

I started to research torture of all kinds: sexual torture, Chinese water torture, and then I found what they'd done to me as an 11-year-old boy. I was furious but relieved as I'd been right all along, knowing this strange treatment had long-lasting effects on me, and had changed my personality for the worst. I now knew why I couldn't shake it off, like I could other punishments I'd received, and think it was 'just' a sexual attack. I'd experienced a prolonged use of CIA torture, by which I mean the extreme interrogation techniques used by the CIA (Central Intelligence Agency) to extract information from their enemies. But I was just a kid!

The Surrey policewoman and I exchanged multiple emails as she delved into the case more. The final email told me that Robinson-Fuller had died and so even though they'd received similar complaints, there was nothing they could do. He would never face justice. She said the assaults should have been reported within six months of them happening, which would have been impossible as I was at boarding school. They were time barred. The rest of my complaints were ignored. It was a big let down.

I rang Paul Corrigan at Farleys Solicitors in Burnley, as he's a specialist in child abuse cases. He said he'd take my case on, on a no-win-no-fee basis, but he advised that I should try and sort it out with the school first. His reasoning was that as there were plenty more victims, some of them must have complained and the school must have somehow satisfied them for this to have been kept quiet for so long. Maybe I'd get a satisfactory response too.

I rang Andrew Latham, an old school friend of mine, the former CEO of the holiday company icelolly.com and the person credited with turning its fortunes around. He was now second in command of the St John Ambulance Brigade, having volunteered there for more than 40 years. I knew he was the type that would always want to help others. I had fond memories of Andrew when, as small boys, we'd walk together down Harestone Valley Road and he'd be on his way to work as a St John Ambulance trainee medic and I was going to work as a volunteer at the St Lawrence

Mental Hospital, and we'd part at the crossroads. He once tried to explain the difference between the Church of England and the Catholic Church and said they were the same as they were both Christians (he failed to tell me the political differences). We were both Christians and both members of the school Christian Club. He even took me to the Protestant church for a couple of services.

After a brief conversation in which I explained the reason for my call, he told me to ring the headmaster of Caterham School, Mr Ceri Jones. Apparently, there was a protocol in place for the children of Mottrams who had suffered abuse and he was horrified that I was one of those children. I told him that I was regularly tortured there and felt the need to do the right thing for all concerned. He told me he couldn't discuss it with me as he was a member of the Caterham School Foundation. He suggested I go through the appropriate channels and to hold off on any legal action until I'd spoken to the headmaster Ceri Jones.

Paula rang Ceri Jones and told him the story. He suggested we come to the school so I could tell him my complaints first hand and he asked Paula if she could accompany me, so we made an appointment. When the time came, I felt very nervous, not knowing how I'd react being back in my nightmare. I was glad Paula was coming although I asked her not to say anything at the meeting. I knew I needed to be careful. Ceri Jones was just the front man and the richer families in the valley controlled the interests of the school. We arrived in Caterham two hours early in order to see what we were walking into (as the saying goes, 'The early bird catches the worm', and I wasn't sure what to expect).

First we drove past the main school to Mottrams. I was surprised to see it was no longer a boarding house and had been turned into a pre-school for very small children who were being collected by their parents. A lot of building work had been done but it was still as scary as ever, although what surprised me was that Paula was very upset. She said she could imagine the small boys walking across to the day school, across the path through the field to the dirty showers where no-one could see them and no-one would hear their screams. Paula thought it was horrific. No wonder I had nightmares.

We went to the main school building and parked the car, not in the visitors' car park but in the parents' area, and then we waited and watched. It wasn't long before I saw plain-clothes police arrive and I realised that my intuitions were right. We were walking into a trap.

Ten minutes before the appointment I walked up to the statue of Rev John Townsend, which was on the lawn outside the headmaster's office, and asked Paula to take some photos of me next to it. As I was being photographed I could see the police in the headmaster's office and they could see me. We went into reception where we had our photos taken for a pass – ridiculous really as we'd already been all round the school. Then a woman we both correctly assumed was a plain-clothes officer, came into reception, looked at us and then escorted us through to a large office, two rooms away from where I'd spotted the plain-clothes policemen. Here we were introduced to Catherine Acton, the head's PA, a pleasant small-framed lady with short blonde hair who offered us coffee which we refused. I didn't want to leave my prints or DNA on anything there. Who knew what they'd frame me for next? I was right to be paranoid.

Catherine showed us to an office next door to the old headmaster's office, and we waited for Ceri Jones. The room was a large, old fashioned- office with brown wood panelling, a very large antique desk with an old-fashioned intercom in its centre – one of those with the switches you press to talk to the secretary, or other rooms. There was a comfy old leather sofa against the wall, on which we were sitting. Moments later, Ceri Jones came in the door, walked straight to the intercom and flicked it down so the secretary or others (or the police?) could hear what was being said in the room. It was obvious he thought we were too stupid to understand what the intercom was for. He told us he was going to take notes and that he was going to manage the meeting alone, which was strange as I was trained at Caterham never to take a meeting or a debate when the other side outnumbers you. They will make themselves right even when they're wrong.

It was obvious he'd taken our Cockney accents as a sign that we weren't smart and he could deal with us irritants alone. My brain was spinning trying to understand what was really going on and my instincts were on red alert. He only wrote about two words on his notepad and then got engrossed in the conversation but, of course, the switch on the intercom was down so it was obvious someone else was listening. My plan was to leave this meeting with an apology from the school for the abuse I'd suffered, and a letter of apology from Graeme Mew for calling my mother sleazy and me a thief.

Ceri Jones was a young charismatic chap about the same age as our daughter, so I already knew it was a mismatch. I was quite upset that he'd invited Paula to come along if the plan was to lure me, and therefore her, into a trap with the police. It seemed like an ungentlemanly thing to do and proved to me that there was no level they wouldn't stoop to. I did, however, understand why the police were there. Maybe they'd had previous complaints from old boys who weren't as civil as me. So I reassured Ceri that I wasn't there to apply East End style pirate law (surprise attack, overwhelming force, no mercy). I was dealing with this situation in the open and as a gentleman. Paula and I both had political hustings experience – he should have Googled us before the meeting.

After introductions, he asked how we wanted to start this. I told him I'd come for something that was mine – my reputation. He didn't seem at all surprised as I recalled my story of torture at the school, and there was no reaction, but when I told him about hillside fights he looked shocked. It was obviously the first time he'd heard about the hillside fights. I thought to myself: 'This is unbelievable. Mass sexual torture, no response, hillside fights, visible shock.' What type of people are we dealing with here?

He asked me if I'd like to come back to the school at a later date and give a talk to the children. I was surprised. Why would they want to listen to someone with an accent like mine? Especially as I had nothing good to say about the school. I asked him if there were any children in the school who spoke like me and he had to stop and think about it. I assumed he thought about lying but then thought I might ask to meet the child, so he had to tell the truth, which was no. I told him the founder of the school, Rev John Townsend, had my accent. He came from the same area as me, and we'd roamed the same streets, albeit 200 years apart.

Now I told him I wanted an apology for publicly calling my mother sleazy and me a thief. He asked how I'd found out about the speech at the East India Club and I told him it was on the internet, to which he said he was going to have it removed. I told him it was a bit late as it had been up there for ages and I already had a copy. I asked if he was a boarder and he said no as he went to a comprehensive school. I asked him how he could know about the boarders' experience then. Had he read it in a book? He said he was a boarding house master for seven years, but it's not the same. You've got to live it to understand how emotionally complicated it is. I told him my story, and how 40 years later, the school was still calling me a thief, and my mother sleazy, in public and publishing it on the internet for all to see. To make matters worse it had been written by the Rt. Hon Canadian Supreme Court Judge Graeme Mew, who not only makes the laws but whose opinion people respect.

Paula went on to tell him how my mother, Carole McQueen, was a school secretary, and then the landlady of the Magpie pub in the City of London for 20 years. She was a very well respected lady throughout the City of London and the East End.

I repeated my demand for an apology and gave him two reasons why. The East India Club had been mired in controversy before. Sir Jacob Rees Mogg had been at the club as a guest of honour at the right-wing Traditional Britain Group in 2013. When he realised it had extreme far-right links, he apologised and disassociated himself from the group of which he'd never been a member or a supporter. When Conservative MP Anne Marie Morris was discussing Brexit at the East India Club, she said that if in two years' time we had a no deal 'we get to the real nigger in the woodpile.' That racist remark got her suspended for a short while, but today she's still the Tory MP for Newton Abbot. She apologised and said it was a figure of speech (in what era?). The difference between Jacob Rees Mogg and Anne Marie Morris is that they both had the decency to apologise. Graeme Mew hadn't apologised.

Ceri Jones had asked me seven times what I wanted, and at this point his voice was raised. I'd already told him numerous times that I wanted 'exoneration, an apology, justice and my reputation back'. I also wanted the school to ask the police to investigate the historic child abuse. Ceri said he had referred it to the police. It was clear to me I was supposed to ask for money as compensation so the police could come crashing in and arrest me for extortion or something. I was aware of the fine line we were treading. Ceri would talk to me then he'd turn to Paula and ask her what we wanted. And she'd say, 'He wants an apology, exoneration and justice.'

I told Ceri Jones I would damage Graeme Mew's reputation just like he'd damaged mine with his defamation of my character, and my late mother's, who wasn't able to defend herself. By this time I was worn out and getting emotional as I'd told him I was haunted by the faces of the other little boys who were sexually abused like I was.

Then, in a loud voice, he said, 'I'll get Graeme Mew on the phone', as if that was supposed to frighten me. His bullying tone made me switch: 'Get goody two shoes on the phone,' I responded officiously, thinking back to the Graeme I knew. The head boy, from one of the wealthy families in the valley, and almost certainly not abused like myself. There's no way he could understand what it was like to be a whipping boy. I said I was going to ruin his reputation. Then Paula, who I'd asked to stay quiet, piped up and said, 'You can't damage a judge's reputation,' to which Ceri nodded.

'Yes I can.'

'No you can't,' she said as Ceri continued to nod. I was getting quite annoyed at this point.

'Why can't I?'

'You can't damage a judge's reputation as I've seen them in the tabloids,' she said. 'Strapped up in torture chambers being sexually whipped by young prostitutes and nothing happens to them. They always keep their jobs.'

I would have fallen on to the floor laughing if it had not been such a serious matter. I then informed Ceri that I will take reputations like a Mohawk takes scalps if I don't get an apology. I wanted a letter of apology absolving me of the crime I was supposed to have committed, and apologising for referring to my late mother's business as sleazy. I told him I was there because I didn't want what I went through – to have been abused and incorrectly branded a thief – to happen to any other children. He said it couldn't happen nowadays as the children are protected now. I said, 'So a day boy can't get into the boarder dorms?' His face told me all I needed to know. There was nothing stopping day boys getting into the dorms. I asked him what security they had to protect the boarders from drugs, as drugs are everywhere. Again, by the look on his face I knew that the boarders weren't protected. What protects them is people like me coming back to complain.

Then Paula said the sexual torture couldn't happen nowadays, to which I disagreed. Whose side is she on? Ceri agreed with her and said, 'That's what it was like back then,' inferring I should just accept it. He then shouted that he had 500 bursaries to give away, expecting me to ask for some but that's where the trap becomes a double-edged-sword. I felt he was offering me a bribe to cover up child sexual abuse, torture, neglect and defamation of character. I told Ceri that I was writing a book on all of this and he'll be writing the last chapter. I'm hoping that Caterham will do the right thing.

The police should have burst in and arrested him for saying he had 500 bursaries to give away but of course they didn't, and now the penny had dropped. These bursaries worth millions are the reason for the collective mass amnesia about child abuse in the valley. Ordinary tax-paying citizens can't get a police officer for love nor money, yet they can have them lying in wait in the next office. Why would senior police officers instruct their staff to frame children? Maybe it's something to do with these bursaries. I then asked if the police still use the sports facilities. He said they didn't and that was enough for me as I'd just finished researching the rugby fixtures of the Metropolitan Police and the Surrey squad and they'd been playing against the Caterham old boys. They're glove in hand with the school, and use the school pitches.

I left it at that. I would take legal action, law permitting. That, I presume, is what a gentleman would do. We left and slipped the trap, or so we thought. As we got up to leave I told him: 'Tell them all,' indicating to the room with the police in, 'And make sure you do tell them all, that it's Pimm's o'clock.' Ceri shook his head, trying not to laugh. At that point the policewoman came in and said Ceri had a meeting.

As we were walking down the corridor, Paula walked in front accompanied by Ceri. Later she said she'd told him there must be scores of children that this awful thing had happened to. He didn't say anything. When we reached the foyer, Paula told Ceri that she couldn't wait for me to go in front of the board, to tell my story. 'That won't be happening,' he said. 'You can't speak to the board.' Paula looked surprised. She said it was important the board know about the power they wield and the devastation it can have on children's lives.

It was a treacherous drive back to London and Paula nearly hit three cars on the way home. The visit had disturbed her and she was unable to get the image of Mottrams, and the path between there and the showers, that I'd walked as a child, out of her mind. Or the smell of the cut grass out of her nostrils.

It wasn't long before I had to admit that going back to that place after 40 years had also affected me. It was surreal, especially with Ceri Jones trying his best to trigger me with psychology and – I felt – trying his best to get me arrested. No wonder people don't come forward. I'm a strong person and it was affecting me. And now it was affecting my wife.

Despite the fact that for the first time in my life, having my honour and reputation restored was a real possibility, I was having nightmares and waking up in a sweaty, upset, angry mess. I decided to contact a counsellor and explained that I'd been unblocking my childhood experiences and had gone to the school to try and resolve my problems. And now I was losing the plot. The counsellor was appalled that the school was doing this to me. She said it was a bad idea to go there and to never go there again. It's thought that writing it down helps but the reality is it makes things clearer. I couldn't stop thinking about it all, and the other children's faces were haunting me, and still are. I needed closure but I don't know if that is actually possible, or if publishing this book will bring closure or extend the pain. Only time will tell.

Ceri had invited us back to the school for a second meeting and said the matter was now with the chair of the trustees, Ed Smith CBE, who was treasurer of Chatham House. But on the advice of my counsellor, we decided not to go. Instead, we researched the board members and sent emails to the trustees whose addresses we could find, as well as Ceri Jones and other members of the school. The email, dated Sunday December 2nd was entitled 'Historical Abuse at Caterham School' and reads as follows:

Without prejudice

Dear Ceri and to whom it may concern,

Please accept Nicholas's apologies for not attending the meeting on 4th December 2018, but after reviewing our minutes from the last meeting, with some consideration he has decided it's not right for him to return to Caterham at this time.

I think your Protocol should be amended because it can't be right that a victim should re-live and re-live their story at the scene of the crime and we know that because of the emotional roller coaster that it has put Nicholas on.

As for looking at the prep school where he suffered prolonged torture at the hands of a Paedophile, in dirty showers, under the school where no-one could hear any screams, I don't think he's ready, for that is his Abu Ghraib. [This refers to the Iraq War when detainees at Abu Ghraib prison were tortured and mistreated by members of the US military.]

I'm glad the police now have a live investigation. As I explained, Surrey Police have already investigated this complaint ref: 4517012803 and have filed Nicholas's complaint alongside other similar complaints made against Caterham School. It appears to me that you have had enough information, but should you need anything further, he would be more than pleased to assist via email. That's not to say if you or the board would like to interview him in London, in the interest of children he will always make himself available for examination when properly called upon. (Chatham house rules or not.)

We are pleased that it's now with Ed Smith CBE (the Chair) who strives for a just world and puts a value on education. Nicholas believes Ed Smith CBE has the wisdom, strength and ability to do what's right for Nicholas and Caterham school.

I would like to point out to you that the CIA at Guantanamo Bay were still, in 2014, using the same torture technique (cold water on the penis) to break the minds of terrorists. (Majid Khan, a known terrorist who was part of a cell who killed eleven people and planned to kill many more, was held in a black site, said interrogators poured ice water on his genitals and threatened to beat him). [by David Rohde June 2nd 2015, Reuters]. Remembering Nicholas's crime as an 11 year old boy was talking in prep, for that he was beaten and given penis torture on a regular basis.

I think it should be known that Nicholas was in a dorm with 4 other boys with housemasters either side of his dorm, opposite his dorm was the maths teacher and the matron's helper. Not one of those four adults ever questioned the Paedophile and it was common knowledge what was going on.

Nicholas was tortured continuously for at least 18 months. Every day the Paedophile (Mr Robinson-Fuller) would take 2 boys, some of the boys were only 8 years old, he stopped when they reached puberty. Nicholas is still haunted by their terrified little faces. On the mornings that he wasn't chosen, he would peer out the window to make sure that the little boys that had gone with Robinson-Fuller came back safely. Their faces have haunted him for most of his life, after his latest visit to Caterham his nightmares have increased. Nicholas received counselling on Thursday 29th November, the counsellor advised him not to return to the school.

He now feels very guilty for not telling his story sooner. As you can see my husband has waived his right to anonymity, in the interest of children. Perhaps you can inform us of the next phase of your protocol?

I look forward to hearing from you.

Yours sincerely,

Mrs Pauline McQueen

There was no reply, and to this day I have no idea what their protocol is. It wasn't until 2021 that we found out what the board would do with regards to this email.

In 2021, Ed Smith stood down as chairman of the board of Caterham

School trustees, as did other trustees (although it interested me that the church member did not stand down). These trustees obviously believed that it was the right thing to do. Ed Smith also stood down as treasurer of Chatham House, which is next door to the East India Club.

Paul Corrigan asked the police for their records about my case and got my medical records to see if he should proceed with the legal case. It took nearly a year before he got what he needed. There was evidence that there were other complaints similar to mine, which goes to prove that I wasn't the only one affected. The police filed the other complaints away. All Mottrams' records were shredded, because Caterham is not a state school and didn't need to follow state law, even though the state's inner London authority forced me to go there. The school has changed its charity number and believes it's not liable, but it still has the same assets and continues to buy up the Surrey countryside and pay little tax.

I'd given the police the names of my ex housemaster John Jones and his second-in-command Jim Seymour. At first Surrey Police said they were going to drag them out of their beds to take them to the police station, then, all of a sudden, their attitude changed. They informed me that the names were so common they couldn't find them, even though I'd furnished them with the address, phone number and email of Mr Jones. They then said they'd investigated the complaint and there was nothing they could do. (The policewoman who couldn't find John Jones' address, and also filed our case with the others, has since been promoted.)

When Paul Corrigan was ready he sent a legal letter to the school.

Their response was to defend themselves saying it was time barred. Robinson-Fuller was dead and because I'd gone to my appointment at the school, my abuse couldn't have affected me. The school knew this would be their defence, which is why they invited me there. If they couldn't incriminate me, break me or bribe me, they could then say abuse didn't affect me. How could it have done if I'd visited the school? And there was no case to answer so the case will not be heard. Caterham did not take responsibility for the abuse of children at Mottrams at the time so why would they take responsibility today? This is something I think about a lot.

I've learnt a lot on my journey since being abused as a child. I realise the effect it has had on my behaviour and the direction my life has taken. I've spent years blocking memories out, trying to stem my emotions, my childhood suicidal thoughts and feelings of worthlessness, my lack of trust in others and feelings of betrayal. I've had ferocious bouts of anger and sleepless nights because every time I close my eyes, I see the faces of children in the showers, or their eyes peering over their bedsheets. I also lost my right to an education, my honour and my reputation. That school tried to take everything away from me and I've had to fight to ensure it didn't happen.

The impact has been considerable. It wasn't until Abu Ghraib was made public that I started to unblock my memories. The mind is a strange thing, the way it protects us. When I saw the pictures of US troops sexually humiliating detainees during the Iraq War in 2004, I started to remember my own abuse and realised I needed to confront my memories and deal with what had happened once and for all. I was definitely suffering from a type of PTSD, which is why I felt the need to drown myself in alcohol just to carry on. I realised my experience shattered me, and I was going to put myself back together no matter what.

In 2015, details about the torture of Majid Khan, a Guantanamo detainee became known. The CIA had used enhanced interrogation techniques (a euphemism for torture) on him, and this included putting ice water on his genitals. He was also given bad food and tied to a pole. The CIA paid two outside contractors $80million to create this interrogation programme, which is not just immoral but illegal.

For Caterham to use enhanced punishment techniques on small children is diabolical. I experienced white torture – sleep deprivation, extreme cold, sexual humiliation, nakedness, ice water on my genitals – and I was made to swim naked for the teachers' entertainment. Not to mention the beatings that I knew were coming later that day, that would draw blood. Yet despite this, the worst thing for me was being made to watch others far younger than myself suffer, and not be able to help them. And I was only 11 years old.

We need greater transparency of the past, more accountability, and not let powerful people use their wealth and position in society to misuse the law and police to deter victims from coming forward. I believe the foundation and trustees have disregarded the values of Caterham, and its founder Rev Townsend, to help keep this scandal covered up. I believe this cover up, and bribery, is perverting the course of justice and this is adding to the pain the victims already have. The culprits should be put in prison for a long time, irrespective of who they are, how much they're worth and where they work.

My story isn't unusual. In 2024, Earl Spencer, the brother of Princess Diana, revealed that he, and other boys, were sexually abused by a female staff member at his boarding school Maidwell Hall, in the 1970s, and this had left him with lifelong 'demons'. He also says the late headmaster of the same school beat the boys bloody with a cane and slipper. The allegations have been referred to the local authority and other victims have been urged to come forward.

If we don't deal with the past, it will continue to happen. And it still does. In 2021, after Ceri Jones told me it wouldn't happen today, William Murdock, headmaster at the private Danes Hill School in Surrey, took his own life rather than face accusations of sexual abuse. At the same time 10,000 children complained on social media about abuse at private schools.

# CHAPTER 24

# Conclusions

In 2016, Professor Alexis Jay OBE was made chair of the government's Independent Inquiry into Child Sex Abuse (IICSA). IICSA was set up following concerns that organisations had failed, and continue to fail, to protect children from sexual abuse. The inquiry would address issues that persist, despite previous complaints and inquiries, and other attempts to reform. This one must not fail.

On May 6th 2021, I rang the IICSA enquiry line to give them an outline of my experience and the information I had. My hope was that they could bring the independent schools in line with state schools, which have a number of safeguarding practices in place. I was asked if I was willing to go public and of course I gave my permission. IICSA set up the Truth Project to give victims of sexual abuse a chance to share their experiences and put forward suggestions for change. I gave evidence via videolink.

That same year, the National Police Chiefs' Council (NPCC) Child Protection and Abuse Investigation (CPAI) set up Operation Hydrant in order to co-ordinate the police response to IICSA. In May 2021, Leon from Surrey Police called me in relation to Operation Hydrant. He said he couldn't help me as my file had been closed by the inspector at Caterham Police Station. Once a file has been closed there's nothing the police can do about it, which gives little hope to any of us who have experienced historical sexual abuse. Leon apologised that he couldn't be of any help. I wasn't surprised.

On October 6th 2021, I sent the Truth Project this email:

To whom it may concern,

My name is Nicholas McQueen My reference is : IICSA-0031170

I gave my evidence by video link on 28th July 2021 at 2pm, my adjudicator was Julia and my support worker was Katie. After the video link I told Katie I didn't think I'd gotten my point across regarding the police attitude towards child abuse laws.

As with electoral laws in Tower Hamlets, 187 laws were broken and the police didn't investigate any. No-one in the police force was held accountable. So no matter how many new laws are brought to the table if the police chose not to investigate we will be no better off.

Katie told me to send an email explaining my point and any recommendations I might have to stop child abuse.

I do believe we can stop all abuse and cruelty within our institutions, but our strategy must encompass changing the minds, attitudes and culture that exists within our boards/trustees/foundations and police forces.

Surrey Police force and Caterham School have scuppered the investigations of the many children who were tortured at Mottrams boarding house. One of my attackers [John Jones, who laughed at my penis after ripping my bedclothes off] who worked at the main school, was still active at the school at the time of my complaint. The policewoman who was handling my complaint was angered by this situation and promised to arrest him. Instead the file was ordered to be closed by her seniors and the policewoman was promoted. These crimes have supposedly been investigated and files closed.

The child protection officer who was told to look into this was informed that the file was closed and there was nothing he could do.

My recommendations are as follows:

(1) A multi-pronged attack on this dire situation would bring about change. Tighter laws, changing attitudes, making sure covering up is a thing of the past. Accountability does not only protect children but it can also bring closure to the previous victims.

The culture of using bursaries as compensation causes mass amnesia around child abuse which is not acceptable and needs to be addressed in order to move forward.

Bursaries are far more valuable than any compensation schemes available. This should be addressed so compensation is more valuable than bursaries in order to stop this amnesia around child abuse.

(2) All bursaries should have government approval and be means tested. Bursaries should not be given to people affiliated with the school. Officers of the Surrey Constabulary should also not be given bursaries, as they use Caterham's school facilities to play rugby and this can cause a conflict of interest if an investigation is necessary.

(3) Public schools should not be allowed to shred records. All Mottrams children's records have been shredded and the boarding of the prep school has been closed with no explanation. There needs to be an independent body that keeps all records of the children that attend these schools.

I have photo documentation of myself attending Mottrams prep school.

Thank you for trying to help but, as with previous investigations I don't hold out much hope for change as this has been going on for many years and as far as I'm aware is still going on today, with perpetrators still working in such establishments.

Yours Hopefully,

Nicholas McQueen

The reply from the Truth Project was as follows:

Dear Nicholas,

Thank you for your email dated 06/10/2021 providing additional information following your session.

I have asked for this information to be shared with Julia the Facilitator who was present with you at your session.

They will ensure this is added to the information you shared with them on the day.

Many thanks for taking the time to share this with us and for your participation in Truth. Your contribution to the work of the Inquiry is greatly valued and your experience will feed into and influence our findings and recommendations with the aim of finding a better way to protect children.

Kind regards,

Truth Project

The Caterham I knew is long gone. Although the motto was 'Perseverance Conquers All', its classist and elitist attitude is still the same 40 years on. The East End and Soho taught me that the only time you look down on someone is when you're helping them up. Their new motto is – laughably – 'Truth Without Fear'. I see little truth, just a cloak of silence. Referring to my mother as sleazy was their biggest mistake.

I nearly became another statistic, another person washed away by the sewer of life, because I'm a Catholic and working class. But I was revitalised when I met Gianni Russo and he told me about the American Dream. The American Dream believes that freedom and equality is open to all, regardless of where you're born; that upward mobility, success and happiness is available to anyone, regardless of class. My counsellor was right – I do feel better. Thanks to Gianni Russo

A hero of mine is the late American politician Senator John McCain. He was tortured for five years during the Vietnam War and earned the Bronze Star, Silver Star, Purple Heart and Distinguished Flying Cross. During his Republican presidential nomination speech, he said a few things that resonated with me, including: 'Nothing in life is more liberating than to fight for a cause larger than yourself, something that encompasses you but is not defined by your existence alone.'

On respect, he said: 'People who hold certain institutional positions should have your respect until they lose it. But the rest of us mortals have to earn it.'

On courage, he said: 'Courage is not the absence of fear, but the capacity to act despite our fears.'

On character, he said: 'It is your character, and your character alone, that will make your life happy or unhappy. That is all that really passes for destiny. And you choose it. No-one else can give it to you or deny it to you. No rival can steal it from you. And no friend can give it to you. Others can encourage you to make the right choices or discourage you. But you choose.'

On losing, he said: 'It's very important to lose gracefully. You know, no bitterness, no anger, no remorse – can't display that.'

The Truth Project concluded its inquiry in October 2021. They interviewed 6,000 victims, making it the biggest investigation into abuse to date. The information gathered will be used for generations to come, making institutions safer for children by putting forward suggestions for change and bringing in tighter laws on child abuse. When I was interviewed they told me some of the children were victims, some were survivors and some were like me, thrivers, throwing themselves into work and challenges and not letting it destroy them.

These institutions need to know we will return to demand an apology. I think that is one way to protect the present children. In recent years criminal convictions have surged but children in boarding situations are still vulnerable due to their isolation. Multiple institutions are implicated when it comes to failing children. Local authorities, police and even school inspectors. The Inner London Education Authority never checked to see if I was OK after ordering me to stay at Caterham. Caterham is named and shamed in the school index of the Truth Report inquiry. Have a look but, beware, it's grim reading. They still haven't apologised to me which indicates that little has changed. The closure of Mottrams and the shredding of records is still a mystery to me. It was my Abu Ghraib, my Robben Island, my Chateau D'if – a black site for kids, where ugly things took place, hidden from view. Caterham stole my dreams and replaced them with nightmares.

***

Operation Lynemouth, the investigation into allegations of election fraud in the 2014 mayoral election in Tower Hamlets, lasted a year, employed 20 detectives and police staff and cost £1.7million. It could have been avoided.

Mr Mawrey (then) QC found several issues. He said you cannot take out a library book without identification but you can vote. (This, of course, changed in The Elections Act 2022, when voter ID rules were brought in.) He also used the term 'ghost voters' for voters who didn't exist. The introduction of postal voting has greatly enhanced the possibility of vote rigging. He also highlighted that we need clearer laws on spiritual influence as clerics were telling Muslims to vote for Lutfur Rahman. He also highlighted bribery by grant, and the huge sums of money given to Muslim charities.

Despite 169 allegations there were no convictions. The Metropolitan Police Service (MPS) said they needed more evidence. I believe the police failed in communication and engagement, and officers should have explained better why the investigations came to nothing. There was a lack of corporate responsibility, lack of training and insufficient resources. In essence, the Metropolitan Police did not consider the election and investigation a priority.

HMICFRS's conclusion of the Lynemouth inquiry, and their recommendations, are as follows:

The Metropolitan Police must guard against complacency even though some things have improved. The following seven points of prioritisation are listed below. These are seven areas for continual consideration, which should reduce risk of recurrence:

1. Prioritisation: the policing of elections and the investigation of electoral offences must be afforded the importance that a democratic society deserves.

2. Leadership: chief officers must provide visible leadership and governance, not only during the election but throughout an investigation such as this, and must ensure evidential opportunities are not overlooked or disregarded.
3. Resources: adequate and suitably trained officers and staff must be made available, both for policing elections and investigating any electoral offences.
4. Consistency: planning (subject to any local leads) and training must be consistent throughout the MPS, to avoid duplication and ensure that officers and the staff can be redeployed to meet demand.
5. Communications: the MPS must communicate and engage with interested parties and, as appropriate, with the wider public, both before, during and after an election and any investigation.
6. Record keeping: the MPS must keep accurate records of allegations, investigations and decisions(with rationale).
7. Legal decisions: the MPS must consult the Crown Prosecution Service about complex legal decisions and, where appropriate, seek early investigative advice.

If an election can be cheated in London, it can be cheated anywhere in the world. In 2022 Lutfur Rahman ran for mayor again, this time representing his new party Aspire, and Conservative peer Lord Hayward called for the Electoral Commission to tackle potential corruption in Tower Hamlets again! In the House of Lords he explained that Rahman had instructed the Bangladeshi carers to collect the votes not campaign for votes. The meeting was held in the Sylheti language. They used the word 'collect' four times (here we go again). In May 2022 the election for executive mayor and councillors took place. Aside from taking up a page in the council mayoral booklet, Rahman did not campaign in any way, while all the other candidates argued about the left and right of politics at hustings and rallies. Rahman swept the board taking control of Tower Hamlets completely.

According to the 2021 census, Tower Hamlets has the largest Bangladeshi population (34.6 per cent) in England and Wales and the largest Muslim population (39.9 per cent). Tower Hamlets is now run by a group of Islamic men, which does not represent the wider community, especially women and the non-religious. When we watch the elections in Bangladesh and see they need the army on the streets, thanks to vote rigging and polling stations being burned down, you can see what's happening here.

A crackdown to prevent voting malpractice is being proposed in parliament following the controversy over the elections in Tower Hamlets.

Lord Hayward is preparing to use a private members bill to try to amend existing electoral laws which would give police clearer powers to stop relatives influencing family members at the ballot box. I'm afraid to say that's locking the stable door after the horse has bolted.

And the problems rumble on. In February 2024, it was announced that government inspectors were being sent into Tower Hamlets Council over concerns about how it is being run by Rahman. They are looking at a range of issues, including how money is spent, 'the policy and practice of grant-making' and senior job appointments.

***

In 2021, Jeffrey Steinberg was sued by a couple in Los Angeles who were given the wrong baby and then breastfed and bonded with a stranger's baby for four months, before it was taken off them. Daphna and Alexander Cardinale thought something was wrong when they noticed the baby girl's skin colour was darker than their own. A DNA test confirmed there had been a mix up and the baby was not related to either of them. The lack of laws around embryos (which, in America, change from state to state) allow these mistakes to happen. The laws are more stringent in Britain and there is little chance of this mistake happening because of the double witness system, which means every time a gamete or embryo is moved from one tube or dish to another, it is monitored to ensure that only one patient is worked on at a time.

We have seven embryos missing. Where are they? Who has them? Will we ever find the answers? They are mine and Paula's children. They need to know about our genetic problems, including my heart failure and Paula's cancer. She now has tumours in her lungs and heart. (The tumour in her heart is stopping her valve from closing: the cardiologist is keeping an eye on it as open-heart surgery is risky at her age.) We now know these tumours are due to a rare disease called Langerhans' Cell Histiocytosis, or LCH. We need to know if we have children and if so where they are so we can pass this information on.

In 2024, Pope Francis called for a global ban on surrogacy, deeming it 'deplorable' as it 'represents a grave violation of the dignity of the woman and the child, based on the exploitation of situations of the mother's material needs. A child's always a gift never the basis of a commercial contract. It's a form of people trafficking and should be banned globally.' I don't agree with everything he says, as he's also against IVF. But I do believe surrogacy allows people to traffic babies like ours.

***

The Brexit argument still lingers but the results are clear. The majority of the UK voted to leave Europe, so we left. Covid and international unrest in Ukraine, and now Israel and Palestine, has affected the economy globally, but in the UK inflation is going down while in the Eurozone it's rising. The UK has less unemployment than Europe. Trade deals are evolving globally, putting us in a better financial position. We have control of our money, land and waters. We've led the world on many things including training more than 60,000 Ukrainian troops in order to help Ukraine and stop Russia's land grab. English is the world's first language and there's a reason for that.

Europe are our neighbours not our friends and that mutual respect should continue. Our true friend is the United States and our relationship is strengthening. In this more dangerous world, Europe will call on us before we call on them. Getting our sovereignty back is the most important issue and there's not a price on it. To be free and unencumbered from our neighbours' views, rules and laws that serve them, and not us, is the greatest part of Brexit. We will excel and lead society as we always have done. It's the reason hundreds of thousands are fleeing Europe, crossing the busiest shipping lanes in the world in small boats to get to us. Our future is brighter than it has been for a long time now that we rule ourselves once again.

***

Truth to me is like water: it will either drip through or come like a flood, but it will get through eventually. Truth is as important to me as it was to Rev Townsend and most of us seek it. This story is not about making money because I've enough money to last me the rest of my life (as long as I die tonight or early in the morning). This is very much about putting the record straight.

Flowers look nice but it can be an ugly business at times. McQueens Shoreditch did an interview with a national newspaper saying they bought the shop from Carole McQueen, Alexander McQueen's aunt, when it was a wilting florist (and they miraculously changed it into a corporate sensation without knowing the business). Let's put the record straight.

Firstly, my mother Carole would not know the difference between a daffodil and a tulip, and the only time she stepped into a flower shop was to visit me. My mother was a huge personality in the City of London, a real lady who ran her pub in a very professional manner. Her cup was overflowing with common sense and there was always someone needing her counsel, and she was great at giving it. She helped so many people see their way through difficult times while sipping a wine or two, so I take offence when anyone tries to give her a fake history. It touches a nerve with me and then nothing else matters.

As for running a florist, not knowing how the flower game is played is very silly, unless it's been set up for you, like McQueens was. Not only will you lose your investment you'll probably have a nervous breakdown on top of it due to the really hard work involved.

McQueens was in good shape when it was handed over for someone to run. It relied on the contracts. It was not a cash sales shop, it had guaranteed income. My corporate brand and business model was well-thought out and tested. It even survived the Black Monday crash which wiped £1.7trillion off the board. This was no wilting florist!

The only negative for people is that it was expensive, but you get what you pay for in this world. It was first class. Aldo Gucci said, 'Quality is remembered long after the price is forgotten.' You'd soon forget the price but you'd never forget the beauty and how long McQueens' flowers lasted. In a short time McQueens swept across London with another two branches opening and new corporate contracts added daily. It was a very fast-growing company. I did feel a bit silly, because I'd been around the world looking for the city paved with gold and it was under my nose the whole time. No more than 100 yards from Petticoat Lane.

I always pop into Claridge's for oysters if I'm passing. They sell the best oysters and the presentation on the silver-tiered trays make it an experience rather than a snack. The wine's pretty good too, but my feelings are always mixed sitting there, remembering Lee's wake and looking at my old flower company, McQueens, which is now based in the foyer.

Now, if you look on the McQueens website you'll see no mention of me, and it says the company started selling flowers in 1991, when of course, it started in the 1980s. McQueens has now gone global, with studios and workshops in London, New York and Seoul and floristry programmes in Australia, Dubai, China and Mexico. Any modern city in the world should have a branch as it unlocks great wealth and is a thrilling business to run. (I told my mum my name would be in lights and so it is, all over the world.) But McQueens florist was one of my children and so erasing me from this history hurts, especially as they still use the same Dutch flowers and one of my suppliers, Dennis. And because legally I own the name.

The whipping boy gets whipped again.

# APPENDIX I

# The East End

The East End is a very special place. It's no more than one square mile and yet there's a certain magic here. Paula and I still live in Albert Gardens, where I lived as a child. No matter where we go around the world, we always come home. The East End is a place that for hundreds of years has changed the way the world thinks, whether you were born here, like myself, or just came to live for a while. For me it's the right side of the tracks.

The following people have either lived or stayed in the East End of London and have made a difference to the way the world thinks:

**The Rev John Townsend**: helped deaf children get an education.

**The Suffragettes:** fought and won the rights for women to vote.

**Clement Attlee:** reformed the welfare state and oversaw the creation of the NHS.

**William Booth:** created The Salvation Army to help the poor.

**Alexander McQueen:** changed the way we look at fashion

**Isambard Kingdom Brunel:** his feats in engineering changed the way we travelled

**Trotsky and Lenin:** responsible for Russia's Red Army which provided the largest land force in the Allied Victory of the Second World War.

**Lutfur Rahman:** (aka The Bangladeshi Fox): masterminded how to cheat an election.

**Nicholas McQueen:** encouraged everyone, especially children, to 'plant the planet, save the world' in 1998. It took a long time to catch on.

# APPENDIX 2

# Cockney Rhyming Slang

Cockney rhyming slang has been around since 1840 and is still used by East End salesmen and in London markets today.

**Loaf of bread** – head
**Bacon and eggs** – legs
**Boat race** – face
**Mutt and Jeff** – deaf
**Scooby Doo** – flu
**Moby Dick** – sick
**Hank Marvin** – starving
**Sky rocket** – pocket
**Boracic lint** – skint
**Dog and bone** – phone
**Septic tank** – Yank
**Currant bun** – sun
**Adam and Eve** – believe
**Pete Tong** – wrong
**Beeswax** – tax
**Barney Rubble** – trouble
**Bubble bath** – laugh
**Joanna** – piano
**Bristol City** – titty
**Ginger beer** – queer
**Whistle and flute** – suit
**Bees and honey** – money
**Apples and pears** – stairs
**Weasel and stoat** – coat
**Duke of York** – fork
**Frog and toad** – road
**Ruby Murray** – curry

**Daisy roots** – boots
**Mince pies** – eyes
**Gregory Peck** – neck
**Plates of meat** – feet
**Raspberry tart** – fart
**Richard the 3rd** – bird
**Dickie Bird** – word
**Lionel Blairs** – flares
**Pen and ink** – stink
**Cream crackered** – knackered
**Jam jar** – car
**Big Ben** – ten
**Baked bean** – Queen
**Oxo cube** – Tube
**Pig's ear** – beer
**Bull and cow** – row
**Rosie Lee** – tea
**Trouble and strife** – wife
**Oxford scholar** – dollar
**Elephant trunk** – drunk
**Jack Jones** – alone
**Farmer Giles** – piles
**Butcher's hook** – look
**Rabbit and pork** – talk
**Tea leaf** – thief
**Pork pie** – lie
**China plate** – mate

**Money**

| | |
|---|---|
| Alan Whicker/Nicker | £1 |
| Bottle of glue | £2 |
| Carpet | £3 |
| Roath | £4 |
| Deep sea diver/Lady Godiva | £5 |
| Cock and hen/Cockle | £10 |
| Score | £20 |
| Pony | £25 |
| Bullseye | £50 |
| Ton | £100 |
| Bag of sand/Grand | £1,000 |

We abbreviate the rhyme so we can talk in front of someone without them knowing what we're talking about.

We had a bubble with the bottle of septics = We had a laugh with the two Americans.

The tea leaf had a butchers at the whistle in the back of the jam jar = The thief took a look at the suit in the back of the car.

Remember, don't get Cockney'd.

# INDEX

Operation Lynemouth,
186–87, 218–220
2015 Mayoral election,
184–87
Bangladeshi community,
175–76, 178–80, 219, 224
name, 135
Tower Hamlets Council
corruption at, 220
Townsend, Rev John, 60–62,
203, 212
Toynbee Hall drama club, 14,
26, 53
Troxy, the, 179, 182
Truman, Jill, 158
truth, 222
Truth Project, 213–17

**U**
UKIP, 171–86
*See also* Brexit; Farage,
Nigel; McQueen, Nicholas:
political career

**V**
Van Nuys Airport, 109–10,
119–20
*Vanity Fair* (magazine), 93
Venice Beach, 105, 126
Vietnam Veteran Crips, 107

**W**
Wales, Sir Robin, 178
Webber, Mark, 175–76, 184
Wentworth Street, 13, 16–17,
54, 64
West End, the, 56, 65–67, 69,
132, 160
*See also* Soho
West Ham United, 13, 26
White Hart pub, 13–14, 23–28,
29–32, 45, 59, 66
Whitechapel, 14, 23–24, 61, 151
Who, The, 50
Wilford, Christopher, 174, 185
Williams, Danny, 139
Wimpy, 29, 48
Wogan, Sir Terry, 168
Woodland Hills, 109–12
Woollahra, 80
working class, 11, 76, 171–72,
216
wreathmaking, 134, 135–36,
150

**X**
XL Tel. *See* Newton, Terry

**Y**
Paula Yates, 136